AN INTRODUCTION TO
FAMILY LAW

Second Edition

GILLIAN DOUGLAS
Cardiff University

OXFORD
UNIVERSITY PRESS

OXFORD
UNIVERSITY PRESS

Great Clarendon Street, Oxford OX2 6DP

Oxford University Press is a department of the University of Oxford.
It furthers the University's objective of excellence in research, scholarship,
and education by publishing worldwide in

Oxford New York

Auckland Bangkok Buenos Aires Cape Town Chennai
Dar es Salaam Delhi Hong Kong Istanbul Karachi Kolkata
Kuala Lumpur Madrid Melbourne Mexico City Mumbai Nairobi
São Paulo Shanghai Taipei Tokyo Toronto

Oxford is a registered trade mark of Oxford University Press
in the UK and in certain other countries

Published in the United States
by Oxford University Press Inc., New York

© Gillian Douglas 2004

The moral rights of the author have been asserted
Database right Oxford University Press (maker)

First published 2001
Second edition 2004

British Library Cataloguing in Publication Data

Data available

Library of Congress Cataloging in Publication Data

Data available

ISBN 0–19–927094–5

1 3 5 7 9 10 8 6 4 2

Typeset in Ehrhardt
by RefineCatch Limited, Bungay, Suffolk
Printed in Great Britain by
Ashford Colour Press Ltd.
Gosport, Hants.

Preface

The aim of the second edition of this book, like the first, is to offer a concise analytical account of how the law is used to regulate families, and family life, in England and Wales. I seek to highlight key issues in the policy debates governing how family law should develop, such as the proper limits of state 'intervention' in family life, the extent to which legal protection should be extended to 'non traditional' family forms, and the balance to be struck between the rights of different family members. I try to set these issues in an appropriate contextual framework of history, social policy and cultural change in which the shape of the law and its development can be properly understood and evaluated.

In the three years since the first edition was published, the pace of legal developments in both the case law and legislation has been relentless. The impact of the Human Rights Act 1998 and the jurisprudence of the European Court of Human Rights are driving legal innovation in both case law and statute. The fact that the European Convention on Human Rights provides but a 'floor' of rights, on which states may build their own edifices of freedoms and protections, is gradually being recognized and leading to the introduction of reforms which are beginning to out-pace the Strasbourg court. New ideas about what is 'fair' when it comes to evaluating family members' claims against one another or in respect of their children are producing shifts in thinking about family relationships and in the outcomes of legislative and judicial decision-making. I have sought to ensure that these developments are considered and critiqued.

All this makes for a stimulating, but frustrating, task for writers trying to comment on and keep up with the ever-evolving body of law governing the family. For example, the current edition has been written during a year in which Parliament has seen the introduction of four Bills directly relevant to the subject-matter of this book, none of which had completed its passage to enactment at the time of writing. The Gender Recognition Bill, the Civil Partnership Bill, the Domestic Violence, Crime and Victims Bill and the Children Bill are all referred to in the text, but since their final shape is unknown, no detailed analysis of their provisions has been attempted, not least because they may be amended out of all existence, or given up completely if the political costs appear to become too high to warrant persevering with them. I have sought, instead, to ensure that the reader understands the aims behind their original introduction and their impact if enacted as intended. Even where legislation receives Royal Assent, delay in its full implementation has become normal, so that, for example, the Adoption and Children Act 2002 will not come fully into force until 2005. The text therefore refers where necessary to both 'old' and 'new' provisions to ensure that the reader can find the relevant law at the time of reading. I have taken account of developments in the law up to July 2004 but the reader should note that, as in the first edition, I have not attempted to provide a comprehensive description of all such developments, focusing instead only on those that I regard as significant in telling the 'story' of family law.

This edition has been written with close attention paid to the views of reviewers of the first. That does not mean that I have necessarily followed all the suggestions made, although I have certainly tried to take many on board. I am grateful to all those commentators who took the time and trouble to read the book with such care.

This edition is dedicated to my 'nuclear' family—Hugh, Isobel, and Duncan Rawlings.

Gillian Douglas

Preface to the First Edition

As family structures, family life, and family policy have become increasingly complicated, so the law governing family relationships has grown in both volume and complexity. An understanding of how the law regulates families must now embrace both marriage and non-marital adult relationships. It must explore the position of children and the role of the state in protecting them from harm within, as well as outside, their family. It must consider the ideological messages that the law may promote regarding how families should be constituted and how family members should behave towards each other. It must do all this against a constantly changing picture of policy initiatives, legal reforms, and judicial developments. It is hardly surprising then, that it is also becoming more and more difficult to obtain an overall picture of how and why family law has developed in England and Wales in the ways that it has.

In this book, I aim to offer a concise overview of family law, which will provide a guide to dealing with this complexity. I seek to discuss the main elements of the subject in sufficient depth to provide a firm grasp of the law, while avoiding the weight of detail that can threaten to overwhelm and confuse the reader. I hope that the text will help the reader to see the linkages between different aspects of the subject and its relationship with other areas of the law and with other disciplines. Most of all, I hope that it will enable the reader to identify and 'tune in' to the main policy issues affecting family law reform and to evaluate policy-makers' and practitioners' responses to these. In order to achieve these aims, I seek throughout to consider how the law may shape, and in turn be shaped by, attitudes and thinking about family life and family relationships, and I discuss cultural, historical, social, and political influences on the law's evolution and current working.

In my view, family law lacks a clear set of organising principles that might form a sufficient structure for a discussion of the subject. It is, however, possible to identify certain key themes that underpin its development. Probably the most significant of these is the extensive change in family structures and in the nature of family relationships that has been witnessed particularly in the last half-century. Alongside, and perhaps flowing from such changes, there has been a growing recognition of the differential impact that law can have on individual members of a family, and of the importance of childhood and gender. In the last twenty years or so, there has also been a realization of the central role played by (judicial) discretion in decision-making in family law, and of the problems this can create; but attempts to move to a more rule-based system have been found to have caused other difficulties. Perhaps ahead of other branches of civil law, family law practitioners and policy-makers have also been aware of the impact of the legal process in determining how the substantive law is experienced by its 'consumers'. Finally, there has long been debate over the proper role of state intervention in family life. I seek to explain and develop these themes in the first chapter of the book and to illustrate them throughout. However, on reflection, I decided that they would not provide an adequate framework for analysing the subject as a whole, and I concluded that I would instead adopt a broad 'family life cycle' approach. After the first chapter then, the book examines the creation of family relationships, traces their legal consequences, and examines their termination and aftermath.

Developments in international law are becoming increasingly significant in influencing thinking in the domestic arena, and inevitably the incorporation of the European Convention on Human Rights into domestic law has heightened awareness of the significance of human rights for the legal regulation of the family. I have therefore sought to ensure that the text reflects the relevance and importance of international law in evaluating English family law.

Because I have not sought to provide a full exposition of the law, I have been highly selective in the legal and other materials cited. I do not refer to every leading case on a topic, nor to the most recent authority that might be available. I do not seek to 'state the law' at a particular date, although I have taken account of the main developments up to the end of June 2001. I include a bibliography of the works that I regard as key sources for the discussion in the text, but these are no more than indicative further reading for those who are interested, and are not intended to be comprehensive.

This book is the product of my reading, discussion with colleagues and students, and reflection over many years. But I am particularly grateful to Chris Barton, Stephen Cretney, and Nigel Lowe, for the care they took in reading the book in draft and for their many helpful suggestions and amendments to the text. I also wish to record my thanks to Cardiff Law School for granting me study leave during the writing of the book.

Siblings, as the following chapters will bear out, receive scant recognition from family law. However, this book is dedicated to my sister, Diane Bryan, who has always been an unfailing source of encouragement and support.

Gillian Douglas

Contents

Table of Cases

Table of Statutes

Table of Conventions and Treaties

I

Introduction: Themes in Family Law

'THE FAMILY' OR 'FAMILIES'?

It might be thought that the concept of 'the family' is clear and well understood. After all, the family appears to have global significance and meaning, appearing in Article 16 of the Universal Declaration of Human Rights where it is proclaimed as 'the natural and fundamental group unit of society', a phrase repeated in other international instruments almost as a mantra. But the meaning of the phrase is not elucidated, providing scope (deliberately, no doubt) to different states with widely differing cultures and societies to attach their own particular understanding to what otherwise looks like a uniform concept. One might therefore expect that the family as understood in the west may conjure up an image radically different from that applying in, say, south east Asia, or the Islamic world.

Even within one society, the 'family' may be a concept open to numerous interpretations, each with a baggage of competing values. Using the definite article, referring to *the* family, suggests a commonly understood notion embodying a certain set of norms, but what picture does it convey? Compare, for example, the picture presented by the term 'single parent family' with that presented by the Royal Family. Qualifying the noun with an adjective suggests that there is something special or different about this particular type of family, that it deviates in some way from the norm. What this norm might be is best gleaned from political discussions of the family. When politicians refer to 'the family', they often seem to have a particular type of family in mind, usually incorporating a married relationship between a man and a woman, with offspring, and a sexual division of labour whereby the husband/father is the primary breadwinner and the wife/mother is primarily responsible for the home and the children. This model, which was the prevailing ideological *and* demographic type of household in the 1950s, has become less typical since then, but remains the aspirational focus of political policies of both left and right, albeit with some concessions to gender equality and economic imperatives requiring the paid labour of both men and women.

The norm of 'the family' may not only be highly contested, but also simply open to question. Does a married couple constitute a 'family', or must they have children to count? How far do ties of blood and marriage underpin what is meant by family, so that the ancestors, descendants, and other relatives marked on a family tree constitute one's 'real' family? If I divorce, do my ex-spouse and his 'family' cease to be part of my family, and if so, do they cease to be part of my children's family too? If I have a same-sex partner, are her parents and siblings now part of my family, and am I part of theirs?

Attempting to understand what constitutes the family is not helped by controversies regarding historical changes to family structure and relationships. Folk wisdom may suggest, for example, that the extended, multi-generational family living in one household has given way to the isolated nuclear family consisting of a maximum of two generations with rarely more than two children. But the extended family household of this type was never the historical norm in England and Wales, where it seems that the nuclear family model has indeed been the prevailing model (which is not to say that a *household* may not have included non-family members, such as servants or lodgers, and have been larger than the modern small household unit).

Furthermore, the family may be constructed from a variety of perspectives including the genetic, focusing upon the blood-tie; social, emphasizing the functions carried out by those standing in a family relationship to each other; psychological, exploring the ties of affect and emotion between individuals; legal, defining the family for the purposes of legally binding decisions and rules; and ideological, promoting a particular form of family structure and behaviour as the desirable norm. These are not necessarily discrete categories—the genetic tie may be used for legal purposes, and ideological notions of the family may be manifested in legal and social policies. It can follow that differing notions of what is meant by the family may be masked by an assumption that we are all talking about the same thing and from the same perspective.

A BODY OF FAMILY LAW?

The family, then, is not a naturally occurring fixed phenomenon but a concept which is constructed in a multiplicity of ways and for a variety of purposes. This plurality of 'ways of seeing' helps to explain why, because of the motivations and policies lying behind their creation at different times, laws may appear to be predicated upon models of the family which not only conflict with non-legal conceptions but which may even be internally inconsistent. Unlike other branches of law, such as trusts or tort, which are clearly legal creations, family law relates, in some way, to an entity—the family—which has meaning, as we have seen, outside the legal domain. This creates a problem of boundary-setting. Which laws can sensibly be described as part of family law? Many different fields of law may have an impact on family members and family life. For example, tax law may distinguish between married and unmarried couples; criminal law may lay down special rules concerning the liability of family members for acts towards each other; housing law may determine rights to succeed to the tenancy of property according to family relationships. But one might not automatically regard these examples as aspects of something called family law. Rather, the essence of family law is that part of the law which is concerned with the recognition and regulation of certain family relationships and the implications of such recognition. Moreover, although this may now be changing, family law in England and Wales has focused primarily on the nuclear family model, with comparatively little attention paid to the existence of other kin. Outside of the context of inheritance and succession there has been little recognition of kinship as giving rise to any legal claims or obligations (even though social and cultural norms may seek to emphasize moral ties arising from such relationships).

In focusing upon *recognition*, we will see that *non-recognition* is equally important to the discussion. The choice of which relationships will be given legal significance and which will be 'left' to other branches of law is a political and ideological one with important ramifications. For example, a lack of any special regime to deal with the property rights of cohabiting couples may betoken a determination to privilege marital relationships over non-marital ones. The imposition of a liability to provide 'child support' for one's biological child, but not one's step-child, may reflect a particular notion of what is a 'real' family. A refusal to countenance marriage between homosexuals may derive from a view of marriage as essentially heterosexual in character. Thus, what is left out may be as important as what is included, in understanding the content of family law and the messages it may send. Nor can the 'peripheral' laws, such as tax, housing, or crime, be completely ignored. To be able to evaluate the impact of law upon families, those parts of law which do not seem central may nonetheless have to be taken into account because they may have significant effects in structuring relationships and influencing modes of behaviour.

PRINCIPLES OR THEMES?

Because family law has emerged as a body of law concerned with regulating a non-legal concept, and because the nature and form of that concept has undergone (and is still undergoing) rapid change, it may appear to lack a set of key coherent principles which consistently shape its development. Rather, it has grown piecemeal in response to perceived social changes, often presented as 'problems' to be tackled. For example, the 'problem' of absent parents who fail to pay adequate maintenance for their children, or the 'crisis' represented by the 'high' divorce rate, are made the subjects of legal reform. These perceived social changes, as we shall see, pull family loyalties in different directions because they are underpinned by different understandings of what should constitute appropriate family behaviour.

Notwithstanding this apparent confusion, it seems to be accepted both internationally (as reflected in the Universal Declaration of Human Rights noted above) and domestically that the goal of all family policy should be the promotion of 'stable family life', which in turn is regarded as the corner-stone of a stable society. The fear of change in family structures and behaviour, and the presentation of the effects of change as 'problems', reflects this belief. Family policy may use economic, social, and cultural means to seek to achieve stability. If it is thought, perhaps, that couples face financial disincentives to marry, then fiscal policy might be used to encourage them to marry, or remain married. The 'approved' roles of parents and children may be reinforced through social stereotypes, such as the obedient child, the responsible father, the caring mother. In the legal sphere, the objective of family stability may be achieved through the promotion of certainty of, and harmony in, family relationships. For example, if it can be established with certainty who is legally related to whom, the legal nature of their relationship can be elucidated and its boundaries determined. 'Appropriate' family behaviour, such as fidelity in marriage can be enforced by clarifying who is married and who is not. Knowledge of the legal consequences of relationships can be used to predict and plan future conduct. Equally importantly, stability may be promoted if relationships are harmonious rather than conflictual. The legal system can seek to limit family members' antagonism towards one another, particularly when relationships are ending. This may be especially important where, although the *adults* may be terminating their relationship with one another, they will continue to have a relationship with their *children* or other family members, and where it will therefore be desirable to preserve or enhance communication with each other. Harmony may also be associated with the privacy of the family. It may be contended that involvement of law and legal processes may worsen difficult family relationships by polarizing positions and magnifying grievances because of the need to express these in the narrow legal language of rights and duties, or fault and innocence. Keeping the family sphere separate from the public world, by denying legal redress to certain types of family disputes, may be promoted as both a means of maintaining the stability of the family as a collective entity, and freedom from state control over how family members choose to behave towards each other.

CHANGES IN FAMILY LIFE

THE STATISTICAL EVIDENCE

It sometimes seems that modern debates on families and law are dominated by statistics which are used to 'prove' that the family is in crisis. It is important to recognize the significance, but also the limitations, of these statistics, and in particular, to unpick the value judgments which may be used in their interpretation. A brief sketch of some of these statistics is presented here, in order to illustrate these points.

Marriage statistics show a fall in the marriage rate throughout the European Union over the past thirty years. Marriage appears to be relatively popular in the United Kingdom, with a rate in 2002 the same as the EU average, at 4.8 marriages per 1,000 population (compared, for example, with the lowest rate of 3.9 in Belgium). Yet the *number* of first marriages in the United Kingdom fell from 459,000 in 1971 to just over 286,000 in 2001. The average age at which men married for the first time rose over the same period from 24.6 years to 30.6, and from 22.6 to 28.4 years for women (ONS, 2004*a*: 31, 32).

What picture emerges from these statistics? Marriage appears to be becoming less attractive, and yet, given the increasing proportion of remarriages, many of those who have tasted it appear ready to try again (nowithstanding the higher rate of failure in such cases). Is marriage merely being postponed, or is it being permanently rejected? Do these figures suggest that there is a social problem to be resolved in some way (higher tax breaks for those marrying, perhaps?) or simply that people's attitudes and conduct are changing? In other words, does it matter that fewer people are getting married?

The same questions need to be asked in response to other changes. For example, the proportion of non-married women under 60 in Great Britain who were cohabiting more than doubled between 1986 and 2002, from 13 per cent to 28 per cent, with nearly a third of divorced women doing so (ONS, 2004a: 32). What significance should be given to this information? By itself, it tells us little. But there may be family law and family policy implications. If large numbers of people are cohabiting instead of marrying, should the law relating to marriage be extended to them so that they can take advantage of its benefits and protections? Or should the disadvantages and penalties of cohabitation be strengthened, in order to deter people from entering into it, and encourage them to marry instead? Does it make a difference if the couple have children, upon whom it may be unjust to impose such burdens? The proportion of children in Great Britain born outside marriage has nearly quadrupled since 1980, to 41 per cent of all live births in 2002. Nearly 64 per cent of these births were jointly registered by parents living at the same address, more than twice the proportion in 1986 (ONS, 2004a: 34). These figures suggest that there is no longer a significant social stigma attached to having a child outside marriage. Given this apparent acceptance of what might previously have been regarded as immoral behaviour, does it make sense for the law to treat children differently because of their parents' marital status?

Now consider the divorce statistics. Divorce has been a major focus of legal attention since the 1950s, with two fundamental changes in the law (discussed in Chapter 6) in 1969 and 1996, although the Government decided not to bring the latter into force. Before the first change, the number of divorces granted in 1968 was 45,036. In 1988, the number had roughly trebled, to 152,139. By 2002, it had fallen back to 143,865 (Lord Chancellor's Department, 2003: Table 5.5). What *cannot* be concluded from these figures is that the rate of *marriage breakdown* has more than trebled over the period, for the number of divorces granted is not a measure of marriage breakdown but only of legal activity. We do not know how many married couples separate but do not divorce, and we do not know how many did so in the past. We cannot therefore say for certain what the rate of marriage failure is, nor whether it is higher than in previous times when divorce was difficult, or impossible, to obtain. For the same reasons, caution must be exercised when comparing the divorce rate in the United Kingdom with that in other countries. While the UK has the second highest divorce rate in the EU at 2.7 per 1,000 population compared with an EU average of 1.9 per 1,000 (ONS, 2004a: Table 2.13), this may be, in part at least, a consequence of the ease of availability of legal divorce and does not show that British marriages are necessarily more prone to fail than in other states.

One final group of statistics should be presented to complete this sketch of family change. The phenomenon most open to attention by policy-makers is the growth in lone parent families. As might be expected from the divorce and birth statistics already presented, the proportion of such families has grown, from 7 per cent in 1972 to 23 per cent in 2003 of all families with dependent children (ONS, 2004a: 27). Around two-thirds of these are headed by divorced or separated mothers, although the fastest growing group are never-married mothers (mainly ex-cohabitants). About 10 per cent of these families are headed by fathers (Haskey, 2002). The concern which attaches to these figures may lie less in their implications for social stability and morality, and more in their cost to the taxpayer, for social security spending on lone parents rose from £2 billion in 1984/85 to £10.4 billion in 1998/99 (Department of Social Security, 1999: 3).

What conclusions can be drawn from these statistics? It does seem that attitudes to family relationships are changing. The assumption that most people will eventually marry and have children and that therefore the law can be predicated on this basis can no longer safely be made. The law, and family policies, may have to encompass a wider, and probably more volatile, range of family structures. A parallel can be drawn with the world of work. The assumptions (no doubt just as mythical as those relating to families) that a man could expect to do one kind of job, possibly with only a handful of employers, throughout his working life, and that a woman could give up work once she was married or had children, have been falsified by changing economic demands. People are now advised to be flexible, to prepare for change and insecurity. The same appears to be true for their family lives and family law may be required to respond to this new (or newly recognized) reality.

THE PURSUIT OF INTIMACY AND PERSONAL FULFILMENT

Another way of presenting these changes is to focus on people's motivations and understandings of their relationships. Again, however, one must be alive to the value judgments which lie behind the accounts. Are people less willing to 'work at' their relationships now? Such an interpretation implies a moral weakness to be contrasted with the stoic acceptance of earlier times. This kind of approach is particularly prevalent in politicians' and media representations of family change, with soundbite references to deadbeat dads and feckless females which may prove highly influential in shaping legal policy. An alternative way of evaluating what is happening is to stress people's continuing search for self-fulfilment and emotional satisfaction from their intimate relationships. Here, the account becomes one of viewing relationships in late modern society as constantly subject to negotiation and re-negotiation as people engage in a 'project of the self' concerned with personal growth (Giddens, 1991; Beck and Beck-Gernsheim, 1995). Traditions and habits no longer constrain actions, and people feel free to move on when dissatisfied. A reluctance to make a long-term commitment for fear that it will prove wanting may underpin delay in entering into marriage, or a turning away from marriage itself; a refusal to accept an unsatisfactory relationship may shed light on the resort to divorce. Even the decline in the birth rate, which is a feature of all developed societies, may reflect a concern for economic improvement and personal comfort. Such attitudes may be regarded, not as selfish, but as manifestations of freedom and equality. While women might once have been constrained by economic dependence and social mores to accept a life lived in a private sphere shaped and controlled by a male head (father or husband), they are now at liberty to pursue their own autonomous goals.

Such analyses appear compelling, but again, caution is called for. They may be presented as demonstrating an—inevitable—progress away from the dark ages of suppression and indifference to emotional well-being toward an enlightened era of tolerance, opportunity, and intimacy. They may assume a degree of personal independence and control actually lacking in many people's lives, especially those of women and children, and they may fail to take into account the ties of dependence created by children and other relatives. While they may trace an increasing emphasis upon having a child as a source of personal emotional satisfaction, who will not prove wanting as another adult might, they do not consider why, if this is the case, many fathers lose contact with their children after their relationship with the mother ends. Nor do they address why economic policies are promoted which appear increasingly to drive parents away from staying at home with their children and out into the workplace.

Regardless of the explanations and theories which might be put forward, the rate and extent of changes from what had become ideologically perceived as the norm of family structure and family life are a constant theme underpinning the development of family law, as will be seen in succeeding chapters.

THE LEGAL NATURE OF FAMILY RELATIONSHIPS

Change has occurred not only in the demographic and social picture, but also in the legal conceptualization of family relationships (Cretney, 2003). Here, one can trace a movement stemming largely from female emancipation in the nineteenth century and the development of human rights thinking in the twentieth (though no doubt underpinned by the same shift to individualism and personal fulfilment outlined above), which has reflected and influenced a reduced emphasis upon stigma, and a growing recognition of the interests and needs of individual family members.

THE DECLINE IN STIGMA

We have noted that the growth of cohabitation and birth outside marriage may well reflect a decreased social stigma associated with these activities. However, cohabitation has received only limited and isolated recognition in English law. For example, it may be possible for a person to succeed to a tenancy which had been in the name of his or her partner before their death, and should their relationship break down, there is now provision for the tenancy to be transferred from one partner to the other. However, if they occupy a home which is owned or being paid for with a mortgage in the name of one partner only, neither remedy is available unless it can be proved that, as a matter of property law, the other is entitled to the home or a share of it. This is because the transfer of *ownership* or a share in the equity value of the home, as a matter of discretionary family law as distinct from property law, is associated with the powers of the court on a divorce, and policy-makers have fought shy of equating marriage and cohabitation for fear of downgrading the significance of marriage.

Where children are concerned, however, the injustice of visiting the sins of the fathers upon their children appears to have led to what may have been the key change in western family law in the twentieth century— the abolition of virtually all of the discriminatory effects of birth outside wedlock. The placing of children in an equal legal position regardless of the marital status of their parents is immensely significant from a symbolic perspective, undermining the centrality of marriage and also shifting the focus of attention from the *adults'* relationship to the position of the *child*.

FROM THE FAMILY TO THE INDIVIDUAL

However constituted or defined, each family is made up of the individuals within it, and their interests may be congruent or diverse. The assumption that the interests of all family members can be identified with that of the 'head' of the family may be productive of the abuse of power or to the detriment of individual welfare. This may be manifested in actions ranging from domestic violence by a husband against his wife, to the refusal of parents to permit life-saving treatment of their child because of their religious beliefs. Much of modern family law is concerned with balancing the interests and needs of different family members, and to resolve conflicts between them; this may necessitate a focus upon individuals, rather than upon the family as a unitary entity.

RIGHTS AND RESPONSIBILITIES

A growing awareness of the position of each individual family member has made it more important, but more complicated, to define the nature and content of their relationships with each other. Traditionally, it was accepted that wives and children were subordinate and subservient to the husband/father, either because of biblical prescription or 'natural' inferiority. Although husband and wife theoretically owed mutual obligations to each other, the power conferred on the husband made the flow of obligation largely one way, with the husband granted extensive rights over the wife's person and property. Legitimate children were subject to the commands of their father, with the mother having no legal right to gainsay him.

The impact of female emancipation improved the position of women, as wives and mothers, during the nineteenth and twentieth centuries, and left them ultimately in an equal legal position with their husbands. Moreover, they were in a superior legal position to *unmarried* fathers, who were denied automatic rights over their children until the Adoption and Children Act 2002 put them in virtually the same legal position as married fathers provided they are named on the child's birth certificate. Equal rights to support, to physical autonomy, and to occupation of the family home, were granted to both spouses from the 1960s onward, as part of a wider international drive towards the recognition of women's rights. This was most explicitly demonstrated in the Convention on the Elimination of All Forms of Discrimination Against Women (1979), to which the United Kingdom is a signatory. Article 16 requires States Parties to 'take all appropriate measures to eliminate discrimination against women in all matters relating to marriage and family relations and in particular. . .[to] ensure, on a basis of equality of men and women' the same family rights and responsibilities.

Protocol 7, Article 5 of the European Convention on Human Rights[1] similarly proclaims that:

Spouses shall enjoy equality of rights and responsibilities of a private law character between them, and in their relations with their children, as to marriage, during marriage and in the event of its dissolution . . .

However, the ambit of this obligation is unclear. Does it require equality of outcome so that the parties emerge from the marriage on an equal footing (and if so, does this mean formal or substantive equality)? One may postulate from it two models of modern marriage, both of which imply some form of equality between the spouses but which view this equality in very different ways. On the one hand, there is what may be called a 'partnership of equals' model. This regards the two spouses as juridical equals and assumes, but does not ensure, that they are also equal economically and culturally. It presupposes that the spouses enter into and live through the marriage on equal terms, even if the reality is different. The alternative model may be called a 'joint enterprise' model. This conceives of marriage as a jointly undertaken project in which the parties assume equal, but possibly different, burdens and have equal rights to the fruits of their labour. To ensure substantive equality, one spouse may have to recompense the other for sacrifices made for the good of the marriage and family unit as a whole. (These two models could of course apply just as well to cohabitation relationships.) It will be seen in the following Chapters that modern English law contains elements of both the partnership of equals and the joint enterprise models, both in relation to marriage and other family relationships.

Simultaneously with the move towards equal rights between husband and wife, their legal position vis-à-vis their children began to change, eventually to be replaced by an emphasis upon the *responsibility* of both parents towards their children. This trend has been part of a general recognition of children as individual rights-bearers and as subjects of the law, and not just its objects. In domestic law, this trend was manifested first by a shift from the assertion of parental (usually paternal) rights to make decisions regarding children, towards reliance upon seeking to ensure the best interests of the child, and to make the child's welfare the 'paramount consideration' when taking decisions affecting that child. With a distinct phase of growing up, through adolescence, emerging as a

---

[1] But the United Kingdom has not ratified this provision because, as will be explained in later Chapters, it is believed that certain rules of English law are incompatible with it.

powerful aspect of twentieth century western culture, came an increased focus upon the exercise by a child of the right to *autonomy* over her own decision-making.

In Hohfeldian terms (1919), a right, properly so-called, possessed by one person requires a correlative duty imposed upon another to permit the right to be enjoyed. Where the adult relationship is concerned, the grant of equal rights to wives also produced a symmetry of obligations. In relation to children, the duties of parenthood came to assume greater ideological significance than the rights, and eventually resulted in the institution of a concept of 'parental responsibility', enshrined in s 3(1) of the Children Act 1989, which encompasses 'all the rights, duties, powers, responsibilities and authority which by law a parent of a child has in relation to the child and his property'.

HUMAN RIGHTS AND THE FAMILY

Inevitably, the growth of human rights doctrine during the second half of the twentieth century contributed to the shattering of the perception of the family as a unit, and to the emergence of each family member as an individual bearer of rights which could be deployed, not just against the state, but also indirectly against other family members. Two key human rights instruments—the European Convention on Human Rights and the United Nations Convention on the Rights of the Child 1989—have an increasingly important part to play here. Most of the rights enshrined in the European Convention were incorporated into English law by the Human Rights Act 1998. The UN Convention has been ratified by the UK, but not enacted into domestic law. Nonetheless, its wide-ranging catalogue of rights for children, covering protection (e.g. from abuse), participation as active members of society, and provision of adequate care, education, and support, provides a yardstick against which aspects of family law such as how far children are consulted regarding arrangements for their upbringing, are increasingly judged (see below).

The European Convention on Human Rights guarantees a number of rights which are of direct relevance to family law and which have begun to influence how the competing interests of family members are to be assessed and how the state should respond to these. Although not drafted with children in mind, it is important to note that *all* family members, including children, may rely on the relevant rights. The re-introduction of the language of rights into the family law arena, after a century of attempting to remove this from the family law lexicon, especially where the parent-child relationship is concerned, has necessitated a new approach to considering how family disputes should be resolved and has re-invigorated arguments based on justice, as distinct from welfare or needs.

Section 3 of the Human Rights Act requires that so far as it is possible to do so, legislation must be read and given effect in a way which is compatible with the Convention rights. Where the High Court or above is unable to interpret the statute so as to render its effect Convention-compliant, it may grant a declaration of incompatibility under s 4. These provisions mean that precedents pre-dating the entry into force of the Act may be ignored (even by the lower courts) where they are incompatible with the terms of the Convention rights, but that where *primary legislation* is found to be incompatible, Parliamentary sovereignty is upheld because a court cannot strike down such legislation. In such a case, s 10 of the Act empowers a Minister of the Crown by order (i.e. subordinate legislation) to make amendments to the legislation.

Although human rights law is usually concerned with the control of state power against the individual and hence is more directly applicable to challenges against state organs (such as a local authority, or central government), the European Convention on Human Rights has what may be described as indirect horizontal effect and may thus be relevant to private family matters too. This is because s 6 of the Act provides that it is unlawful for a public authority (which includes a court) to act in a way that is incompatible with Convention rights. This means that even where a court is handling what looks like a private matter, for example, a dispute between divorcing parents over the contact arrangements to be made regarding their child, the court is bound to ensure that its decision is compliant with the requirements of the Convention. The decision it reaches will thus indirectly enforce the right of one family member against that of another. Consider, for example, Article 8 of the Convention, which appears most relevant to family issues. This guarantees that:

(1) Everyone has the right to respect for his private and family life, his home and his correspondence.
(2) There shall be no interference by a public authority with the exercise of this right except such as is in accordance with the law and is necessary in a democratic society. . .for the protection of health or morals, or for the protection of the rights and freedoms of others.

If a mother does not wish the father to see their child, because she fears this will disrupt her relationship with her new husband, she may argue that if the court upholds the father's claim to have contact, it will be infringing her right to respect for the family life she has with her husband and the family unit they have created with the child. Equally, the father may argue that a refusal of contact infringes his right to an ongoing relationship with his child. The child may also have her own views on the matter. The court, as a public authority within s 6, will have to determine the dispute by balancing the family members'competing rights and deciding in whose favour that balance should be struck (see Chapter 5 for discussion of how it attempts to do this).

Article 8 imposes both positive and negative duties on the state. On the one hand, the state must not interfere with the exercise of the right except where this is 'necessary in a democratic society' in order, *inter alia*, to protect the rights and freedoms of others (in such a case thus immediately requiring a comparison, and weighing, of the rights of one family member against another). Determining when such interference is 'necessary' will usually require a consideration of whether it was a 'proportionate' response to the situation. For example, a decision by a local authority to remove a child from her parents because of a risk of abuse will be proportionate if the perceived risk to the child is sufficiently great and there is no lesser means of protecting the child than by her removal. In this example, the parents' right to respect for their family life with the child must be subordinated to the child's right to life or bodily integrity (under Articles 2 and 3).

On the other hand, the right to respect for family life may require a state to take positive measures to recognize and foster relationships, for example, by enabling legal ties to be made between a child born outside marriage and her blood relatives,[2] by ensuring that parents are able to participate fully in decisions taken by courts or administrative bodies affecting their child,[3] or by seeking to reunite a parent with her child where the other parent has failed to return the child after a contact visit.[4] This positive sphere of responsibility enables arguments for family law reform to embrace the Convention rights as a further justification for action—for example, as will be discussed in Chapter 2, to recognize a person's gender reassignment so that they can marry in their new gender.

This fragmentation of the family into its constituent members is controversial. It may be argued that a focus upon rights and duties ignores the essence of family life, which is the undertaking of tasks out of love

[2] *Marckx v Belgium* (1979) 2 EHRR 330.
[3] *W, R, O, B and H v United Kingdom* [1988] 2 FLR 445.
[4] *Hansen v Turkey* [2004] 1 FLR 142.

and affection, rather than because of legal constraint. It may pit one family member against another, and undermine feelings of security and trust. The extent to which the individual, as distinct from the family, should be the focus of policy is a difficult and continuing problem for family law.

FROM STATUS TO CONTRACT?

We have already seen how the decline in stigmatic associations of certain family structures has been mirrored in legal developments. This trend, and the increased focus on the individual, should be compared with the identification of a movement in legal history 'from status to contract' as identified by Sir Henry Maine. Maine argued that whereas in earlier times, one's legal personality and the resulting rights and obligations derived from one's religious and familial status, in modern society, these depend upon one's entry into freely negotiated contracts. A contractual model of family relationships appears to fit nicely the new emphasis upon reciprocal rights and duties. Entry into marriage, for example, can be seen as the acceptance of a contract which sets out the terms which will govern the spouses' behaviour. Marriage has indeed been viewed as a type of contract in Judaeo-Christian doctrine, and in modern law, there is a clear drive towards permitting couples to shape their relationship through contractual terms which will be given legal effect, although this has tended to impact upon broken relationships rather than continuing ones (see Chapters 3 and 6). On the other hand, the introduction of a new legal status, 'civil partnership', for same-sex couples, suggests that the acquisition of a publicly-recognized status still carries its attractions (see Chapter 2).

The progression (and Maine certainly viewed the trend as progressive) from status to contract may be more difficult to discern in the parent/child relationship. It is true that the abolition of the discriminatory effects of illegitimacy (and the eventual recognition of forms of cohabitation) reflects a rejection of status as the determinant of legal identity. However, it is more difficult to see the scope for a contractual model here, since the child can scarcely be regarded as having contracted with her parents for forms of support and obligation. But the relationship between the parents, qua parents, may be viewed in this way to a limited extent, and we will see how agreements regarding the care and upbringing of children are also strongly encouraged by the modern legal system (see Chapters 3 and 5).

STATE INTERVENTION IN FAMILY LIFE

THE MEANING OF 'INTERVENTION'

Alongside the emergence of a contractual model of family relationships, the eighteenth and nineteenth centuries also saw the development of a liberal conception of the family as a private sphere beyond the reach of state interference. From this stems the attitude that the state should not tell parents how to bring up their children, or that violence within the family is 'domestic' and somehow deserving of different treatment from violence between strangers. Much agonizing may be expressed by reformers regarding the 'acceptable' limits of state intervention in family life, but such debates take place in apparent ignorance of two fundamental points. First, the state has long 'interfered' in family life by laying down expectations of behaviour, ranging from the obligations of marriage (demonstrated, if only negatively, by the historical grounds for separation or divorce) to the requirement, since 1870, that parents ensure their children receive education. Secondly, it ignores the fact that what goes on 'in the private sphere' is thereby *endorsed* by the state's willingness to allow it to take place. Thus, by declining to 'tell parents that they cannot hit their children', the state sanctions their corporal punishment. It is not that there is no law forbidding such punishment, but that there is a law permitting it. On this basis, there is no such thing as 'non-intervention' in family life, because where law and policy draw a line, they mark a judgment on what is to be regarded as acceptable behaviour between family members.

Arguments that state intervention is somehow 'wrong' may conjure up images of a totalitarian state which directs how children are to be brought up and indoctrinates them regardless of parental preferences. The extent to which people may live their lives and bring up their children according to their own beliefs and value systems is indeed one of the tests of a free society, and is reflected in Article 8 of the European Convention on Human Rights (see above) which guarantees the right to respect for both one's private and family life. The juxtaposition of the concepts of privacy and family is significant and reflects classical liberal thinking.

POSITIVE AND NEGATIVE INTERVENTION

It should not be thought that all overt state intervention is coercive. The creation of a welfare state might be criticized by some right-wing commentators as destructive of individual and family responsibility and autonomy, but it may also be viewed as the collective expression of concern for all members of society and a factor which can facilitate and strengthen family relationships. The balance between encouraging welfare dependency and breaking family ties is a difficult one which continues to exercise those responsible for social policy. Few nowadays would argue that the provision of a comprehensive health service undermines family solidarity by removing the onus of caring for one's relatives, but the debate concerning who should care for family members when a relationship ends retains strong echoes of such sentiments. The question whether the state should support an ex-wife, or mother and children, or whether her former husband and the children's father should do so is a key issue in family law reform, with a pendulum effect caused by political and economic spending priorities and complicated by ideological and moral arguments, producing now a swing towards state support, now a return to individual obligation.

Where intervention *is* coercive, difficult decisions may have to be taken and again, the underlying values influencing them need to be recognized. Should parents, for example, be permitted to withdraw their child from sex education or religious education in school because these are incompatible with their own beliefs? Protocol 1, Article 2 of the European Convention provides that 'the state shall respect the right of parents to ensure. . .education and teaching [provided by the state is] in conformity with their own religious and philosophical convictions'. This therefore supports the right of parents to withdraw their children, although this is not a completely unfettered right. Yet the Article also guarantees that '[no] person shall be denied the right to education'. Can a child therefore insist that she attend lessons deemed unsuitable by her parents? This example demonstrates clearly how rights assumed to offer protection against a coercive state may come to be claimed in effect against other individual family members, with the state inevitably deemed by some to be acting coercively if it upholds either the right of the parents, or of the child, against the other.

Should the child be *removed* from the family, because of beliefs or practices deemed unacceptable in modern western society? Cases of physical, emotional, and sexual abuse might appear clear-cut situations where the state must act to protect the child, but at what point do 'firm discipline' or cultural norms regarding early marriage become regarded as abusive and therefore warranting intervention? At what point should social workers cease the attempt to 'rehabilitate' a child with her birth family after she has been abused, and resolve instead to find her a permanent substitute home, perhaps through adoption? Would the answer be different if, for example, the child was a Balkan refugee, displaced because of war and brought to this country by well-meaning volunteers who then decide that they can bring her up in a far better way than would be possible in an orphanage or refugee camp? What if her parents or other relatives are discovered, perhaps some years later, by which time the child can no longer remember her native language and has become closely attached to her carers?[5] The courts may be faced with the difficult task of somehow balancing the child's right to know of her origins (guaranteed by Article 7 of the United Nations Convention on the Rights of the Child) with welfare concerns which might argue for keeping her in a settled and loving environment to which she has become adapted, and further with the right of her relatives under Article 8 of the European Convention on Human Rights to respect for *their* family life with her. Is the court's decision an interference in family life if it compels the carers to hand the child back to her relatives, or if it permits the child to remain with them? Is it to be categorized as state interference at all, or simply as the resolution of a problem?

THE SIGNIFICANCE OF DISCRETION IN FAMILY LAW DECISION-MAKING

BREADTH OF DISCRETION

The main task undertaken by the courts dealing with family law is to handle disputes between family members, usually arising from divorce. These disputes focus upon two issues; the financial and property arrangements to be made, and the arrangements for the children. In each case, the court is given a broad discretion to reach a decision which is tailor-made for the parties, albeit with some limited guidance, in the form of a check-list of factors to bear in mind in so doing.

If called upon to decide, for example, with which parent a child should live after their divorce, the court is placed under a duty, under s 1(1) of the Children Act 1989, to treat the child's welfare as its paramount consideration. In exercising this judgment, the court is guided by a range of issues which it must take into account, including the child's ascertainable wishes and feelings, any risk of harm, the child's age, sex, and background, and so on. But there is no guidance on how to rank these in order

---

[5] See *Re K (Adoption and Wardship)* [1997] 2 FLR 221, CA.

of importance. While in some cases, the decision may be straightforward, in others, value judgments may inevitably affect the outcome. For example, suppose that the two parents have shared the care and upbringing of the child, who is now aged 18 months, because each has worked part-time. One judge may consider, influenced by assumptions about appropriate parental roles for men and women, that a child of this age would be best off with the child's mother. The judge would not be upholding the *right* of the mother to have the child live with her, but would be deciding that the child's *welfare* required this outcome. Another judge may reject this view as outmoded, but be left pondering how to decide the dispute. If each parent is apparently as well able to care for the child as the other, and the child enjoys a good relationship with both, the judge might as well toss a coin. Since this would be regarded as unprincipled, the judge is compelled to find *some* difference between the two upon which to justify a decision, but the statute does not provide a ready answer to the dilemma, and even the case law inevitably stresses the individuality of each decision and its application to its own particular facts.

Similarly, in deciding on the financial arrangements to be made when spouses divorce, the court is directed by s 25(1) of the Matrimonial Causes Act 1973 to 'have regard to all the circumstances of the case' and, if the couple have minor children, to give first consideration (not paramount) to *their* welfare. The court is then obliged to consider a list of matters, including the parties' financial resources, needs, age, standard of living, and conduct. The only other 'steer' that the court receives from the statute as to what would be a desirable outcome, is the obligation under s 25A to consider whether a 'clean break', in the sense of no continuing financial obligations between the spouses, can be achieved, either immediately, or after a fixed duration of time.

Nonetheless, *trends* in the case law, governing both financial arrangements and disputes concerning children, provide some guidance to lawyers who must advise clients on whether a case is worth pursuing, and they will also rely upon their knowledge of what the judges in their local courts tend to prefer, and manoeuvre their clients accordingly.

'BARGAINING IN THE SHADOW OF THE LAW'

Rules of thumb have therefore had to be evolved because of the overriding demand of the system to dispose of cases as quickly and effortlessly (as far as the *courts* are concerned), as possible. The chief way of achieving this goal is to encourage the parties to settle the dispute themselves, rather than to expect the court to arrive at a solution for them, and in fact, the vast majority of financial and children's arrangements are *not* adjudicated by a judge, but are settled after negotiation between the parties, often (but not always) with the help of their lawyers. Encouragement can be positive, and negative. On the positive side, it may be suggested that the parties attempt mediation, whereby a neutral third party helps them to talk through with each other the arrangements that they would like to make and move towards a compromise. Where lawyers are retained, their knowledge of the system and of the likely outcome of disputes if they do proceed to adjudication, can enable them to advise their clients and steer them towards a realization that the deal being offered through negotiation is the best which can be achieved. Such a process has been dubbed 'bargaining in the shadow of the law' (Mnookin and Kornhauser, 1979), because the law provides a framework within which the parties themselves can, and indeed are expected to, reach a mutually acceptable solution.

But there are many more negative incentives to settle, which are also associated with this model. Chief among these are the costs and delays apparently inherent in the legal system. These can turn the negotiating process into a poker game to be won by the party who is most prepared to tough it out and wait for the other to blink. A spouse who needs to resolve the question of what will happen to the matrimonial home, because, for example, he cannot afford to support a mortgage *and* pay rent, may feel compelled to agree to a settlement more favourable to the other spouse in order to divest himself of the mortgage sooner rather than hang on in the hope of a better deal later. Similarly, the 'shadow' of the law may be so vague and murky that it is impossible for the lawyer to predict with any accuracy the likely outcome of an adjudication.

In a discretionary system which may depend upon the lawyers' local knowledge of how things are viewed and handled, or, as Sarat and Felstiner put it, 'knowledge of the ropes, not knowledge of the rules' (1995: 106), the task for the lawyer may be to negotiate, not so much with the other side, as with her own client, to educate the client into these local norms and to persuade her to agree to the proposals being put. If the lawyer is actually wrong in her assessment of the system and the likely outcome, the client may obtain a poor deal.

Even if the lawyer predicts accurately the decision which the local judge will make, the likelihood is that different judges, although guided by the generalized rules of thumb, will reach different decisions. A point may be reached when the benefit of individualized justice with solutions tailored to particular family circumstances, which underpins the rationale of discretion, is outweighed by the disadvantage of inconsistency and its potential for injustice between different litigants in different locations.

A FORMULA INSTEAD?

It may be that, if these problems, important though they are, had not had implications for public finance, then nothing much would have been done to deal with them. However, public money is affected directly by them in two different ways. First, there are the costs of providing access to a legal system which processes disputes according to this discretionary model, both through the Community Legal Service (formerly legal aid), and the costs connected with staffing the courts. Secondly, the extent to which individual couples reach settlements (either negotiated or court-imposed) that do not meet their full living costs will impact upon the social security system which may be required to meet the shortfall. For example, when a clean break settlement is reached so that a former spouse is not required to make continuing maintenance payments to the other, her on-going financial needs will either be met from her own resources or from her entitlement to welfare benefits such as income support. We have seen that the growth in the amount spent on such benefits for lone parent families has increased as the number of such families has risen, and the majority of these families are headed by divorced or separated mothers whom one would expect would be supported by their former spouses. It is clear and indeed, was well understood (as we will see in Chapter 6), that the social security system has been used to make up any difference between the amount of money needed to live on and that forthcoming from the other spouse. Once these drains on public expenditure became politically controversial, policy-makers looked for a cheaper solution.

Their attempted remedy was to produce an alternative approach which, by increasing the certainty of the eventual outcome, would both encourage early settlement and provide a degree of consistency between different decision-makers. The scope for such an approach appears to have been greater in the financial sphere than when dealing with children cases, perhaps because there is a natural reluctance to reduce the needs of children to a set of automatic nostrums. However, where the allocation of money and property is at stake, there is less concern. Accordingly, the calculation of the amount of money which should be spent on supporting children, or the assessment of the appropriate division of property on divorce have been made subject, in many jurisdictions including this one, to the application of a formulaic approach. The United Kingdom Child Support scheme, enacted in 1991, is discussed further in Chapters 3 and

6, but here it may be noted as a clear attempt to introduce an 'expert system' into the family law sphere. Its failure may be attributable, in part, to the ultimate impossibility of providing a 'just' system dependent upon fixed rules to be applied to a very wide range of circumstances. But the Governmental decision to reform, rather than abandon it suggests that the effectively untrammelled discretion which characterized the matrimonial and children's jurisdiction until the 1990s is not now regarded as acceptable or affordable. The continuing search for the third way between discretion and rules is a key feature of modern family law.

PROCESS AND EXPERTISE

THE FAMILY JUSTICE SYSTEM

Since family disputes may raise non-legal issues, such as what is going to be in a child's long-term physical and psychological best interests, they may require non-legal expertise to arrive at the best solution. Further, even where the dispute is strictly legal, it is likely to have additional dimensions for the parties, in terms of their emotional well-being. A couple ostensibly arguing over whether the marital home should be sold on their divorce, for example, may in fact be more consumed by feelings of rejection or loss caused by the end of the marriage, and the legal dispute may be a means of expressing those feelings. Awareness of these non-legal dimensions has prompted both practitioners and policy-makers to seek alternative means of dealing with family disputes. Such alternatives cover a wide spectrum. At one level, there have been attempts to make the legal process more 'user-friendly', such as by providing court rooms which are less formal and frightening than criminal courts, and abandoning open court hearings and the need to recite unpleasant and distressing allegations when these are undefended anyway. Additionally, family lawyers have been exhorted, by policy-makers and through professional codes of practice, to adopt a 'conciliatory' approach to negotiations in family matters, which seeks to minimize antagonism between the parties and to foster constructive communication so as to promote good relationships after the end of the legal process. 'Collaborative law', as practised by some lawyers in the United States, entails lawyers for both parties undertaking not to resort to court proceedings but to work to facilitate settlement between their clients. Should negotiations fail, the parties must instruct new lawyers to represent them. In some jurisdictions, a special 'Family Court' has been established, to provide facilities of a legal and non-legal nature so that all the issues can be resolved in one forum. This has not been adopted in England and Wales. Instead, courts at all levels have a greater or lesser jurisdiction over family matters, although a considerable degree of special expertise has been developed within them and, to some extent, it could be said that there does exist a family court, albeit one which operates across the civil court structure.

Because English family law grew in a piecemeal fashion, powers to administer different parts of it were granted to different courts for different purposes, with overlaps in certain areas, and gaps in others. The basic structure at present is that the lowest level of courts, the magistrates' court, hears cases relating to children, domestic violence, and (though this is now rare) adult maintenance, sitting in what are called 'family proceedings courts'. The county court handles children cases, domestic violence, and divorce. Different judges within the county court, the District Judges and Circuit Judges, exercise different jurisdiction according to the complexity of the case, depending upon their degree of training and specialism. The Family Division of the High Court deals with especially complicated or serious cases, and acts as an appeal court from the family proceedings court. The Court of Appeal hears appeals from the county court and High Court, and the House of Lords hears appeals on family matters from the Court of Appeal.

Cases concerning children may usefully be divided into two categories—'private law' and 'public law'. The former relate to disputes between family members, while the latter concern disputes between the family and the state, usually in the guise of a local authority taking child protection proceedings. Generally speaking, it is left to the applicant in a private law case to decide in which level of court to commence proceedings (subject to requirements imposed where the litigation is publicly funded, and jurisdictional limitations), while public law cases are usually begun in the family proceedings court. All cases may be transferred either sideways or upwards in the hierarchy, either to speed up proceedings or to match the degree of complexity with the appropriate level of judicial expertise.

THE USE OF FAMILY MEDIATION

The suspicion that the legal process may be iatrogenic—that is, that it may, in itself, cause further dispute and disharmony within the family— coupled with recognition of the fact that many family disputes have non-legal causes and ramifications, has led to the search for an alternative process of family dispute resolution, through mediation, which has received strong Governmental support in recent years. Mediation may be distinguished from lawyer-negotiation because the mediator acts as a neutral facilitator of discussion between the parties. Furthermore, rather than leave the decision-making to the lawyers or to the judge, in mediation, decisions are reached by the parties themselves. Mediation services in England and Wales began as local initiatives by lawyers and social workers (including those attached to the courts) keen to provide an alternative to the traditional system. They were initially concerned primarily with disputes relating to children, and mediators were usually social workers or counsellors by background. Gradually, mediation has been extended to other types of family disputes, such as those concerning property, and lawyers have begun to qualify as mediators and offer mediation themselves, as an alternative to negotiation and representation. The attempted colonization of family law by mediators, and the consequential attempted capture of mediation by family lawyers has been a major feature of the British family justice system since the 1980s. Mediation is now an inherent part of the legal process in cases concerning children or financial relief on divorce. The desirability of resolving disputes through mediation, its limitations and its opportunities, is a continuing matter for debate.

THE CONTRIBUTION OF NON-LAWYERS

Whereas a family court might employ non-legal experts as part of the adjudicatory process, in the English court system, non-legal expertise is obtained through the use of other professionals acting as officers of the court, as expert witnesses for the parties, or as the providers of non-legal services to clients going through family problems. This is most evident in cases concerning children. Where, for example, parents are in dispute over their child's future, the court may direct an officer to investigate and file a report. The officer is a social worker by training, attached to the Children and Family Court Advisory and Support Service (known as CAFCASS). Such officers, known, in private law cases, as 'children and family reporters' are encouraged to make recommendations to the court on what they regard as in the child's best interests, and their recommendations carry considerable weight, to the extent that a court disagreeing with the officer's opinion must clearly explain and justify this.

A slightly different role is played by the officer, known as a 'children's guardian' when acting in public law cases. Here, the guardian is appointed by the court to represent the interests of the child who is the subject of the proceedings. The guardian is a party to the case and may be legally represented, but also prepares a report for the court. Where the guardian's view of what is best for the child clashes with the child's own wishes, then if the child is of sufficient understanding, the court may permit her to be represented by the lawyer previously instructed by the guardian, who may seek alternative legal representation or is obliged (and has rights of audience) to act as advocate on her own behalf.

Other non-legal personnel may become involved in legal matters affecting a child by appointment as experts in the proceedings, either jointly instructed by both sides, or as competing experts retained by each party. They can range from paediatricians diagnosing abuse from physical findings when a child is taken to hospital, to child psychiatrists asked to advise on the likely outcome for a child of a particular placement or change of carer. Reliance upon experts is not unproblematic. Different experts may disagree in their interpretation of evidence, be it relating to the case at hand, or pertaining to their discipline in general. For example, major controversies have arisen over the diagnosis of child sexual abuse (Butler-Sloss, 1988), 'Munchausen's Syndrome by Proxy', also known as fabricated illness syndrome, where a parent or carer is alleged deliberately to make a child ill in order to attract attention to themselves,[6] and 'parental alienation syndrome', whereby a parent is alleged to influence a child so that he or she refuses any continuing contact with the non-resident parent (Bruch, 2002). Judges and lawyers, possessing only a lay understanding of such matters, may be ill-equipped to choose between competing expert opinions and metaphorically 'blinded by science', especially when one expert is particularly highly renowned and the court relies on his or her evidence without adequate scrutiny (see Chapter 5).

Outside the courts, a multi-disciplinary group may be summoned to a child protection conference by a local authority dealing with allegations of abuse or neglect, to consider whether action needs to be taken. The group may include the child's teacher, General Practitioner, health visitor, and any police who are involved in the case, as well as social workers, lawyers, and child health experts. The point is to examine the child's needs from a variety of perspectives in order to arrive at the best informed decision, and to avoid too narrow a conception of the problems facing the child which might arise should the decision be a purely legal one.

---

[6] See *R v Cannings* [2004] EWCA Crim 1, [2004] 1 All ER 725, *Re U (Serious Injury: Standard of Proof); Re B* [2004] EWCA Civ 567, [2004] 2 FLR 263.

Outside the sphere of legal action relating to children, the involvement of non-lawyers is likely to be confined to the giving of advice or assistance, or expert testimony, rather than extend to decision-making. Accountants, actuaries, and valuers may all be called upon to give their opinions on financial and property matters, for example, as to the likely cost of providing a certain standard of living for a divorced wife for the remainder of her life, or the likely sale price obtainable on the matrimonial home.

Finally, in some areas, solicitors are funded by the Legal Services Commission to act as a point of referral to other services which can help a client facing a marriage breakdown or family problem. Under the FAInS initiative (or Family Advice and Information Networks), the solicitor assesses the new client's needs and may refer him or her to mediation, counselling or medical services or may refer their child to specialist support services. The aim is to enable the client to resolve the non-legal difficulties he or she is facing whilst involved with the legal system. This pilot scheme has been set up in recognition that a client may have many non-legal problems to face alongside the legal process of divorce and that the legal system itself cannot be expected to resolve these. The view that what initially looks like a legal problem may in fact be much more multi-faceted is an important development in the approach to family issues by policy-makers in this field.

THE VOICE OF THE CHILD

As noted above, the rise of individualism has resulted in a greater perception of the needs and rights of individual family members and has culminated in the recognition of the concept of 'children's rights'. For the legal system, the most significant of these is Article 12 of the UN Convention on the Rights of the Child:

(1) States Parties shall assure to the child who is capable of forming his or her own views the right to express those views freely in all matters affecting the child, the views of the child being given due weight in accordance with the age and maturity of the child.

(2) For this purpose, the child shall in particular be provided the opportunity to be heard in any judicial and administrative proceedings affecting the child, either directly, or through a representative or an appropriate body, in a manner consistent with the procedural rules of national law.

This provision presents major challenges to the legal (and indeed the political) system. The establishment of a Children's Commissioner whose role is to oversee the political, social, and legal position of children within the state and to investigate processes and events which appear to undermine children's rights, has been adopted as a means for taking forward the United Kingdom's commitment to Article 12. Wales, then Northern Ireland, Scotland, and finally, in future, England, each has a commissioner, with varying jurisdiction and powers, to fulfill this function. There are also mechanisms (discussed in Chapter 5) enabling children to initiate proceedings to resolve issues concerning them, but they are difficult for children to make use of and depend upon the willingness of adults to facilitate their availability. They are also limited to exceptional circumstances. It has yet to be resolved how far 'run of the mill' cases involving children should be opened up to children's participation. For example, should a child, who is inevitably going to be affected by the parents' divorce, be permitted to join in the proceedings? A court may direct that an officer of CAFCASS, such as is appointed in public law cases, should represent the child in private law proceedings[7] but the state could not finance this in the case of all the children (some 150,000 per annum) whose parents divorce each year nor, in most cases, would it probably be necessary. But how a child's voice can best be 'heard' in legal proceedings is a continuing dilemma.

THE INTERNATIONAL DIMENSION

With increased international mobility, immigration, and globalization, a growing number of families contain members who have moved to the UK from elsewhere, or who are from different national or cultural backgrounds. Encouragement of mass immigration from the Indian sub-continent and the Caribbean in the middle of the last century, the facilitation, under European law, of movement of workers from one member state to another, and a growing awareness of the circumstances of those in the third world, have all resulted in a need for family law and policy to recognize the diversity of family backgrounds and to manage the problems that may arise. For example, a cultural norm of arranged marriage and submission to parental choice of partner in south Asian societies may come into conflict with the norm in the UK of freedom of

---

[7] Family Proceedings Rules 1991 r 9.5 (as amended). Sections 41(6A) and 93(2)(bb) of the Children Act 1989 (as amended) make further provision for rules of court to specify when children may be separately represented in relevant proceedings.

choice of partner based on romantic rather than family considerations. A marriage between partners of different nationalities who may have lived in the home country of each for a time, may require consideration of which jurisdiction's courts should handle their divorce if the marriage subsequently breaks down. A shortage of babies available for adoption in the UK may prompt a search in a third world country for a needy orphan to bring home to adopt. Legal responses to these problems may require action at a number of different policy levels. It may be sufficient to ensure that the domestic law caters for the situation—so that, in the first example, the law may need to spell out that *forced* marriage, as distinct from an arranged match, is not binding on the couple. Concerted international action may be required to provide uniform rules of jurisdiction and enforcement to deal with cases such as the second example, to avoid 'forum shopping' whereby each partner attempts to invoke the jurisdiction of a system which they hope will be more advantageous to their case. In cases involving couples from European Union states, a complex European code on jurisdiction,[8] lays down rules to deal with the problem. Finally, the problems caused by inter-country adoption such as the potential for corruption, the danger of babies being sold to rich Westerners by impoverished parents, and the difficulties of adjustment of seriously disturbed children adopted from very poor circumstances have produced an international Convention (the Hague Convention on Inter-country Adoption, 1993) intended to control the movement of children, to ensure their adequate protection in both their home country and that to which they are brought, and to prevent the exploitation of their parents.

All three mechanisms—amendment of domestic law to grapple with issues raised by cultural diversity, adoption of uniform rules across borders, and the development of shared norms of procedure on an international basis—are a growing feature of the family law world.

CONCLUSION

Family law, then, may be seen as a mirror reflecting social, cultural, and political developments in the face of change in 'late modern' society. The lack of a consistent set of principles underpinning the law is hardly

---

[8] Council Regulation (EC) 1347/2000 on Jurisdiction and the Recognition and Enforcement of Judgments in Matrimonial Matters and in Matters of Parental Responsibility for Children of Both Spouses [2000] OJ L160/19.

surprising, given the lack of consensus on the role of the law, the form of relationships deserving of its recognition, and the roles of the parties within these relationships. Ways must be found of conceiving family relationships and of managing their formation and termination, to achieve the ultimate goal of promoting and enhancing social, and family, stability. The following Chapters explore how the law has been used to respond to these challenges.

2

Formation of Family Relationships

FORM *VERSUS* CONTENT

The legal recognition of family relationships can be seen as serving one basic purpose. This is to enable the state to identify particular relationships to which it can attach certain legal consequences. The question then arises as to why the state might wish to do this. It might be argued that it facilitates state control over people's individual choices and preferences. On a more pragmatic level, it makes it easier to organize the necessary functions of the state if it is relatively straightforward to determine who is legally linked to whom. For example, financial support obligations can be imposed on and enforced against those deemed by law to be 'related'.

These objectives are not necessarily *sinister* manifestations of 'state intervention in family life', although they should nonetheless be recognized as examples of such intervention. Determining who is legally related to whom can be protective. For example, it might be less likely that a person will marry someone who already has a spouse if there is an effective system of public marriage registration which enables the authorities, if not the potential victim, to discover whether this is the case in advance of the wedding. A child who might otherwise have to be cared for by strangers may be found a home with relatives if these are legally recognized as being linked to the child. (However, this is not to ignore the possibility that such protection does not *in fact* result from the legal regime governing family relationships.)

Historically, there have been two ways in which family relationships have been identified by law—through marriage and through the blood tie. The first was more important in practice, although the second was as important ideologically, largely because of the difficulty, until modern scientific techniques resolved the problem, of determining conclusively who was actually genetically related to whom. Although marriage is in some senses a contract, it has also bestowed a status upon those who enter into it and the most important legal consequence of this status was the right to regard children born from the union as themselves possessing a highly significant legal status—that of legitimacy. The advantages of this status were historically many and profound. The corresponding disadvantages of birth outside marriage were serious and onerous.

Modern social attitudes, as noted in Chapter 1, have downgraded the stigmatic associations of illegitimacy and the desirability of marriage. The reality of changing demographics has forced a realization that the state is no longer capable of constraining people into making the 'acceptable' choice of forming intimate ties only through marriage. It has become more common to approach family relationships with a greater emphasis upon their content and the functions they fulfil rather than upon the form of their creation. This is beginning to affect how the law determines which of these relationships should be given legal recognition.

THE RIGHT TO MARRY AND FOUND A FAMILY AND THE RIGHT TO RESPECT FOR FAMILY LIFE

This dichotomy between what may be classed as 'old' and 'new' foundations of legal recognition is epitomized by the inclusion of two different 'fundamental human rights' in the European Convention on Human Rights. On the one hand, Article 12 provides that:

Men and women of marriageable age have the right to marry and to found a family according to the national laws governing the exercise of this right.

This Article has been interpreted by the European Court of Human Rights as being 'mainly concerned to protect marriage as the basis of the family' thus establishing only one right—to marry and found a family.[1] In other words, there is no right, as so far understood, to found a family *outside* marriage. By contrast, Article 9 of the Charter of Fundamental Rights of the European Union asserts 'The right to marry *and* the right to found a family shall be guaranteed' (emphasis added).

However, as we saw in Chapter 1, Article 8(1) of the Convention guarantees that

Everyone has the right to respect for his private and family life, his home and his correspondence.

In the case law of the European Commission and European Court on this

---

[1] *Sheffield and Horsham v United Kingdom* (1999) 27 EHRR 163.

provision, a much broader understanding of what can constitute a 'family' life and hence a 'family' has been accepted. Unmarried parents, cohabiting couples with children, homosexual parents, and transsexual couples with children have all been acknowledged as having a right to respect for their family life under this Article[2] (although the Court has held that Article 8 does not itself guarantee the right to *found* a family—which is contained in Article 12—and hence there was no breach of Article 8 when a single homosexual was denied permission to adopt a child under French law.)[3]

These two Articles, now incorporated into domestic law through the Human Rights Act 1998, provide the benchmarks against which English law must be assessed in discussing how it currently gives legal recognition to family relationships. The following discussion first considers the 'old' basis of such recognition deriving from marriage as an institution focused on form and status, and then examines the 'new' foundation based on family life identified through the quality and nature of the relationship and the functions it fulfils for those within it.

RECOGNITION BASED ON MARRIAGE

It can be seen that the right contained in Article 12 is limited in at least two ways. First, men and women must be of 'marriageable age'. Secondly, the right may only be exercised in accordance with 'national laws'. These two qualifications allow different states to assert their own cultural and social conceptions of marriage. States have the freedom to set down, for example, the minimum age ('marriageable age') at which people can marry; how many spouses one may have at the same time; whether marriage is terminable before death; and whom amongst one's relatives one can marry.

THE CONCEPT OF MARRIAGE IN ENGLISH LAW

The traditional starting point for any discussion of the English law of marriage is the view put forward in *Hyde v Hyde*[4] that marriage is 'the voluntary union for life of one man and one woman to the exclusion of all others'. This must be considered by reference to both statute and case law which explain and expand its meaning. In particular, the rules governing

---

[2] *Marckx v Belgium* (1979) 2 EHRR 330; *Johnston v Ireland* (1986) 9 EHRR 203; *Salgueiro da Silva Mouta v Portugal* [2001] 1 FCR 653; *X, Y and Z v United Kingdom* (1997) 24 EHRR 143.
[3] *Fretté v France* (2004) 38 EHRR 21.   [4] (1866) LR 1 P & D 130, 133.

what conditions must be satisfied to create a valid marriage shed light on what marriage is *for* and the rules governing exit from marriage through divorce have, historically at least, illuminated what kinds of behaviour are expected to take place within a marriage. (But we will see in Chapter 6 that this may no longer be the case, as divorce increasingly becomes a procedural/bureaucratic legal process.)

The rules concerning the validity of marriage themselves divide into two categories. Some requirements are so fundamental that failure to comply with them is contrary to public policy and renders a marriage *void*, i.e. regarded as never having come into lawful existence. Although court proceedings may be taken to declare that this is the case, they are not essential, and anyone can seek to impugn the marriage, perhaps years after the parties to it have died. For other requirements, however, only the parties to the marriage are given the right to determine whether non-compliance should result in the marriage being declared invalid. Such marriages are known as *voidable* marriages and can only be annulled by court decree granted during the parties' lifetimes.

Marriage as a heterosexual union

English law, deriving from the Judaeo-Christian tradition, requires that marriage be a relationship between two parties of the opposite sex. Section 11(c) of the Matrimonial Causes Act 1973 provides that a marriage is void unless the parties to it are male and female. This was justifiable in times when the demands of the inheritance laws and family economic imperatives made the production of heirs within the confines of an identifiable marital relationship of paramount significance in society. But it needs express justification today. It reflects an assumption that one of the purposes, if not the main purpose, of marriage, is still the procreation of children. This assumption is now outmoded. Although Article 12 of the European Convention on Human Rights creates, as noted above, one right 'to marry and to found a family', the inability or failure to reproduce has never been a ground for annulling or terminating a marriage and no state lays down an *upper* limit for 'marriageable age'. The European Court recognized this in *Goodwin v United Kingdom* where it stated that 'the inability of any couple to conceive or parent a child cannot be regarded as *per se* removing their right to enjoy [the right to marry]'.[5]

The requirement for a relationship between persons of the opposite sex may also underscore a concern to confine—and promote—sexual

---

[5] (2002) 35 EHRR 18 at para 98.

conduct within marriage. As Ormrod J stated in *Corbett v Corbett* (*otherwise Ashley*):[6]

sex is clearly an essential determinant of the relationship called marriage because it is and always has been recognised as the union of man and woman. It is the institution on which the family is built, and in which the capacity for natural heterosexual intercourse is an essential element.

The rules relating to *voidable* marriages support the argument that heterosexual sex is an important element, if not the purpose, of marriage. Under s 12(a) and (b) of the Matrimonial Causes Act 1973, where there is an inability or wilful refusal on the part of one spouse to consummate the marriage, then the marriage may be annulled by the court. Non-consummation is not, of itself, a ground for nullity, but only where it derives from an inability or refusal to consummate. It is therefore clear that it is the spouses' own expectations and wishes that determine whether a lack of sexual relations is to be crucial to the continuation of the marriage and a 'companionate' marriage, where the parties agree not to have intercourse, may be valid. That the intercourse must be heterosexual is made clear by the courts' definition of 'consummation' as the penetration of the vagina by the penis[7]—other forms of sexual activity are irrelevant.

The current requirement for marriage to involve a male and a female rules out the possibility of homosexuals entering into a lawful marriage with each other (although it may be noted that other states, including Belgium, the Netherlands, and the US state of Massachusetts have begun to permit same-sex marriage and Article 9 of the Charter of Fundamental Rights of the European Union noted above omits any reference to 'men and women' as having the right to marry). But the question of what is meant in law by a male and a female immediately arises. Where people undergo gender reassignment treatment and act as if of the opposite sex, can they marry someone of the same sex as that to which they were assigned at birth? A negative answer was given by Ormrod J in *Corbett v Corbett*, where he held that a person's sex, for the purposes of marriage, must be biologically determined:

for even the most extreme degree of transsexualism in a male or the most severe hormonal imbalance which can exist in a person with male chromosomes, male

---

[6] [1971] P 83, 105H.   [7] *D-E v A-G* (1845) 1 Rob Eccl 279.

gonads and male genitalia, cannot reproduce a person who is naturally capable of performing the essential role of a woman in marriage.[8]

Several cases were brought in the European Court of Human Rights to challenge this ruling, finally proving successful in *Goodwin v United Kingdom* and *I v United Kingdom*.[9] The European Court considered that, since the male-to-female applicant in each case had no possibility of marriage to a man, yet lived as a woman, was in a relationship with a man, and wished only to marry a man, 'the very essence' of her right to marry under Article 12 had been infringed and there was no competing justification for barring her from enjoying that right. The Court's decision placed the onus on the United Kingdom to reform the law. An opportunity to do so via case law was rejected by the House of Lords in *Bellinger v Bellinger*,[10] on the basis that the complications and ramifications of a change in the law could not be adequately dealt with via statutory interpretation of s 11(c) alone, but necessitated public consultation and Parliamentary action. The court instead made a declaration of incompatibility under s 4 of the Human Rights Act 1998 (see Chapter 1). A Gender Recognition Act was accordingly passed by Parliament in 2004. It will enable a person who has gender dysphoria and who has lived in their acquired gender for the preceding two years to acquire a gender recognition certificate, to be issued by a Gender Recognition Panel consisting of at least one legally and one medically qualified member. The general legal effect will be to recognize the person as of his or her acquired gender for all purposes.

Notwithstanding the Government's willingness (though in the face of the European Court's ruling, it had little choice) to recognize gender reassignment, it does not follow that the legislation marks the abandonment of a heterosexual model of marriage. To the contrary, a marriage contracted in ignorance of the fact that a person has undergone such treatment will be voidable, and a married person will be denied a full gender recognition certificate until they have terminated their existing marriage. Marriage will thus continue to be limited to couples who are legally of opposite sexes, and there are no plans apparently to permit same-sex marriages. This stance derives from an ideological rather than a logical

---

[8] At 106D. In the case of an 'inter-sex', i.e. a person with ambiguous sexual characteristics, psychological factors may also be relevant: *W v W (Nullity: Gender)* [2001] Fam 111. [1999] 2 FLR 542, 548E.

[9] (2002) 35 EHRR 18, (2003) 36 EHRR 53.

[10] [2003] UKHL 21, [2003] 2 AC 467.

imperative. It is simply not yet felt to be socially, culturally, or politically right to permit people of the same sex to marry.

Marriageable age

Under English law, the minimum age for contracting a valid marriage is 16 for both men and women. In the now comparatively rare case where a person under 18 wishes to marry, they must have parental consent or, if this is refused, the consent of the court. Although 16 appears rather young in today's social climate where people are marrying later and later, the minimum age was in fact raised in 1929 from the former common law ages of 12 for a girl and 14 for a boy, which were the presumed ages of puberty. The linking of the age of marriage with that of sexual maturity reinforces the sexual and reproductive rationale behind traditional marriage. The increase in the age reflected an attitude that childhood and adolescence are periods of life distinct from adulthood during which the person should be shielded from the usual responsibilities and concerns of adults. In particular, it was felt that sexual activity should be discouraged among the very young. Changing social attitudes have meant that while it may now be thought undesirable for young people to marry, it is accepted that it is unlikely that they will refrain from sex. Thus, in public policy terms, it may be undesirable to separate the 'age of consent' to sexual intercourse and the age at which a person can marry, as to do so would appear to endorse sexual activity outside, but not inside, marriage.

An exclusive union

English law does not permit a person to have more than one spouse at a time. A bigamous marriage is void under s 11(b) of the Matrimonial Causes Act 1973 and bigamy is a crime under s 57 of the Offences against the Person Act 1861. In *Whiston v Whiston*[11] it was said that 'bigamy strikes at the very heart of the institution of marriage' although it is hard to see why this is more so than a breach of any of the other fundamental conditions for a valid marriage. Large parts of the world permit the taking of more than one *wife* at a time, although polyandry is much rarer, and within England and Wales, the phenomenon of taking several spouses one after the other is facilitated by the relative ease of modern divorce law. The abhorrence of bigamy appears to stem again from the traditional view of marriage as the exclusive locus for a sexual relationship and from a reluctance to contemplate such a relationship involving multiple partners.

---

[11] [1995] Fam 198, CA, per Russell LJ at 208.

A voluntary union

Lord Penzance in *Hyde v Hyde* described marriage as a *voluntary* union. The idea of marriage as a contract facilitates the notion that it must be entered into by mutual agreement. Under canon law, from which the common law of marriage was derived, the essence of marriage was the consent of the parties and a lack of consent rendered the marriage *void*. Under modern English law, however, a lack of consent only renders a marriage *voidable*. As with the issue of non-consummation, this enables the parties themselves to decide whether to affirm their commitment to the marriage or not. A party to the marriage may therefore seek a decree of nullity under s 12(c) of the Matrimonial Causes Act 1973 if either party did not validly consent to the marriage, 'whether in consequence of duress, mistake, unsoundness of mind or otherwise'. Lack of consent is most likely to arise today as a consequence of a marriage arranged within an ethnic minority community. In such cases, there may be a clash of wills between the parents who are seeking to uphold the traditional values of their community, and the child who is influenced by western norms and seeks to make his or her own choice of partner. For example, in *P v R (Forced Marriage: Annulment: Procedure)*[12] a 20 year old woman, who had formed an attachment with a man of whom her parents disapproved, was persuaded to go to Pakistan to attend her sister's funeral. Once there, she was told a marriage had been arranged for her and that her refusal to go through the ceremony would bring shame on the family. She reluctantly did so, and was later able to get help to return to the UK. In such a case, the Court of Appeal has held that, where the petitioner can show 'that the pressure. . .is such as to destroy the reality of consent and overbears the will of the individual', a decree can be granted on the basis of duress.[13] The court therefore granted her petition of nullity holding that her consent had been vitiated by force and by the enormous emotional and other pressure the family had brought to bear upon her. Whether making a marriage based on lack of consent only *voidable* provides sufficient protection to those at risk of forced marriage is open to doubt. In a multicultural society, it is important to recognize that people may hold different views on the virtues of arranged marriages. But by placing the onus on the unhappy party to have the marriage annulled in the event of coercion, the law arguably legitimates the pressure which may be put on a vulnerable person to comply with familial expectations.

---

[12] [2003] 1 FLR 661.
[13] *Hirani v Hirani* (1983) 4 FLR 232, CA per Ormrod LJ at 234G.

As with other types of contract, a mistake may suffice to show a lack of consent to the bargain. However, case law has limited this to cases where there is a fundamental mistake, either as to the very identity of the person one is marrying, or as to the nature of the ceremony. A mistake as to the attributes of the other spouse (e.g. that he is wealthy when in fact he is poor) is insufficient according to the courts. Legislation was enacted to ensure that injustice was not done to a person duped or misled into marrying in certain circumstances. These, however, are limited to specific situations raised in cases where the courts had denied a remedy. Under the Matrimonial Causes Act 1973, s 12(d), (e) or (f), a spouse can seek an annulment where the other was suffering from mental disorder or venereal disease, and a man can seek a decree where the woman was pregnant by someone else at the time of the marriage. Where there is a more general incompatibility or disappointment with the other spouse, the remedy lies in divorce.

A union for life

Canon law did not permit divorce as distinct from annulment (although the term 'divorce' was used even when nullity was in issue). However, Parliament could pass any law it chose and a practice evolved, between the sixteenth and nineteenth centuries, for the very wealthy to obtain a divorce by private Act of Parliament. This was superseded in 1857 when it became possible to terminate a valid marriage by divorce granted by a court. Thus, when *Hyde v Hyde* was decided, its definition of marriage was already inaccurate. A marriage, while *expected* to last for life, could in fact be ended at the suit of either party. Today, with the frequency of divorce, this is well understood. But it is worth noting that, even in the case of a 'marriage of convenience' where the parties know from the outset that they will part immediately after the ceremony, they can nonetheless only end the marriage by going through the usual divorce process. This is because, at present, the terms of the marriage contract are fixed by law and cannot be varied by the parties themselves. There is only one type of marriage recognized in law, and that is one of indefinite duration.

Marriage according to national laws

English law lays down additional requirements governing the entry into marriage, which advance its understanding of the concept of marriage. For example, under the First Schedule to the Marriage Act 1949, there are restrictions (known as 'prohibited degrees') on marriage between close relatives, whether by blood or marriage. These stem originally from biblical prohibitions and are to be found in most if not all societies in one form or another. Yet even very similar societies may vary quite significantly in the details of their restrictions, for example, regarding marriage between cousins and across the generations. Once more, the sexual and reproductive rationale of marriage underlies such rules, it being regarded as undesirable and potentially genetically dangerous for people in the same family to have a full sexual relationship. But there is little clear logic to how the restrictions have been drawn up, especially where marriage between in-laws is concerned.

The other set of laws governing formation of marriage concerns the formalities that must be completed to seal the marriage. At common law, no religious ceremony was required; nor need there have been any witnesses. It sufficed that the parties declared that they took each other as husband and wife. This casual approach to marriage occasioned scope for uncertainty, secrecy, and fraud which became a problem for those families seeking to secure their estates through arranged marriages, and the danger of the 'clandestine marriage' was a real one. But it was not until 1753 that rules governing the form of marriage were imposed by statute. Apart from in the case of Jews and Quakers, who were allowed to marry according to their own rites, only the Anglican ceremony was deemed to give rise to a valid marriage. Notice of intention to marry had to be given by each party in their home parish (usually by publication of banns in the church), and the ceremony had to be performed in public.

Subsequent religious toleration and acceptance that some people might prefer a purely secular ceremony led to a proliferation of rules to cater for personal preferences. The *purpose* of requiring formalities to be completed now lies less in the need to prevent secret marriages taking place and more in a concern to spell out to the parties, through the dignity and ritual of the occasion, the seriousness of the commitment that they are making to each other. Couples may choose to marry according to religious rites, which, if conducted according to the appropriate rules, will create a valid marriage in English law as well as one recognized by the religion concerned. Alternatively, they may undergo a civil ceremony, either with or without an additional religious ceremony which would have significance only to the adherents and carry no civil legal consequences.

At one time, with very rare exceptions, civil ceremonies could only be conducted in register offices but these vary in charm and attractiveness and so the Marriage Act 1994 permits civil weddings to be conducted in other premises provided that these are approved by the local authority.

Marriage at home is not permitted, but marriage in a coal mine or in the Brighton Pavilion is perfectly legal. The Government (General Register Office, 2003) have proposed further liberalizing the rules to permit couples to marry anywhere they choose (subject to the agreement of the person performing the ceremony and to national minimum standards of suitability). Civil weddings now outnumber religious ceremonies, reflecting both a decline in religious observance and a preference for a wedding which can fulfil the couple's romantic fantasies.

In accommodating the parties' wishes in this way, the modern law attempts to reflect a view of marriage as a relationship designed to provide emotional satisfaction to the couple, through sexual intimacy in most cases and through the procreation of children in many. Yet the continuing conception of legal marriage as a traditional union means that many couples now try, or are compelled, to achieve these objectives outside marriage, through 'new' forms of relationship which nonetheless provide them with a 'family life'. These will be explored later in this Chapter, after we have considered how the law reinforces the traditional model of marriage through its rules regarding parentage of children.

THE ATTRIBUTION OF PARENTAGE

Through its rules governing the attribution of parentage and the concept of legitimacy, English law traditionally upheld the European Convention conception of the right to found a family as one grounded in marriage. These rules were ultimately concerned with enabling men to identify those of their children on whom they wished to bestow their name and rights of succession. Unless the man determined otherwise through a will, any children born outside his lawful marriage were regarded as having no legal relationship with him at all (although support obligations could be enforced by the parish under the Poor Law). The corollary was that birth to a wife apparently within a lawful marriage gave rise to a powerful presumption that the child was indeed the genetic offspring of her husband and that legal presumption remains the starting-point for establishing paternity in modern law. An unmarried mother, like an unmarried father, had no legal relationship to the child at common law.

In a society in which marriage and birth within marriage were the only socially acceptable forms of family-building, the marital presumption provided a means, albeit subject to problems of proof in a state of limited scientific understanding, of establishing which relationships would give rise to particular legal consequences. It preserved a sense of stability by aligning and equating the supposed (but ultimately unprovable) genetic link between a man and a child with the clearly established fact of his marriage. Unless he had suspicions regarding the fidelity of his wife, he would take on the rights and responsibilities of fatherhood on the assumption that they were being exercised in respect of 'his own' children. Equally, except where they were dependent on the parish for poor relief, he could ignore the claims of other children who sought to assert a relationship with him, unless he *chose* to recognize them. Even then, English law, unlike many civil law systems, provided no *formal* method of acknowledgement of his paternity of such children.

The establishment of paternity based on the fact of marriage

Until egg donation became feasible, as long as the fact that a woman had given birth to a child could be proved, usually by the presence of witnesses, there could be no doubt that this woman was also the genetic mother. If she was married, then the law presumed that her husband was the genetic father of the child. Genetic parenthood was thus regarded as congruent with the fact of the parents' marriage. It was for the husband to disprove his paternity. At one time, the stigma of illegitimacy for the child was such that the standard of proof required of him was beyond a reasonable doubt. However, the Family Law Reform Act 1969, s 26 provides that the presumption may be rebutted on the balance of probabilities. In fact, as testing has become more reliable with the availability of DNA analysis, the precise standard of proof has probably become academic because the fact that a person is, or is *not* genetically related to another can be established with virtual certainty.

Directing a test to determine paternity

Where a child's paternity is in issue, samples will be required from the alleged father, the mother, and the child in order to carry out the DNA analysis. The court may *direct* that a test be conducted but cannot force a party who declines to be tested to submit.[14] However, under s 23(1) of the Family Law Reform Act 1969, in such a case, the court may draw such inferences as appear proper, including adverse inferences. Thus, a man refusing to be tested may find that the court rules that his refusal thereby establishes his paternity.

The extent to which social attitudes and behaviour have changed in recent years is reflected in the way the courts exercise their discretion whether to direct a test and in the context in which paternity tests

---

[14] Family Law Act 1969, ss 20, 21.

commonly become an issue in modern litigation. According to the House of Lords, a court should direct a test unless it is satisfied that this would be against the child's interests.[15] The courts no longer accept that there is a stigma attached to a finding that a child has been born outside marriage. Rather, they attach considerable importance to the right of the child, enshrined in Article 7 of the UN Convention on the Rights of the Child, 'as far as possible, to know and be cared for by his or her parents'.

Traditionally, one might have expected that the issue of paternity would normally arise where a man was seeking to show that he was *not* the father of a child. This might be in the context of a divorce based on his wife's adultery or where an unmarried woman was seeking financial support from him for the child. In modern times, there may still be substantial numbers of cases where men seek to avoid a finding of paternity, especially where they are being pursued to pay child support.

By contrast to this position of attempting to *disclaim* paternity, recent years have also seen an increase in reported case law in the number of cases where paternity is *claimed* by a man who is not married to the mother. Such cases may arise where the woman has terminated her relationship with the man but he wishes to establish or assert his relationship with her child. Until legislation reversed the position, the courts had no power to force a woman to permit her child to be tested. This situation was criticized as undermining the child's right to know his genetic identity, which may be regarded as an aspect of his right to respect for his *private* life under Article 8, and, furthermore, as potentially infringing the man's right under Article 8 to respect for his *family* life.[16]

Where the child is settled into another family unit with the mother and her husband, the man asserting his parentage has both to rebut the marital presumption and establish his genetic link to the child. The courts have appeared less certain in such cases whether they should uphold the traditional family by applying the marital presumption or pursue the genetic truth but the strong trend in recent years has been to regard the 'truth' about the child's parentage as having a greater value than the continuation of a 'cover up' intended to preserve the existing social family unit in which the child is being raised.[17] In this regard, the courts have moved the law away from its preference for marriage as the

---

[15] *S v S; W v Official Solicitor (or W)* [1972] AC 24.

[16] *Re O and J (Children) (Blood Tests: Constraint)* [2000] Fam 139, reversed by s 82, Child Support, Pensions and Social Security Act 2000 (inserting revised s 21(3) into the Family Law Reform Act 1969).

[17] *Re H (a minor) (blood test: parental rights)* [1996] 4 All ER 28, CA per Ward LJ at 42j.

foundation of the family and towards a recognition that family relationships may in fact be established in other ways.

Creating a parent/child relationship without a genetic link

Where couples are unable to conceive children of their own, they may seek to establish a family through other means. The practice of adoption in the sense of taking a child into the family and bringing her up as one's own has probably always been carried out. Modern methods of assisted reproduction, which enable genetic material to be donated to others, provide a new means of creating a family without a genetic link between 'parents' and child. The demand for and resort to these services forced legal changes whereby the social relationship could be given recognition regardless of the absence of any genetic tie. Adoption was recognized as a legal procedure in 1926 and the attribution of parentage via assisted reproduction was made the subject of comprehensive legislation in 1990. These legal mechanisms still reflect vestiges of a notion of the family as being ideally based on the marital relationship (or at least the stable cohabitation) of the adult 'parents'. It is not possible, under English law, for a child to have more than two legal 'parents' at a time. In each case therefore, the rules supplant whoever would originally have been deemed by law to be the parents of the child, by the substitution of new parents. The child ceases to be legally recognized as part of the birth parents' family, and becomes completely absorbed within that of the new parents (subject to the rules on offences relating to sex with an adult relative and prohibited degrees of marriage, which continue to apply to the birth family).

Adoption

Adoption was the subject of major reform in the Adoption and Children Act 2002, intended to modernize the law and to recognize the significant social changes which have affected the concept in recent times. The law[18] provides for the adoption of a child under the age of 18, either by one person or a couple, who must usually be aged at least 21. Section 144(4) of the 2002 Act provides that a couple consists either of a married couple or 'two people (whether of different sexes or the same sex) living as partners in an enduring family relationship'. This expanded definition, enabling same-sex partners as well as cohabiting couples to adopt, represents a significant move away from the view that the need of the child for

---

[18] To be brought into force by 2005; the Adoption Act 1976, ss 14 and 15 permits adoption only by a single person or a married couple.

a stable family life is best reflected by requiring adopting couples to be married, as was previously the case. Parliament took the view instead that it is the 'enduring' nature of the adults' relationship with each other that provides the necessary security for the child, not the legal form of that relationship, and in so doing, it took an important step towards adopting the more functional approach to families and their regulation enshrined in Article 8.

The stereotype image of adoption is of an infertile couple adopting a baby but this kind of adoption is now very much the exception. Few babies are available for adoption in this country, as contraception and abortion on the one hand, and greater social tolerance of having children outside marriage, have grown. There are now two main kinds of adoption. First, there are those that may be described as *reconstituting* a family, as in the case of adoption by step-parents or relatives of the child. Here, the aim is to redraw the family's boundaries by substituting a new 'parent' or parents for a birth parent, while preserving the child's ties with one side of her family tree. Secondly, there are adoptions which *create* a family tie where none existed before. These involve the adoption of a child unrelated to the adopters. The main source of such children lies, in this country, in the child care system where it may be decided that a child's best interests will be served by placement in a new family because of the inadequacies of her birth family. An alternative source which can provide babies to would-be adopters lies in inter-country adoption, with mainly poorer countries providing a seemingly unlimited number of sometimes severely disadvantaged children who could be better cared for in the affluent west.[19] Only 'baby' adoption can really enable the adopters to construct a family akin to the classical nuclear model based on marriage with the child being brought up virtually from her birth by the adoptive parents. Even then, in inter-country adoption this is achieved at the cost of transplanting the child from her home culture to what will usually be a very different type of society, with consequential problems of emotional adjustment when (and if) the child comes to appreciate what has happened to her. The adoption of a child from care is likely to involve an older child with memories of her birth family and increasingly, the adopters will be expected to agree to the child continuing to have some limited contact with that family. The step-parent or within

---

[19] The Hague Convention on Intercountry Adoption 1993, attempts to set out clear rules and procedures governing intercountry adoption. The Adoption (Intercountry Aspects) Act 1999 and the Adoption and Children Act 2002 incorporate most of its provisions into English law.

family adoption, while attempting to (re)constitute a nuclear family based on marriage or stable cohabitation, does so at the cost of incidentally (and deliberately) wiping out the legal status of the other birth parent.

Assisted reproduction

Perhaps it is not surprising that, faced with such problems, many couples may prefer to create a family through assisted reproduction treatment. Such a couple may undergo fertility treatment using donated gametes so that the woman can give birth herself and thus establish a gestational, if not a genetic link to the child. Sperm or eggs, or both, may be donated and transferred to the woman's womb through a variety of techniques including insemination with the sperm and in vitro fertilization. Where the woman is unable to carry the child, a surrogate mother may be used, who may either simply provide her womb for the purpose or also provide the egg, making her the genetic *and* gestational mother of the child.

Until the advent of egg donation, the genetic and gestational roles of motherhood could not be separated and it was never established definitively by the common law whether legal motherhood was based on the blood tie or on the fact of giving birth. When legislation was enacted to cater for assisted reproduction, it was assumed that donation of eggs would generally take place in order to enable an infertile woman to give birth to a child whom she would raise as her own. It was also intended that the practice of surrogacy should be discouraged. Accordingly, s 27 of the Human Fertilisation and Embryology Act 1990 provides that it is the woman who carries the child who is to be treated as the legal mother.[20]

Under s 28(2) of the same Act, where a married woman gives birth to a child as a result of receiving donated *sperm* (or an embryo created using donated sperm), her husband will be treated as the father of the child. In this way, the law continues to enable the man to establish a legal link with those children whom he wishes to acknowledge as 'his'. He can seek to avoid the ascription of paternity by showing that he did not consent to his wife undergoing the treatment. However, in such a case, the marital presumption still applies and he must go on to rebut the

---

[20] The commissioning parents in a surrogacy arrangement may apply for a parental order under s 30 of the Human Fertilisation and Embryology Act 1990 to acquire parental status where a surrogate has been used, provided that at least one of them has a genetic link to the child (i.e. has provided either the egg or sperm).

46   *An Introduction to Family Law*

presumption through the use of DNA testing to show that he is not the genetic father.

Section 28(3) also enables an unmarried man to acquire parental status even though he has no genetic link to a child. It provides that where donated sperm, or an embryo created with donated sperm, are provided as part of treatment services for a woman and a man together, that man will be treated as the father of the resulting child. However, the legislation shows a preference for married couples. It provides that a man married to the mother acquires parental status even where the treatment (in practice, only donor insemination) was not performed in a clinic licensed under the Act. In the case of an unmarried man, by contrast, s 28(3) applies only to treatments carried out under a licence.

RECOGNITION OF FAMILY RELATIONSHIPS BASED ON 'FAMILY LIFE'

The foregoing discussion has shown that there are still many features of the law which reflect the importance attached to the formation of family relationships within the framework of marriage. But it is also clear that recent legal changes have attempted to recognize and give legal effect to the reality of an increasing trend towards the creation of relationships which fall outside marriage but which nonetheless are seen to merit the description of being 'family' relationships.

The starting point is to examine the concept of 'family life' as laid down by the European Court of Human Rights. The use of this term permits a 'modern' conception of family relationships to be adopted in order to reflect a recognition that the content and substance of family life may be at least as significant as that of the form in which it is established. We have seen that it is not easy to elucidate the 'essence' of the supposedly well-understood concept of marriage. At least, however, the law can establish clear rules governing entry into the marriage relationship even if their logic may be open to challenge. It is much more difficult to define 'family life' so as to embrace a variety of other relationships which can somehow be regarded as sufficiently similar in their content or purpose to those traditionally viewed as 'familial'.

THE CONCEPT OF 'FAMILY LIFE' UNDER THE EUROPEAN CONVENTION ON HUMAN RIGHTS

What is clear from the Strasbourg jurisprudence is that the marriage bond will always give rise to 'family life', including where the bond is legally ended by divorce.[21] But in the absence of a marital relationship, something more than the blood tie, per se, will be required.[22] In so holding, one may see an attempt both to follow the traditional legal emphasis upon marriage as the basis of family relationships *and* to recognize the modern focus on the content rather than bare form of such relationships.

The easiest way of determining whether a non-marital relationship can be said to create a 'family life' may be to compare it with the traditional notion of the family established by marriage. The European Court of Human Rights appears to rely on this reasoning by analogy in reaching its conclusions on this issue. It has held that the relationship between parents and child clearly constitutes a bond amounting to family life regardless of whether it is based on marriage, but in establishing the factual basis for such a claim, regard must be had to a number of factors. Consideration must be given to whether the parties live or have lived together, the length of their relationship and whether they have 'demonstrated their commitment to each other by having children together or by any other means'.[23] However, although, in *Keegan v Ireland*,[24] it said that '[t]he notion of "the family". . .is not confined solely to marriage-based relationships and may encompass other de facto "family" ties where the parties are living together outside of marriage' it was there dealing with a case involving a parent/child relationship. It has also held[25] that a family unit created by the partnership of a female to male transsexual, his female cohabitant, and their children born after donor insemination constituted a de facto family life, but there again, the essence of the case concerned the relationship between 'parent' and child. The Court has not yet ruled on whether a cohabiting relationship between adult partners can of itself constitute a family life. English law, by contrast, has had to wrestle with this problem, both in statute and case law.

COHABITING RELATIONSHIPS BETWEEN HETEROSEXUAL COUPLES

Contrary to frequent misconception, there is no concept of 'common law marriage' in English law whereby an unmarried couple might somehow,

---

[21] *Berrehab v Netherlands* (1988) 11 EHRR 322.
[22] *G v Netherlands* (1993) 16 EHRR CD 38 European Commission of Human Rights (gamete donor).
[23] *X, Y and Z v United Kingdom* (1997) 24 EHRR 143, para 36.
[24] (1994) 18 EHRR 342, para 44. [25] *X, Y and Z v United Kingdom* above n 23.

perhaps by effluxion of time, acquire some status akin to marriage with all the consequences which flow from the latter. Traditionally, cohabitation was regarded as immoral since it involved extra-marital sexual intercourse and the judges might use scathing words to describe those who engaged in it. In *Gammans v Ekins*, for example, Asquith LJ said 'To say of two people, masquerading, as these two were, as husband and wife (there being no children to complicate the picture) that they were members of the same family, seems to me an abuse of the English language'.[26]

As social attitudes have become more tolerant, the legal approach towards cohabitants has also softened. Other jurisdictions, both in the common law and civil law worlds, have legislated to recognize certain types of cohabiting relationship and to clothe these with all, or most, of the consequences attached to marriage. By contrast, the strategy of English law has been to extend some of the legal benefits of marriage to cohabiting (or formerly cohabiting) couples, according to specific subject matter and social need. It has been possible since 1976, for instance, for a cohabitant to seek protection under legislation governing domestic violence whereby the court may order the other party to refrain from 'molesting' the applicant, or even to leave the family home (see further in Chapter 4). Since 1997, this protection may be extended to the permanent transfer of the rented tenancy of the home to the applicant from the tenant partner, by order of the court. A person who was cohabiting with another may also succeed to some sorts of tenancy on the partner's death. Provided they lived together for at least two years immediately before the death, a surviving partner has been able, since 1995, to claim provision from the deceased partner's estate under the Inheritance (Provision for Family and Dependants) Act 1975. The same qualifying period applies to a claim by a cohabitant under the Fatal Accidents Act 1976. Yet it can be seen that in these examples the law only appears to have recognized the 'status' of cohabitation when it has come to an end or at least is under strain. The state's respect for the 'family life' of the cohabiting parties is given only when that family life has ended. It has hitherto only been in the case of social security legislation that currently cohabiting couples are treated as if they are married. Here, however, the motivation behind the law is to enable the state to avoid having to support a person who may in practice (though not in law, as discussed in Chapter 3) expect her partner to meet her financial needs. Ironically, although adoption and assisted reproduction law now permit unmarried couples to adopt or obtain

[26] [1950] 2 KB 328, 331, CA.

parental status after fertility treatment, it is not actually necessary for such couples to show they are cohabiting (although it may be difficult for a non-cohabiting couple to succeed in persuading decision-makers to grant them access to adoption or treatment).

Defining cohabitation

Sometimes the courts have felt able to extend statutory protections to unmarried couples by broadly defining qualifying words. For example, they eventually held,[27] when deciding who should succeed to a person's tenancy, that his cohabiting partner was as much 'a member of his family' as his child or siblings. Parliament caught up with such rulings by then expressly enacting provisions relating to those living, or who have lived 'with each other as husband and wife'. In using this formulation, one can see that the strategy is to utilize marriage as the benchmark against which to compare the cohabiting relationship and to determine whether the latter is sufficiently similar to the former to warrant recognition. As with Strasbourg, so the courts and other decision-makers, such as the social security authorities, who have to interpret these words, have relied on various factual elements that are assumed to be present in a marriage and hence can be taken as giving rise to a marriage-like relationship. Although they have stressed that these are not an exhaustive list, it appears that they do spell out the basic questions to be investigated.

Membership of the same household
The first question to ask is whether the couple actually share the same household; in other words, do they live under the same roof, albeit not all of the time? This can obviously be difficult to determine where a couple may each have their own property but spend most of their time together.

Shared daily life
A way of resolving the dilemma posed by this example is to ask how far they share tasks connected with their daily lives and how they manage their affairs. As one judge has put it, is there 'a mutuality in the daily round'?[28]

Finances
One way of establishing such mutuality is to examine how the couple arrange their finances. Where they pool their resources and share expenses, it may be easier to conclude that they are cohabiting as husband

---

[27] *Dyson Holdings Ltd v Fox* [1976] QB 503, CA.
[28] *K v K (Enforcement)* [2000] 1 FLR 383.

and wife. However, there is a considerable element of possibly outdated stereotyping here. Many married couples today may seek to keep their finances separate and divide up responsibilities for different expenses in such a way that it may be hard to distinguish them from flat-mates. This particular criterion may in fact owe much to the use of this test in the social security context where the concern is to limit the state's responsibility to support one of the partners.

Stability
Inevitably, relationships outside marriage may range from those that are over in a matter of days to those lasting longer than many marriages. Since it is unlikely that the benefits of marriage are intended by policy-makers to be bestowed on those enjoying a holiday romance or a 'temporary fling', the duration of the relationship and its sense of permanence may be an important consideration.

A sexual relationship
We have seen that a sexual relationship is a presumed but not a necessary condition of marriage. The same is true of cohabitation, although the absence of sexual relations must inevitably strengthen the claim of a couple who argue that they are *not* cohabiting 'as husband and wife'.

Children
Many cohabiting couples do not have children but may be living together first to test out the strength of their relationship, so the absence of children cannot be a determining factor. Where the couple *do* have a child, we have seen that the European Court of Human Rights will readily find that they share a family life and the same approach applies domestically. However, one could conceive of a divorced couple who live in the same house so as to preserve the relationship with their child, while leading separate lives vis-à-vis each other. Further, where the partner takes on the role of substitute or step-parent to the child, a court may conclude that this is evidence going towards establishing that the couple are cohabiting.

Intention and motivation
Where two people are living under the same roof, their reasons for doing so must be explored. In one case,[29] a woman who had been injured in an accident was being cared for by a male friend with whom she *had* formerly cohabited. It was eventually held that they were not living together as husband and wife because this was not now their intention.

[29] *Butterworth v Supplementary Benefits Commission* [1982] 1 All ER 498.

Appearance to the outside world

At one time, the stigma attached to extra-marital cohabitation resulted in couples holding themselves out as married, with the woman adopting the man's surname. This is less likely to happen nowadays, perhaps, but where a couple appear—or could be taken to appear—to outsiders as if they are cohabiting in a quasi-marital relationship, this may be taken into account.

Qualifying cohabitation relationships

Even where it may be concluded that a couple are 'cohabiting', the law may still choose to withhold the particular benefit of marriage which is being sought from those who are felt not to deserve it because, for example, the relationship has not lasted long enough. The difficulty is in determining what is long enough. The median length of cohabitation is increasing, and is currently about four years, after which it tends either to progress into marriage or to dissolve (Barlow et al, 2003). On this basis, the use of a two-year qualifying period for an inheritance claim appears if anything to be generous. Clearly, any defined length will be arbitrary and lead to hard cases which deserve recognition but fall on the wrong side of the line. It is not surprising then, that legislators may prefer to leave it to the courts and others to 'take into account' the duration of the particular relationship in issue and decide on the particular facts and in the light of all the circumstances whether it has been 'long enough' to deserve recognition.

COHABITING RELATIONSHIPS BETWEEN SAME-SEX COUPLES

The European Court of Human Rights has yet to regard same-sex relationships as giving rise to a 'family life'. So far, it appears to have regarded homosexual *conduct* as an aspect of a person's 'private' life but to have failed to see homosexual cohabitation as familial.[30] This may, to some extent, stem from its focus on the parent/child relationship rather than adult partnerships. It has, for example, been prepared to accept homosexual parents as having a family life with children with whom they are genetically related.[31]

Again, the issue has had to be tackled in domestic law. We have seen that the English concept of marriage implies a heterosexual union. The

---

[30] *Kerkhoven v Netherlands*, Application 15666/89 (1992, unreported).
[31] *Salgueiro da Silva Mouta v Portugal* (2001) 31 EHRR 47.

52   *An Introduction to Family Law*

solution, in several European states (ranging from Denmark to the region of Catalonia), has been to legislate specifically for same-sex unions through the concept of the 'registered partnership'. This generally extends to the couple all the usual consequences and benefits of marriage, save for the freedom to adopt or seek access to assisted reproduction treatment. These limitations suggest that states using this mechanism wish to stop short of viewing same-sex cohabitation as functionally equivalent to marriage by denying it the same scope for creating a legal family. They thus underscore the same distinction drawn in the European Convention between Article 12—the right to marry *and* found a family—and Article 8—the right to family life.

English law-makers have belatedly sought to catch up with these developments and indeed to overtake them. A Civil Partnership Bill was introduced into Parliament in 2003. If enacted, it would permit same-sex couples to register their partnership and thereby obtain virtually identical rights to those of spouses. The same rules regarding minimum age, prohibited degrees and sexual exclusivity would apply as they do to marriage. The same rights and responsibilities as pertain to spouses would apply equally to registered partners. Dissolution of the partnership would be treated in the same way as a divorce. The English law would be more inclusive than that operating in other European countries, since same-sex partners will in any case be able to adopt under the terms of the Adoption and Children Act noted above.

The move towards all-encompassing legislation of this kind was encouraged by the increasing willingness of the courts to chip away at the concept of the family to include homosexual 'family life' within its ambit. The major breakthrough came in *Fitzpatrick v Sterling Housing Association Ltd.*[32] The issue in the case was whether the surviving partner in a same-sex couple could succeed to a protected tenancy previously held in the name of the deceased partner. The Rent Act 1977 (as amended) provided that 'a person who was a member of the original tenant's family' could succeed to the tenancy. A majority of the House of Lords held that a homosexual partner could indeed be regarded as a member of the other's family. As Lord Slynn explained, the intention of Parliament in enacting the original legislation, dating back as far as 1920, was to enable not just a legal spouse but other members of the family unit occupying the property to qualify for succession. The hallmarks of the relationship were essentially that there should be a degree of mutual interdependence,

[32] [2001] 1 AC 27, HL.

of the sharing of lives, of caring and love, of commitment and support. In respect of legal relationships these are presumed, though evidently are not always present as the family law and criminal courts know only too well. In de facto relationships these are capable, if proved, of creating membership of the tenant's family.[33] In so holding, their Lordships took note of the change in social attitudes towards family relationships which has taken place over the years and held that, since Parliament had chosen not to define the word 'family' in the legislation, it was open to the courts to find its meaning in accord with current social developments.

The Rent Act also provides that a spouse (and a person living with the original tenant as husband or wife) may succeed to the tenancy, and the appellant had argued that he should have been regarded as such a person and have succeeded on that basis (which would have resulted in a tenancy with greater security having been awarded). Their Lordships unanimously rejected this argument. However, in *Ghaidan v Godin-Mendoza*[34] the House re-interpreted the provision in the light of the Human Rights Act (which was not in force at the time of their earlier ruling) and held that it was appropriate to include same-sex couples within the definition of a 'couple living together as husband and wife'. Their Lordships reasoned that the appellant's right to respect for his home under Article 8 was engaged by the attempt to evict him and that, since he was being treated differently to a heterosexual partner, Article 14 (the right to non-discriminatory treatment) was in issue. The House could see no objective and reasonable justification for this difference in treatment and the majority accordingly ruled that it must interpret the legislation so as to give effect to the appellant's Convention rights. The European Court of Human Rights ruled to like effect shortly earlier in a similar case brought against Austria.[35]

In rejecting the argument that to uphold the rights of same-sex partners would undermine the traditional family, both the domestic and European court reflected once again the growing preference for examining the content and functions of the given relationship rather than relying on its outward form. The European judgment is particularly important. Notwithstanding the advent of the Human Rights Act, the English courts must still give effect to the meaning of the words used in the statute being interpreted. There may be no room for manoeuvre with some existing

[33] Ibid at 38.   [34] [2004] UKHL 30, [2004] 3 WLR 113.
[35] *Karner v Austria* (2004) 38 EHRR 24.

legislative formulations of cohabitation. For example, s 62(1) of the Family Law Act 1996 defined cohabitants, for the purposes of domestic violence protection, as 'a man and a woman who, although not married to each other, are living together as husband and wife'. *Karner v Austria* lends support to the argument that such a provision is incompatible with the terms of the Convention and indeed this provision will be amended to enable same-sex couples to be included (see Chapter 4).

RELATIONSHIP BETWEEN PARENT AND CHILD

We have seen that both European and domestic jurisprudence place increasing emphasis upon the relationship between parent and child as giving rise to a familial bond which should be given appropriate recognition by the state. In an early and important European Convention on Human Rights case, *Marckx v Belgium*,[36] it was held that such recognition may require positive obligations to be performed by the state to enable the proper exercise of the right to respect for family life, and not just the avoidance of interference with that right. The law may therefore have to provide effective means whereby parents and children can assert their relationship with each other without unnecessary restrictions and barriers being placed in the way. In the Belgian case, this meant that the requirement that the mother formally acknowledge her child was unduly restrictive. However, the Court has not yet categorically held that limitations on the right of an unmarried *father* to establish his relationship to his child are necessarily a similar breach. In *Sahin v Germany; Sommerfeld v Germany*[37] it held that a German law, which gave mothers the right to determine whether the unmarried father could have contact with his child unless he could satisfy a court that this was in the child's best interests, was discriminatory under Article 14 since no such limitation applied to married fathers. It considered that in the case of a child born of a relationship where the parents had lived together, no sufficiently weighty reasons had been put forward to discriminate on the ground of the father's status. On this basis, it seems that the law should not be applied in such a way as to prevent the genetic tie between parent and child being used as the basis for legal recognition, at least where this is bolstered by evidence of social parenthood and the establishment of a 'real' family unit. However, the Court has also held, in determining whether automatic rights should accrue to the father based on his genetic

[36] (1979) 2 EHRR 330.   [37] [2003] 2 FLR 671 at para 94.

parenthood, that it is permissible for the law to distinguish between married and unmarried fathers and thus to deny the latter the same rights bestowed on the former. This is because a state may wish to limit the benefits of legal fatherhood to 'meritorious' unmarried fathers and may do so by requiring them to prove their 'fitness'—such as the fact that they have lived in a close stable relationship indistinguishable from the conventional family unit based on marriage—before granting them equal rights.[38] It seems that, in this particular part of its jurisprudence at least, the European Court views cohabitation as functionally equivalent to marriage and a sufficient qualification to require the equal treatment of the father with those who are married.

The legal position of the child born outside marriage

In English law, a legal tie between the child and the *mother* was recognized during the nineteenth century. At a time when (see Chapter 3) the law gave *married* mothers few rights over their children, the unmarried mother gradually came to be regarded as possessing most, if not all, of the same legal rights as a married father over his legitimate children. However, these were of little or no value—the reason for attaching legal recognition to the mother was to reinforce the stigma of her misconduct and to force her to support the child financially or to name and shame the father so that proceedings could be taken against him. There was no concern for the child's position—rather, the child was intended to suffer a similar stigma to that of the mother. It was not until the late twentieth century that a more sympathetic attitude led to a gradual improvement of the legal position of children born outside marriage. This was accomplished by a diminution in the significance attached to the status of the child's parents by abolishing most of the distinguishing features of 'legitimacy' and 'illegitimacy'. The process began in 1969 with the virtual equalization of children's inheritance rights. The Law Commission (1979, 1982) subsequently reviewed the law, taking into account developments in Europe including both the *Marckx* case and the drafting of a European Convention on the Status of Children Born Outside Wedlock 1975. Their efforts resulted in the law concerning parental rights and duties towards children being amended in 1987 and finally overhauled by the major reform of all child law enacted in the Children Act 1989.

The strategy for improvement was twofold. First, s 1 of the Family Law Reform Act 1987 requires that legislation be construed without

---

[38] *B v United Kingdom* [2000] 1 FLR 1.

regard to whether a child's parents (or anyone else through whom a relationship is deduced) are or have been married to each other, unless the contrary intention appears. This means that, unless legislation clearly requires, the question of whether a child is born or descended from married or unmarried parents is irrelevant in establishing the child's legal rights and obligations. For example, all children may inherit under a clause in a will referring to 'my children' and all children are entitled to financial support from their parents.

The second means whereby the position of these children was to be enhanced lay in improving the position of the father. It may be argued that it is in a child's interests to have both parents legally empowered to take decisions and actions in respect of the child, and that it may place a child in a vulnerable legal position if this is not the case. For example, if a child's unmarried mother is killed in a car accident, having made no will naming a guardian, there may be no one with the right to take over the care of the child. Although legal proceedings may be taken, this could cause delay and expense and why, if the child has always lived in a family unit with the mother and father, should such legal proceedings have to be taken to formalize the reality of the position? Legislation was therefore enacted to reduce the need to take such proceedings, although the law currently still stops short of treating all fathers alike, regardless of their marital status.

THE POSITION OF UNMARRIED FATHERS IN ENGLISH LAW

Acquiring parental status through birth registration

We saw earlier that the starting point in English law is to presume that a married man is the father of his wife's children. There is no equivalent presumption in the case of unmarried men, even where they are cohabiting with the mother. Inclusion of the man's name on the birth register as the child's father is prima facie evidence of his paternity. However, an unmarried father cannot *insist* on such registration against the mother's will, unless a court has first made an order (for parental responsibility or imposing financial liability) recognizing him as the legal father. In this way, the mother's autonomy is preserved, although she may be compelled to recognize the father's position if a court had determined it first.

Parental responsibility and the unmarried father

In 2002, around 82 per cent of births outside marriage were in fact registered jointly by both parents (ONS, 2004c). This may be taken to represent a degree of recognition by both parents of the father's role in the child's life. Furthermore, of these jointly registering parents, 77 per cent recorded that they lived at the same address, apparently signifying a continuing cohabiting relationship. The trend towards increased joint registration underpinned by apparent cohabitation influenced the Government to propose that such men should now be accorded not only the status of father by virtue of registration but also the rights, powers, and obligations which might be assumed to go with parental status, in other words, what is termed 'parental responsibility' (Lord Chancellor's Department, 1998). This was accomplished by the Adoption and Children Act 2002, discussed further below.[39]

The concept of parental responsibility (discussed fully in Chapter 3), is a shorthand expression for what, in s 3(1) of the Children Act 1989, are described as 'all the rights, duties, powers, responsibilities and authority which by law a parent of a child has in relation to the child and his property'. The use of the label *responsibility* is a deliberate shift of emphasis away from a focus on *rights*, intended to reinforce the view that parents (should) exercise their powers for the benefit of their children and not for themselves. Nonetheless, the label cannot disguise the legal reality that, until the 2002 Act, the *obligation* to support his child could be imposed upon the unmarried father even though he lacked any corresponding *rights* in respect of that child. On the other hand, parental responsibility undoubtedly brings with it the right, privilege, or freedom (albeit sometimes subject to the consent of any other holder of parental responsibility and to the overriding control of the courts) to make decisions about the child's future, including important issues such as how the child is to be educated, what surname the child should bear, and what medical treatment the child should undergo. Given this significance, it is not surprising that debate concerning how unmarried fathers should be treated in law has revolved around whether they should be entitled to parental responsibility—and hence parental rights—or not. Yet it is ironical that the debate has taken place at the same time as the law has more generally shifted its focus away from the *rights* of parents towards the interests of the child.

It is clear that several of the arguments in favour of improving the position of unmarried fathers have little to do with the interests of children. Rather, they are concerned fundamentally with doing away with the discrimination that unmarried fathers have undoubtedly faced, both

[39] Section 111 amending s 4 of the Children Act 1989.

compared with unmarried *mothers* and *married* fathers. As the Scottish Law Commission (1992: paras 2.38ff) explained, to deny a man the right to play a full legal part in his child's life may be unfair, especially if, for example, the mother refuses to marry him. The rationale for refusing equality of position lies in the assumption, held, as we have seen, by the European Court, that some unmarried fathers are 'unmeritorious' and must be denied legal rights over their children. Yet *married* fathers may be irresponsible and uncaring but are not denied their legal rights (although they can be restricted from exercising them where, for example, a court makes a residence order determining that the child is to live with the mother). Those opposing the grant of equal rights have argued that this places the mother in a difficult position if she does not wish to continue (or acknowledge) a relationship with the man. Further-more, it may provide a means whereby the man can control her care of the child and, indirectly, her own freedom of action. But this is equally true where the parents are divorced. At one time, the situation was graphically illustrated by postulating the hypothetical example of a rapist impregnat-ing a woman and then insisting on exercising parental rights over the resulting child. This example influenced the English Law Commission to reject the option of granting automatic parental responsibility to all unmarried fathers, but it was dismissed by their Scots counterpart as lacking a basis in reality and hardly significant enough to justify tarring *all* unmarried fathers with the same brush.

A halfway house was found by adopting a twofold solution. First, by enacting (in the Family Law Reform Act 1987, s 1) that legislation must be read without regard to marital status, it was provided that most refer-ences to a 'parent' will encompass the unmarried father. For example, such a father must usually, if traceable, be included in any child protec-tion proceedings; he is also given the same right as a married father to seek orders in respect of the child in private law proceedings (see Chapter 5). In these important instances therefore, he has the same par-ental *status* as a married father. Secondly, and perhaps more significantly, it was made easier for the unmarried father to acquire full parental responsibility and thus equal rights and powers with the mother to decide how the child is to be brought up.[40]

---

[40] Unmarried fathers who acquire parental responsibility remain, in one respect, different from mothers and married fathers, in that their parental responsibility may be removed by court order: s 4(2A) of the Children Act 1989 as amended by the Adoption and Children Act 2002, s 111.

Automatic parental responsibility upon registration of the father on the birth certificate
In order to ensure that the majority of children born outside marriage will have both parents in possession of parental responsibility, the Adoption and Children Act 2002 amended the Children Act 1989, s 4(1)(a) to provide that when the father becomes registered as such on the child's birth certificate, he acquires parental responsibility. The reform puts English law ahead of the European Convention jurisprudence which, as we have seen, may still permit discrimination where the parents have not lived together. No such cohabitation requirement is imposed by the 2002 Act. It represents a clear indication of the trend towards recognizing the *fact* of family relationship rather than its form and provides yet a further impetus towards regarding 'family life' rather than marriage, as the foundation of legal family relationships in English law.

The 2002 reform eliminates the need, for the vast majority of cases, for either party to do anything extra to establish the father's legal position. However, in cases where, for some reason, the father is not registered on the birth certificate (in 2002, some 43,000 children: ONS, 2004*c*), s 4 of the Children Act lays down two means of enabling him to acquire parental responsibility, either by agreement with the mother, or by court order.

Parental responsibility agreements
Section 4(1)(b) states that unmarried parents may by agreement provide for the father to have parental responsibility for the child which he then shares with the mother. To guard against forgery of the mother's signature by the father, the agreement must be witnessed by a justice of the peace, justices' clerk, or court official and registered with the Principal Registry of the Family Division. But there is no other requirement of outside scrutiny and no attempt to check whether the agreement is in the interests of the child. However, relatively few such agreements appear to have been registered. The main reason for the low take-up is lack of knowledge of the procedure, but research (Pickford, 1999) suggests that inertia and a diffidence about raising the issue with the child's mother may also play a part. The new option of acquisition of parental responsibility by joint registration, which already reflects the general practice, is likely to make such agreements even rarer than they currently are.

Parental responsibility orders
Where an unmarried father is determined to acquire parental responsibility in the teeth of the mother's objection, he may apply to the court under

s 4(1)(c) for an order to like effect. But the take-up of this opportunity has also been relatively low, with only 8,240 orders made in 2002, for example (Lord Chancellor's Department, 2003: Table 5.3). Furthermore, taking proceedings for an order is likely to be a hostile act, signifying the break-down of the relationship with the mother, and this creates a difficulty for the court hearing the case. What is to be the rationale for granting parental responsibility to the father in such a case? It might be to uphold the right to respect for his and the child's 'family life' and to recognize the reality of the family unit created between parents and child and enable him to exercise the same powers as a married father. But if so, what is the point of making an order if this unit has now broken down and he is not living with (indeed, may never have lived with) the child? It might instead be to recognize the role the father can play in the child's life, regardless of the quality or state of the parental relationship. If so, how far can or should the court control the freedom of action thereby granted so as to ensure that the mother's position as primary carer of the child is not jeopardized? The courts have attempted to steer through these difficulties first, by setting out basic criteria which should be satisfied before an order should be made and secondly, by downplaying the legal significance of the order.

As to the first of these, the basic test which demonstrates the father's 'merit' or qualification for being granted parental responsibility requires him to satisfy the court as to the degree of commitment he has shown towards the child, the degree of attachment existing between him and the child, and the validity of his reasons for seeking an order.[41] Satisfaction of this test does not raise a presumption that the order should be granted,[42] but the usual approach of the courts has been to grant an order unless there are strong reasons, such as violence shown against the child, to refuse it. This has been so even where it is clear that the father can play only a minimal role in the child's future life (including the situation where the child is about to be adopted by strangers). In taking this stance, the courts have laid great stress on the assumption that it is in a child's interests to 'know' his father (or at least know that his father has acknowledged him). They have also relied on the second mechanism of minimizing the legal importance of the order so as to reassure the mother that her position will not be undermined. As Ward LJ put it in *Re S (Parental Responsibility)*:[43]

---

[41] *Re H (Minors) (Local Authority: Parental Rights) (No 3)* [1991] Fam 151, CA.
[42] *Re H (Parental Responsibility)* [1998] 1 FLR 855, CA.
[43] [1995] 2 FLR 648, 657, CA.

It is wrong to place undue and therefore false emphasis on the rights and duties and the powers comprised in 'parental responsibility' and not to concentrate on the fact that what is at issue is conferring upon a committed father the status of parenthood for which nature has already ordained that he must bear responsibility.

The problem with this explanation is that, as noted above, the father already has 'the status of parenthood' by virtue of being recognized as the father—parental responsibility is intended to flesh out this status by granting precisely the rights, duties, and powers which Ward LJ seeks to dismiss. Why, one might ask, would the father otherwise bother to acquire it?

THE POSITION OF STEP-PARENTS

Increasing divorce and increasing cohabitation (which is statistically more likely to break down than marriage) have meant that not only has the number of lone parent families risen in the past twenty-five years but the number of step-families has also grown. It has been estimated that around 10 per cent of children (at least one million) are living in step families (ONS, 2002: 18), over 90 per cent of which consist of a couple with at least one child from a former relationship of the *mother*. Contrary to the old fairy tales then, a child these days is much more likely to live with a step father, than with a step mother. The experience of step-relationships can be a difficult one for adults and children alike. How far the step-parent is to assume the role of the absent parent is particularly problematic. Uncertainty about the legal position of the step-parent may compound the difficulties. The mere fact of being married to, or cohabiting with, the birth parent does not give rise to any legal relationship between the step-parent and the child. However, there is provision to allow orders (both in relation to financial provision and the child's upbringing) in respect of the child to be made in favour of, or against, a step-parent who is *married* to the birth parent, where the child is regarded as a 'child of the family'. This phrase includes a child, 'who has been treated by both of [the spouses] as a child of their family'.[44] Such 'treatment' is a question of fact, to be judged objectively.[45]

---

[44] Matrimonial Causes Act 1973, s 52; Domestic Proceedings and Magistrates' Courts Act 1978, s 88; Children Act 1989, s 105(1).

[45] It is not limited to step-parents but may apply to other quasi-parental relationships. See, e.g. *Re A (Child of the Family)* [1998]1 FLR 347, CA—grandparents looking after their teenaged daughter's child. When the grandparents' own marriage broke down, it was held that their care for the child had gone beyond what might be normally be expected of grandparents and the child was effectively part of 'their' family.

A step-parent may also apply to adopt the child, in which case he or she legally takes the place of the 'missing' parent. These kinds of adoptions have been disapproved as distorting the true family relationship but they still form around 25 per cent of all adoptions (Lord Chancellor's Department, 2003: Table 5.4). Alternatively, the step-parent may acquire and share parental responsibility with the birth parents. This may be done by obtaining a residence order under s 8 of the Children Act 1989, but this may be artificial since the main point of such an order is to settle the arrangements as to where the child is to live, and parental responsibility is bestowed as an adjunct to this rather than being the main point of the order. Instead, (but only if the step-parent is married to the birth parent), he or she will, under a change introduced by the Adoption and Children Act 2002, be able to obtain parental responsibility *simpliciter*, under the Children Act 1989, s 4A, by making an agreement with the birth parents or by applying for a court order, in the same way as an unmarried father may do.

'FAMILY LIFE' OUTSIDE THE PARENT/CHILD RELATIONSHIP

To conclude this survey of how the law recognizes the formation of family relationships, it is necessary to say a little about non-parental ties.

It has been seen that for the purposes of succession to a tenancy, the term 'family' was interpreted flexibly to include same-sex partners. This exercise in statutory construction reflected how, in everyday discourse, one may, depending upon the context, include or exclude within one's family those to whom one regards oneself as 'related' in some way. Strasbourg jurisprudence has only scratched the surface of this reality. It has recognized the position of those outside the parent/child or spousal relationship, in upholding the right to respect for family life of grandparents in *Marckx v Belgium*, but it has not yet given the same clear recognition in relation to other family ties. English law, however, has long acknowledged such ties. For example, in the absence of a will, the Administration of Estates Act 1925, as amended, provides for distribution of the deceased's estate to, in order of priority, children, parents, siblings, nieces and nephews, half-siblings, grandparents, and uncles and aunts (see further, Chapter 6). It can be seen that all these are related by blood. Adoption legislation is broader; it includes these (apart from nieces and nephews) within the term 'relative' (as in the context of adoption of a child by a 'relative') and applies this equally to those related by marriage.

In these examples, the law follows its traditional approach based on the blood or marriage tie. But the law is even more flexible than this. A parent, or the court, may appoint an adult to act as the child's guardian in the event of his or her death. Where the parent makes the appointment, there is no check on the person's suitability to act, but if the appointment takes effect, that person is immediately vested with parental responsibility for the child.[46] Under the Children Act 1989, *any* person may apply to the court for leave to seek an order relating to the child. In particular, the court may grant a 'residence order' which, as seen above, settles where the child will live and also vests parental responsibility in the applicant for its duration.[47] The grant of a residence order to a third party, although of temporary duration and subject to revocation, creates a substantial legal tie between the adult and the child and solidifies their Article 8 right to respect for family life. It also enables legal recognition to be given to a broad range of family structures and relationships. For example, the allocation of parental responsibility to a third party does not thereby result in its removal from the parents; instead, it is shared with them. It is therefore possible for more than two people to have parental responsibility for a child at the same time, breaking the normative model of 'parenting' implicitly based on the heterosexual two-parent family. In *G v F (Contact and Shared Residence: Applications for Leave)*,[48] for instance, the applicant had played a full part in caring for and raising the child of her lesbian partner during their cohabitation. The court granted her leave to seek a shared residence order, which would vest her with parental responsibility for the child, to be shared with the birth mother (and, potentially, with the birth father as well).

Special guardianship

In the case of older children especially, it has been recognized that adoption may be an unsuitable device for providing permanence where they need the stability of a long-term substitute family. Cutting off the child from all legal links with her birth family may be undesirable and draconian, especially where contact with a parent, siblings or other birth relatives is to continue even after the placement (see Chapter 5). The Adoption and Children Act 2002 accordingly inserted s 14A into the Children Act 1989, which introduced the concept of 'special guardianship'

---

[46] Children Act 1989, s 5. This is discussed further in Chapter 3.
[47] Sections 8(1), 10, and 12(2), discussed further in Chapter 5.
[48] [1998] 2 FLR 799.

as a measure intended to be a kind of extra-secure form of residence order. Any person (other than a parent) may apply for such an order, either as of right or with leave. Unlike a normal residence order, under s 14C, special guardianship gives the holder the right to exercise parental responsibility to the exclusion of anyone else with parental responsibility (except where any enactment or rule of law requires the consent of more than one person with such responsibility in a matter affecting the child). The aim is to permit foster carers to obtain legal authority to determine the child's upbringing, free from day-to-day interference from the birth parent, without creating the 'new' legal family brought about by adoption. This kind of legal mechanism has existed before; 'custodianship' was abolished by the Children Act 1989 because it appeared to be viewed by potential applicants as an inferior form of security of their relationship to the child compared with adoption. It is unclear whether 'special guardianship' will prove more attractive.

Other 'family' ties

Finally, more recent legislation has attempted to encompass an even broader group of people with whom one may be said to have some kind of 'family life'. In s 63(1) of the Family Law Act 1996 (as amended), for example, in addition to all those mentioned above, 'relative' is defined as including step-parents and step-children; grandchildren; aunts, uncles, nieces, nephews, and first cousins of the half-blood or by marriage; and all such included relatives of a former spouse or cohabitant. Even such a broad range may exclude still others in respect of whom a person can claim a quasi-family or domestic relationship. The legislation accordingly also provides that persons 'associated' with the applicant include fiancés (present or past), persons who 'have or have had an intimate personal relationship with each other which is or was of significant duration,'[49] and those who live or have lived in the same household 'otherwise than merely by reason of one of them being the other's employee, tenant, lodger or boarder'. The purpose of such an expansive definition is to enable a person facing violence or other behaviour amounting to 'molestation' to obtain an order to prohibit its repetition (see Chapter 4). It therefore makes sense to define the class of those concerned broadly and it would be wrong to claim that all of these are to be legally regarded as if they

---

[49] Added to s 62(3) by the Domestic Violence, Crime and Victims Bill 2003–4. See also s 27 of the Sexual Offences Act 2003 for an expansive definition of 'family relationships' in relation to familial child sex offences.

were members of the applicant's 'family'. Nonetheless, the protection was not intended to be completely open-ended and is expressed to be limited to those in respect of whom one might say there is a close personal relationship or avowed family bond.

In drawing the boundary so widely, Parliament can be said to have been demonstrating how modern family relationships may have more to do with family *behaviour* than with family *ties*. As some sociologists have argued (Morgan, 1996; Smart and Neale, 1999), understanding what is meant by 'family' may be more a question of exploring what people 'do' together that can be classed as 'familial', than considering the narrower issue of with whom they do it. It is what people 'do' in family life which forms the subject-matter of the following Chapter.

3

Rights and Responsibilities within the Family

INTRODUCTION

How far the law should be used to lay down norms of behaviour for family members to follow in their relationships with each other causes problems for liberal societies. First, there is the problem of the public/private divide. In classic liberal thinking, as noted in Chapter 1, the family belongs to the private sphere and the mark of a free society is the reluctance of the state to interfere in that sphere. On that basis, it might be argued that the law should not be used as a tool to regulate family relationships because to do so is to undermine people's freedom and to restrict how they choose to live their private lives. Secondly, are not family relationships marked out from others by their altruism? Family relationships depend upon the 'higher' motivations and feelings of love, care, and affection rather than upon self-advancement and obligation. Within our families at least, we can 'be ourselves' and can show unconditional love to those around us without having to be coerced by the state into fulfilling our obligations to each other. We take on such obligations willingly, not because the law tells us to do so. So it might be concluded that there is limited scope for the law to play in the fully functioning family, and it is only when the relationship is in crisis and has broken down that it might be called upon to intervene, precisely because family members can at that point no longer rely upon each other's goodwill.

This is certainly the traditional way of looking at how the law regulates family relationships. Family law at one time focused primarily on entry into and exit from marriage, with most attention paid to the consequences of divorce. What went on in between the wedding and the divorce was of comparatively little interest. This was not surprising, since it did not give rise to many problems that could be brought to lawyers and courts to resolve—or at least, to lawyers and courts applying common law and equity. But it did not follow from this that the law had no interest in internal family problems. Rather, it upheld a status quo that vested decision-making authority and coercive power in the husband/father in the family, and expected the wife/mother and children to submit to him, whatever their own wishes and feelings might have been. Generally, women and children could not use the law to protect them from the demands of the male head of household, however unjust these might be, not because the law had nothing to say about them, but precisely because it upheld his right to enforce these demands. In this way, the law was used to regulate family relationships just as comprehensively as if it had laid down in a detailed code precise instructions on who could do what and to whom as was common in those countries influenced by the Code Napoléon (Glendon: Chapter 3).

Nor is the law's inability to require people to love each other ultimately a real problem. While *feelings* cannot be prescribed by law, *behaviour* can still be controlled. Until recently, spouses' behaviour could ultimately be controlled (or at least, be subject to sanction) by the operation of divorce law. Equally, while parents cannot be made to love their children, they *can* be limited by the law in how far they can use physical punishment to discipline a child. As discussed below in Chapter 6, rules governing marital misconduct now have limited significance, and it has been argued by some right-wing politicians that their diminution has weakened the marriage bond. Significantly, the politicians who tend to support the argument that marriage is being weakened by the state's reluctance to lay down clear norms of *marital* behaviour are often those most keen to 'keep the state out' when it comes to prescribing *parental* conduct towards children, especially as regards punishment. This suggests that what is at stake here, as many feminists understood when they began the struggle for women's emancipation in the nineteenth century, is a struggle for power within the family.

RIGHTS AND RESPONSIBILITIES

Conduct within relationships is translated into law through the concepts of rights and responsibilities. Sometimes, these are interpreted narrowly to mean that a person possesses a right that places another under a corresponding duty to act, or refrain from acting, in order to allow the right-holder to exercise his right (Hohfeld, 1919). Such a definition could perhaps be used to characterize the rights given to men under the common law as husbands and fathers. They had a right, for example, to determine where the family would live and the standard of living it would enjoy. Wives and children had a duty to follow the man and obey his demands. Wives had a similar claim right to be maintained by their husbands, and husbands had a corresponding duty to support their wives. Unfortunately, wives had no direct means of enforcing their right through the courts, because they could not sue their husbands to enforce it, so its practical utility was minimal. The only way a wife could seek to enforce the husband's duty was to pledge his credit for goods and services (if a trader would agree), with the trader then permitted to sue the husband for non-payment. In this way, the law upheld, at an ideological level, the privacy of the family unit by refusing to 'interfere' in the relationship between husband and wife, and the primacy of the male head, by refusing to permit his actions to be questioned by his wife. The marital relationship, while proclaimed as a 'contract' at the point of entry, was not recognized as a legally enforceable contract regarding its ongoing terms and conditions. At the same time, the law could be used to enforce the commercial arrangement—as a contract—between the trader and the husband, thus upholding the demands of the public—market—sphere.

One of the key features of change in family law over the past 150 years, reflecting much broader changes in social attitudes, has been the emancipation, first of women as mothers and wives, and more recently of children, from this position of subservience to the male head of their family and their recognition in law as independent and individual rights-bearers. But when more than one person has the same rights, questions then arise as to how these are to be balanced and when one rather than another will prevail. One way round this problem, which was used in family law until the enactment of the Human Rights Act 1998, was to apply principles which overrode mere 'rights', and could be used to determine the matter. Whether this will continue to work so easily in a human rights-dominated ethos must be considered in this Chapter as we look at how the current law has evolved.

THE MARITAL RELATIONSHIP

THE COMMON LAW LEGACY

The nature and content of the marital relationship in English law is based on two notions, the 'doctrine of unity' and the concept of 'consortium', which now have little real significance. This is a reflection of the diminution in the importance of marriage, and of the adult relationship as the focus of attention for family law and policy. The general trend has been twofold: to equalize the position of men and women within marriage and to reduce the differences between marriage and other relationships.

The doctrine of unity

At common law, marriage might have been seen as reflecting the 'joint enterprise' model outlined in Chapter 1, because it was said that, on marriage, husband and wife became one legal unit. However, that one was the husband and there was no suggestion that, once the marriage had been entered into, the parties were intended to be regarded as equals. The 'doctrine of unity' operated to suspend a woman's legal personality for the duration of the marriage; she could not sue or be sued in her own right but must be joined in the action by her husband. The more practical significance of the doctrine was that, on marriage, all the wife's property (barring that held on trust for her) vested in the husband. This included any property or earnings she subsequently acquired. It was because the effect of this rule could leave the wife totally destitute that the law imposed a duty on the husband to provide a home and maintenance for the wife. Wealthy families used settlements and trusts to secure to the wife some independence from her husband, but their motivation was as much to protect the family wealth for the benefit of future generations as to secure the wife's own position. The wife remained dependent on the trustees and could not control the property herself. It is not surprising, therefore, that reforms to matrimonial property law were among the earliest fruits of the agitation for female emancipation.

The most important legislative amendment, the Married Women's Property Act 1882, established that married women would henceforward retain and acquire property as their separate property, in the same way as a single woman, and all men. *Formal* equality was therefore granted to married women, marking the first step on the way to regarding marriage as a 'partnership of equals'. But subsequent generations of feminists have pondered whether this was the correct remedy to have sought. It ignores the fact that women earn less then men and therefore have less ability to acquire property on an equal footing with their husbands, so that, at the end of the marriage (be it by death or divorce) the married woman may be significantly worse off than the man. It means that, where a couple intend that they should share their property, they must take additional steps to ensure that this intention is given legal effect, otherwise again, the wife may find herself unprotected. And, for those who regard marriage as a key institution to be promoted by the state, it detracts from its significance by removing any property consequences flowing from the fact of marriage alone.

In other jurisdictions based on civil law, marriage (or sometimes cohabitation) may give rise to a 'community of property' whereby, depending upon the precise terms of the system applying, property acquired during the relationship is shared by the couple and divided equally between them at its end. Strict equality of division may not resolve the problem of the substantive inequality of women, and there is usually provision to allow couples to opt out of the system, but if nothing else, the community model sends a message that marriage is a joint enterprise which has consequences not attached to other relationships.

The concept of consortium

The other distinguishing feature of marriage at common law, which also implied a joint enterprise, was that it gave rise to the concept of 'consortium'. This archaic-sounding notion means no more than 'living together as husband and wife with all the incidents that flow from that relationship' (Lowe and Douglas, 1998: 55). The concept did not imply equality of the spouses. It did, it is true, lay down mutual rights and obligations but, as with the doctrine of unity, the balance of advantage was heavily weighted on the husband's side. He was enabled to enforce the wife's obligations by recourse to law; she was not. It is doubtful whether it still makes sense to think of the content of marriage in terms of 'consortium'. No one seems very sure what the 'incidents' flowing from the relationship consist of. In this respect, consortium resembles the concept of parental responsibility governing the relationship between parent and child which, as noted later in this Chapter, has also been regarded as incapable of precise definition. However, certain key aspects of the marital relationship can be elucidated and do require discussion.

KEY ASPECTS OF THE MODERN MARITAL RELATIONSHIP[1]

Physical autonomy

Until the House of Lords ruled otherwise, in *R v R (rape: marital exemption)*,[2] it appeared that a husband could not be convicted of rape of his wife, because, according to Hale,

---

[1] Except where otherwise specified in the text, the rules relating to marriage are expected to apply equally to civil registered partnerships if legislation introducing these is enacted.

[2] [1992] 1 AC 599. The Sexual Offences Act 2003, s 1 amends the definition of rape to exclude any reference to the offence requiring 'unlawful' sexual intercourse, which had, prior to the House of Lords' decision, been thought to connote extra-marital intercourse.

by their mutual matrimonial consent and contract the wife hath given up herself in this kind unto her husband which she cannot retract.[3]

On this basis, marriage could be seen as giving the husband a right to his wife's sexual services and imposing a duty upon her to provide them. Since a sexual relationship lies at the heart of the legal concept of marriage, as discussed in Chapter 2, this is perhaps not surprising. The law on adultery and legitimacy also helped to reinforce the exclusivity attached to the sexual services of a wife, by permitting divorce if she proved unfaithful, and by bastardizing any children born outside marriage. This argument might be countered by noting that husbands too could be divorced for adultery, thus implying that the duty to be faithful applied to both sexes. However, only in 1923, in the wake of the general political emancipation of women at that time, did the law allow a wife to divorce her husband simply on the ground of his adultery. Moreover, the consequences of being found to have committed adultery remained graver for women, both in terms of stigma and financial hardship, than for men. A remnant of the sexual obligation of marriage may remain in the current divorce law. Either spouse may seek to rely upon the other's excessive demands or refusals to have sexual intercourse (or other types of sexual practice) as behaviour that he or she cannot reasonably be expected to live with (see further Chapter 6).

Interestingly, some years before the courts had finally ruled that husbands have no immunity from prosecution for marital rape, they had already recognized that wives have physical autonomy from their husbands in regard to control over child-bearing. In *Paton v BPAS*, Sir George Baker P refused to grant an injunction to a husband who wished to prevent his wife from having an abortion. The President, echoing liberal arguments regarding the private sphere and the altruistic basis of family obligations, considered that '[p]ersonal family relationships in marriage cannot be enforced by the order of a court'.[4] This approach appears to ignore the extent to which the courts, by refusing to punish a husband for rape, for example, in effect enabled men to enforce their wives' marital obligations. However, it is compatible with other twentieth century decisions to the effect that a husband cannot insist that his wife use, or refrain from using, contraception—and neither can the wife.[5] The modern position regarding physical autonomy is therefore that just as with the concept of separate property, marriage has ceased to have any

---

[3] 1 Hale PC 629.   [4] [1979] QB 276, 280F.
[5] *Baxter v Baxter* [1948] AC 274, HL.

particular consequences; each spouse has the same rights to physical protection as any other person, regardless of their relationship.

Surname

A similar lack of significance attached to marriage can be seen in the law concerning the use of a surname by married persons. There is no legal rule requiring a woman to take her husband's surname on marriage, although by convention many women do this. Similarly, if a marriage ends, whether by death or in divorce, the woman may retain her married surname. This flexibility regarding surnames extends to unmarried cohabitants where, at least when a stigma was still attached to living together, the woman might have taken the man's name so as to cover up the fact that they were not in fact married. So long as there is no intent to defraud others, choice of surname is entirely a matter for the individual. The position is rather different where the surname of children is concerned, as will be considered later in this Chapter.

The right to occupy the family home

At common law, consortium appears to have imposed upon the spouses a mutual duty to live together—if either left without just cause, he or she would be 'in desertion' (which remains a basis for divorce). The husband could apparently enforce the wife's duty to live with him by resort to physical restraint, at least until this was clearly prohibited at the end of the nineteenth century.[6] The legacy of this licence to restrain a wife from leaving can be seen in a reluctance, until recently, to take the problem of domestic violence seriously, as is discussed in Chapter 4. However, by corollary, the husband had a reciprocal duty to provide a home for the wife to live in with him, so long as she did not commit a matrimonial offence (such as adultery). At common law, this right was only enforceable as against him. The wife could prevent her husband from evicting her, but if he left her and sold the property to a third party, or relinquished his tenancy to the landlord, she could not rely on her right as against the husband to prevent the third party from gaining possession of the property.[7] Of course, if she herself was entitled to occupy the property, either because it was her separate property or she and the husband were joint tenants, then she could rely on her own property rights against the third party. But until the 1960s it was relatively uncommon for

[6] *R v Jackson* [1891] 1 QB 671, CA.
[7] *National Provincial Bank Limited v Ainsworth* [1965] AC 1175, HL.

spouses to own or rent property jointly and even rarer for a woman to own a home herself.

Legislation was enacted to remedy this problem, and the current law is contained in Part IV of the Family Law Act 1996. Unlike the common law, it applies to either husband or wife (but it is assumed in the discussion below that the wife is the vulnerable party). Since a spouse who already has property rights in the home (as owner or tenant, for example) does not need special protection, s 30 vests 'matrimonial home rights' only in a spouse who lacks such property rights (and does not extend these rights to cohabitants at all). Such a spouse has a right not to be evicted from the property by the other spouse without a court order and a right, if not in occupation, to enter and occupy it. The rights attach only to a property that was, or was intended to be, the parties' matrimonial home; a spouse may not claim a right of entry to a property acquired by the other subsequent to their separation. Where the spouse who is the owner or tenant leaves the home and stops paying the mortgage or rent, then the spouse relying on matrimonial home rights has the right to make the payments in lieu to the mortgagee or landlord and can resist possession proceedings. In this way, her right to occupy can be protected, although if she lacks the means to pay the outgoings on the property, either out of her own earnings or through social security, for example, she may ultimately have to move anyway.

To prevent the spouse with property rights from disposing of the property to a bona fide purchaser without notice of the other's matrimonial home rights, s 31 enables the wife to register her rights as a charge against the property. In practice, this is usually only done when the parties are in the throes of divorce and the wife needs to ensure that the property can be dealt with as part of the divorce settlement.

The statutory right to occupy the marital home may be seen as an example of the 'joint enterprise' model of marriage. It grants a right by virtue of marital status but recognizes that the parties are not necessarily economically equal. It is also a symbol of the state's regard for marriage. However, it cannot be seen as a significant *advantage* of marriage over cohabitation any more, because, as we will see in Chapter 4, the courts have power to grant similar protection (albeit based on discretion rather than by virtue of a statutory right) to a cohabitant.

The right to be maintained

A sharper distinction between married and unmarried couples can be drawn when it comes to considering the modern application of the right to be maintained. We saw above that at common law, the wife could not enforce her right directly against her husband. However, the ecclesiastical courts could order a husband to pay alimony (maintenance) to a wife seeking a separation from him. When judicial divorce was introduced in 1857, the Divorce Court was given power to order maintenance in favour of an innocent wife who was granted a divorce. In 1878, the magistrates' courts were given jurisdiction to grant a separation order where a husband had been convicted of assault of his wife, and to order him to pay her maintenance. The grounds for an award of maintenance were eventually widened to include a failure to provide reasonable maintenance and to apply equally to husbands and wives.[8] In practice, this jurisdiction is now rarely used. It has been largely superseded by the more comprehensive powers available on a divorce, and by the focus upon support for children which reflects the broader trend towards concern with the parent/child relationship. These are discussed below and in Chapter 6.

It was not only the private law that imposed an obligation to support. Since the end of the sixteenth century, the Poor Law had imposed a duty to maintain upon spouses, parents, grandparents, and children that could be enforced by the Parish if a person became dependent upon it for Relief. Underpinning this approach is a view of the family (and not just the married couple) on the joint enterprise model—a collective grouping working for each other and recognized as a unit by the outside world. When the Poor Law was replaced by the establishment of the welfare state in the 1940s and the development of social security, the obligation to support was limited to spouses and parents, reflecting a shift in focus to the nuclear rather than wider family unit. Now, under the Social Security Administration Act 1992, s 78(6), men and women are liable to maintain their spouses during the marriage. Where a claimant is married and living with her spouse, he[9] will be expected to support her and any children in the family unit and their resources will be 'aggregated' and regarded as available to meet the needs of the whole family (even if he gives her nothing). Tax credits may operate to boost a family's income otherwise derived only from low wages, to the amount the state regards as necessary for their support. But if the husband's earnings are high, and he is simply mean with his money, the wife is unable to claim in her own right. Where the spouses separate, she will be able to claim for herself and any children

---

[8] The relevant provisions are currently contained in the Matrimonial Causes Act 1973, s 27 and the Domestic Proceedings and Magistrates' Courts Act 1978, s 1.
[9] The obligation is reciprocal.

living with her, and social security benefits are a primary source of income for separated wives with dependent children in this country.

Yet, as with physical protection and occupation of the home, the law has expanded beyond the scope of marriage to provide similar rights and limitations in respect of cohabiting couples. Where a woman is cohabiting with a partner 'as husband and wife', they will be regarded as if they were married for the purpose of claiming means-tested benefits even though s 78(6) does not impose a duty upon cohabitants to support each other. The motivation for the policy is to prevent each cohabiting partner from being able to claim benefit as if living alone rather than as a joint unit. If cohabitants were not treated in this way, they would have a financial advantage over married couples. Same-sex cohabitants currently enjoy exactly this advantage, since they are not regarded as living together 'as husband and wife'.

Contracts between the spouses

At common law, a wife could not make binding contracts with her spouse, or with anyone else. She was given contractual capacity in the property reforms of the nineteenth century, and one might have expected that the courts would henceforward enforce contractual arrangements made between the spouses, since each was to be regarded as an autonomous individual in charge of his or her own property. But again, the liberal ideology of the private sphere and the altruism of family relationships provided a justification for continuing to refuse to recognize marital contracts. In *Balfour v Balfour*,[10] Atkin LJ proclaimed that 'each house is a domain into which the King's writ does not seek to run, and to which his officers do not seek to be admitted'. The Court accordingly declined to enforce an agreement that a husband would pay his wife an allowance while he was overseas, holding that there had been no intent to create legal relations and therefore no contract. The decision remains an authority for what might well be regarded as the 'common sense' proposition that couples make many arrangements and agreements together which they never contemplate as being legally binding, and that therefore it is right for the law to be wary of enforcing marital agreements too readily. As Lord Hodson put it in *Pettitt v Pettitt*,[11] '[t]he conception of a normal married couple spending the long winter evenings hammering out agreements about their possessions appears grotesque. . .' though whether this should apply to the case of a financial allowance is open to

---

[10] [1919] 2 KB 571, 579, CA.   [11] [1970] AC 777, 810F, HL.

question. Certainly, once the spouses have separated, there is no bar to enforcing an agreement because they are regarded as having negotiated it at arm's length. However, they cannot by agreement exclude the court from exercising its jurisdiction to make financial and property orders in the event of divorce; see Chapter 6.

Marital property

Although the courts declined to enforce contracts made between cohabiting spouses, they did not show the same reluctance to attach legal consequences to arrangements made by married couples regarding the ownership of their property. In *Pettitt v Pettitt*, Lord Diplock explained the difference on the basis that *Balfour v Balfour* concerned the non-performance of a promise in the realm of contract law. By contrast, once acts are performed, they cannot be deprived of their legal consequences in the sphere of property law. It is in determining this issue that the question of whether marriage should be viewed as a partnership of equals or joint enterprise arises most acutely. For most married couples, the problem will arise only when the marriage is over and then the law of divorce or family provision is sufficiently flexible to fulfil either model, as will be seen in Chapter 6. But the ownership of property may fall to be determined in other contexts, particularly where a spouse is facing bankruptcy and the prospect of having all 'his' property seized by the trustee in bankruptcy. In such a situation, determining who actually owns the property that is occupied and enjoyed by the family will be crucial. The basic position regarding family property is discussed here, but because of its practical and symbolic importance to the life of the family, the detailed rules governing ownership and occupation of the family *home* are discussed in Chapter 4.

The separate property concept enacted in 1882 means that even where property is brought into the family for joint use or occupation, it does not thereby become regarded as jointly owned. There is no concept of 'family assets' in English law. This does not, however, mean that property cannot be co-owned. It is the parties' intention which ultimately determines whether any item of 'family property', be it a house, personal property, or an investment, can be regarded as jointly owned. In taking this approach, the courts may be regarded as having utilized the joint enterprise model of marriage, by giving recognition to the spouses' view of their property rights as based on their sharing of the benefits and burdens of the marriage relationship. But they have done so on the basis of factual evidence and individual circumstances rather than the status of the parties' relationship. The same rules therefore apply, apart from some limited exceptions explained below, to cohabitants as well as to spouses.

Indeed, marriage might now be said to have only a limited bearing in determining property ownership. Most importantly, the courts may be readier to infer that a married couple intended to share their property with each other than an unmarried couple.[12] Additionally, there are three, now rarely used, statutory provisions which apply to married couples' property rights. The first[13] of these is s 17 of the Married Women's Property Act 1882. This provides that 'in any question between husband and wife as to the title to or possession of property' either spouse may apply to the High Court or a county court and the judge may make such order 'as he thinks fit'. At one time it was argued that this section bestowed a discretion on the judge to allocate property between the spouses in any proportions he thought appropriate. However, in *Pettitt v Pettitt*, the House of Lords ruled that the section only provides a procedural mechanism for resolving the question of ownership. This need for a discretionary jurisdiction, at least for married couples, was met once divorce law was reformed in 1970, giving the courts a wide jurisdiction to adjust the spouses' property rights (see Chapter 6).

Personal property
Where spouses put their earnings into a joint bank account, they will be regarded as co-owners of the account.[14] If only one spouse pays money in, it will be a question of fact as to whether the account was intended to be for joint use. Where the account is in the name of one spouse only, the other may be regarded as entitled to a share, again if it can be shown that they intended this result. Where property is acquired by one spouse with money withdrawn from the account, it is presumed that it is owned by that spouse alone, unless, once more, an intention that it be jointly owned can be established.[15]

However, where one spouse gives money to the other to be spent on particular purposes, such as where a husband gives his wife housekeeping money, it was held that the money remains his and any savings made by the wife as a result of her good management accrue to him.[16] The unfairness to the wife of this ruling was intended to be alleviated by the

---

[12] *Bernard v Josephs* [1982] Ch 391, CA.
[13] The second is discussed below at p 78, and the third (s 37 of the Matrimonial Proceedings and Property Act 1970) is discussed in Chapter 4.
[14] *Jones v Maynard* [1951] Ch 572.   [15] *Re Bishop* [1965] Ch 450.
[16] *Blackwell v Blackwell* [1943] 2 All ER 579, CA.

Married Women's Property Act 1964. This provides that where a husband makes an allowance to the wife (but not vice versa) 'for the expenses of the matrimonial home or for similar purposes', any money derived from the allowance or property acquired out of such money shall be treated as belonging to them both in equal shares. Although this provision may be said to follow the joint enterprise model of marriage, by using the parties' marital status as justifying a special approach, it is regarded as flawed. First, it provides that the money is to be held in equal shares rather than jointly. This means that, on the death of one of the parties, the survivor does not take the whole amount, as would be the case where property is jointly owned, but only a half share. The other half forms part of the deceased's estate and may be willed away from the surviving spouse, thus reinforcing the separate property approach. Secondly, the Act is outmoded because it presumes a stereotyped division of labour and responsibility in the household. By referring to an 'allowance' to cover the 'expenses' of the home, it appears to cover only money handed over to a wife for weekly housekeeping. It is unclear—but doubtful—whether, if the wife paid the mortgage instalments from the allowance, she would thereby acquire an interest in the matrimonial home. Nor does the Act envisage that a wife might support her husband, who takes care of the home instead of her. The Law Commission has recommended that the Act be repealed, and replaced by a statutory presumption (subject to exceptions, including property acquired by gift or inheritance) that property bought for the joint use or benefit of spouses should belong to them jointly (Law Commission, 1985). No legislation has resulted, but the Government has accepted that the current law is incompatible with Protocol 7, Article 5 to the European Convention on Human Rights (discussed in Chapter 1).

THE PARENT/CHILD RELATIONSHIP

PARENTING AS A 'JOINT ENTERPRISE'

'Parenting' is increasingly seen as an exercise to be engaged in by both parents with the goal of 'producing' a well-adjusted adult who is able to contribute to the well-being of society. Each parent has an equal part to play in this endeavour, although this may entail undertaking different roles. There is ambivalence in social and cultural attitudes regarding whether mothers and fathers should be interchangeable 'parents', or whether they have distinctive contributions as role models for their children, the father as bread-winner and exemplar of 'manly' values, the mother as carer and epitome of 'feminine' attributes. Of course, such gendered conceptions of parenting reinforce traditional family—and marriage—norms. In this process, as explained below, the law has moved both towards formal equality—a partnership of equals—and towards a joint enterprise model.

CHILDREN AS THE FOCUS OF ATTENTION

Legal and social interest in children has gone through three phases of development. The first, in the nineteenth century, arose from a fear that lack of parental control was leading to increased *delinquency* and public disorder among the children of the poor. Society's self-interest therefore required that attention be paid to the education and discipline of children which, if the parents proved unable to provide voluntarily, the state would have to coerce. In practice, this meant that only the parents of the working classes would be at risk of any 'state interference' in how they brought up their children, since only they failed to conform to the dominant middle-class norms of appropriate parenting. Toward the end of the nineteenth century the 'discovery' of child cruelty and neglect brought a new concern for the *welfare* of children, again focused on the children of the poor. During the twentieth century, child welfare emerged periodically as a social problem to be tackled by the welfare state. But this time, the focus was only partly upon the children of the lower classes, with attempts to tackle child poverty through the social security system, and child abuse through the criminal and care systems. The increasingly influential discipline of psychology broadened the concept of welfare to encompass a child's psychological and emotional as well as physical well-being. With changing family structures and the growth of divorce and birth outside marriage permeating all social classes, those in the higher social classes whose family problems came before the courts were also brought within the reach of social attention.

Most recently, the focus has shifted again. The influence of human rights discourse has produced an international recognition of the *rights* of children, embracing civil and political rights on the one hand and social, cultural, and economic rights on the other. Such rights, brought together in the United Nations Convention on the Rights of the Child in 1989, include both the same rights as those of adults such as the right to freedom of expression, and rights special to children, such as the right to know and be brought up by one's parents. These specifically child-orientated rights include rights that can be categorized as, on the one hand, welfare rights, such as a right to education and to safety from abuse and, on the other, autonomy or participation rights, such as a right to be heard in proceedings affecting the child. This international recognition of children as rights-bearers occurred at the same time as domestic legal developments were taking place. They were both underpinned by a growing view of children as social actors and as participants in family life, rather than as 'objects of concern' (Butler-Sloss, 1988) and passive victims of forces and adult actions. How far incorporation of the European Convention on Human Rights into United Kingdom domestic law will reinforce this trend depends on the willingness of the courts to view children's interests in autonomy or participation rights terms, rather than to reconceptualize them simply as rights to welfare, as explained below.

The increasing state 'intervention' in the family which has been the consequence of each of these three phases of legal development, has been easier to justify, even in a liberal society, when considering the interests of a child than in the case of adults. The state has a legitimate interest in the welfare of all its citizens, including children who will form the next generation of workers, taxpayers, and leaders. The 'discovery' of child abuse, even more than that of spousal violence, led to a realization that family members, and especially the adults, may not always behave with love and altruism towards those weaker than themselves. A child may be unable to protect him- or herself from abusive parents and there may be no one other than the state to do so for the child. Adults may be expected, to an extent at least, to fend for themselves and to find means of protecting their own autonomy (although as will be seen in Chapter 4, this is not always so in practice).

FROM PATERNAL RIGHTS TO PARENTAL RESPONSIBILITY

Ironically, at the same time that arguments based on equal or human rights were being used to improve the legal position of women and children in family law, there was a concerted effort to reject the whole notion of rights in favour of a focus upon obligations and responsibilities when describing the position of parents.

The position of unmarried mothers was discussed in Chapter 2. Since the nineteenth century, they alone have had automatic parental rights and responsibility for their children, although unmarried fathers have been liable to pay financial support in respect of their children and have, since the 1980s, been able to acquire parental responsibility by order or agreement and now, by registration on the birth certificate.

The position of married women as regards their children was enhanced during the nineteenth and twentieth centuries, by putting them in an equal position with that of their husbands when it came to determining how a child was to be brought up. First, a series of nineteenth century statutes wrested away from married fathers the absolute authority over their children granted by the common law, by permitting mothers to seek custody of and access to their children against the father's wishes. Then, the Guardianship of Infants Act 1925 laid down that in any proceedings, neither the father nor the mother should be regarded as having a claim superior to the other in respect of the custody or upbringing of the child. It also granted the mother the right, previously exclusive to the father, to appoint a guardian for her children in her will. Yet it was not until the Guardianship Act 1973 that statute gave each parent equal *and* separately exercisable rights over a legitimate child. Remarkably, not until the Children Act 1989 was the last vestige of patriarchal superiority finally removed (with the abolition of an archaic rule that a father was the sole guardian of his legitimate child during his lifetime).

However, if parents are to stand equal when determining the upbringing of their child, who is to have the final say in the event of a disagreement? If they cannot agree, how is a court to resolve the matter? The 1925 Act made clear that the child's welfare was the 'first and paramount consideration'. This formulation helped consolidate a new emphasis on and concern for the child's interests, occasioned by greater awareness of and sensitivity to children's psychological needs. This became reflected in a general approach, culminating in the 1980s, which sought to undermine any sense that children are the *possessions* of their parents. Parental rights and authority were now understood as existing, not for the parents' own benefit, but 'for the benefit of the child and they are justified only in so far as they enable the parent to perform his duties towards the child'.[17] To reinforce this message, the Law Commission (1988) recommended that the phrase, 'parental rights and duties', which appeared in the Children Act 1975, should be replaced by the concept of 'parental responsibility' and this was duly enacted in s 3(1) of the Children Act 1989. But it would be a mistake to assume from this that parents are no longer regarded as having *any* possessory rights in their children. On the contrary, there is still a clear emphasis upon parents as having the primary interest in, as

---

[17] Per Lord Fraser in *Gillick v West Norfolk and Wisbech Area Health Authority* [1986] AC 112, 170D, HL.

82   *An Introduction to Family Law*

well as responsibility for, their children, and the state is still wary of 'interfering' too readily in how parents choose to raise their child. Furthermore, the incorporation of the European Convention on Human Rights has served to reinvigorate the concept of parental rights, by requiring public authorities to ensure that they do not infringe parents' as well as children's Article 8 right to respect for their family life.

RECOGNIZING THE CHILD'S RIGHT TO DECIDE

Where the parents and child are in dispute with each other, the courts have been prepared to uphold the child's right to autonomy, if they consider that the child is mature enough to take the decision and that so doing will not damage her long-term welfare. In *Gillick v West Norfolk and Wisbech Area Health Authority*[18] a mother of four daughters argued that such action would infringe her parental right to control medical treatment for her children, at least while they were under the age of 16 (at which age, s 8 of the Family Law Reform Act 1969 provides that a child may validly consent to medical treatment herself). The House of Lords ruled that it was not unlawful for a health authority to advise doctors that they could give contraceptive advice and treatment to girls under the age of 16, without the parents' knowledge or consent. A majority of the House ruled that parents have no absolute authority over a child and that, once a child reaches a sufficient understanding and intelligence to be capable of making a decision (although the requisite degree of understanding may be substantial), the child can give a valid consent. Lord Scarman went further and considered that once that point is reached, the parent's right 'yields' to that of the child and is terminated.

The *Gillick* decision therefore established that, once a child is sufficiently mature to decide for herself, she may give a valid consent to issues such as deciding whether to have medical treatment, regardless of her chronological age and regardless of the opposition of her parents. '*Gillick* competence' has become the shorthand expression encapsulating the issue of whether a child has the appropriate degree of maturity and understanding to be allowed to take a particular decision (not just those concerning medical treatment) for herself. It mirrors international thinking on children's rights and in particular, Article 12(1) of the UN Convention on the Rights of the Child, which provides that States Parties

[18] [1986] AC 112.

shall assure to the child who is capable of forming his or her own views the right to express those views freely in all matters affecting the child, the view of the child being given due weight in accordance with the age and maturity of the child.

This kind of test has the advantage of flexibility over fixed age limits. It recognizes that a child considerably below the age of 16 or the age of majority may yet be mature enough to appreciate the consequences of decisions and actions affecting her life. It also enables a full consideration of a child's individual circumstances to be taken into account by the person, be they a doctor, judge, or other adult, who must respond to the child's wishes. But this flexibility also bestows a wide discretion on such adults in determining whether the child is indeed sufficiently 'competent'. There is a danger that where adults happen to disagree with the child's view, they may simply conclude that the child must be insufficiently mature and hence not competent to decide for herself. In this way, although the *Gillick* test is set within a context of children's autonomy rights, it may be used as another manifestation of upholding the child's *welfare*.

Indeed, this appears to be what has happened, at least in cases concerning medical treatment. Subsequent decisions have made clear that although a *Gillick* competent child may give a valid *consent* to such treatment, her *refusal* to undergo it may be overridden by the High Court exercising its inherent jurisdiction and by anyone with parental responsibility. This will usually be a parent, of course, but, as explained in Chapters 2 and 5, it could also include a guardian, a special guardian, a person who has a residence order in respect of the child, or a local authority in whose care the child has been placed by court order. The distinction between consent and refusal was established in two Court of Appeal decisions, both concerning girls with significant mental problems. In *Re R (A Minor) (Wardship: Medical Treatment)*[19] a 15-year-old girl who had become suicidal was placed in an adolescent psychiatric unit. She refused to take the drugs prescribed for her and was made a ward of court. The Court of Appeal ruled that she was not *Gillick* competent because of her fluctuating mental capacity. However, Lord Donaldson MR went on to hold (contrary to the view of Lord Scarman, noted above, that parental rights terminate once the child has become competent) that those with parental responsibility retain the power to consent even where the child is competent to give a valid consent herself. Thus, in his view, they could consent to treatment in the exercise of their parental responsibility and

[19] [1992] Fam 11.

override the child's refusal. The Court of Appeal followed this approach in a subsequent decision, *Re W (A Minor) (Medical Treatment: Court's Jurisdiction)*.[20] There, a 16-year-old girl, suffering from anorexia, was refusing treatment and was close to death. Section 8 of the Family Law Reform Act 1969 made clear that she could give a valid consent to treatment, but the Court held that neither this nor *Gillick* gave her a right of veto over such treatment.

The case has been followed on several occasions subsequently and it seems reasonably clear that a court will not permit a child under 18 to 'martyr himself' (in the words of Ward J in *Re E (A Minor) (Wardship: Medical Treatment)*.[21] It may seem right that where a child is mentally disturbed, her refusal of treatment should be overridden because, when she is recovered as a result of the treatment, she will probably be grateful for what was done. But where the refusal, although apparently irrational, is the product of sincere belief, the court's decision may subject the child to emotional suffering. In *Re E*, a 15-year-old boy who was suffering from leukaemia refused a blood transfusion, because he was a Jehovah's Witness. His parents also refused their consent to the treatment, and the High Court overrode their refusal. He survived as the result of being treated, but on becoming 18, refused further transfusions and died. His case highlights the illogicality of the law's distinction between adults and minors—while a competent child can be kept alive in her best interests, as soon as she reaches adulthood, her refusal of further treatment becomes effective.

THE CONTENT OF PARENTAL RESPONSIBILITY

The Law Commission (1988, para 2.6) rejected laying down a statutory definition of parental responsibility, arguing that a comprehensive list of its incidents would become outmoded and would have to vary depending upon the age and maturity of the particular child. Section 3(1) of the Children Act 1989 accordingly simply defines the concept as:

all the rights, duties, powers, responsibility and authority which by law a parent of a child has in relation to the child and his property.

This unhelpful and self-referential formulation means that, as with the concept of consortium in marriage, one can only discover the content of parental responsibility by reference to extensive case law and other statutory provisions. Such reference produces quite a long list, which may be

----

[20] [1993] Fam 64.   [21] [1993] 1 FLR 386.

divided into three aspects of parenting: possession, upbringing, and protection. It will be seen that, notwithstanding modern rhetoric, the notion of parental *rights* (or in Hohfeldian terms, privileges or powers) remains important in this analysis. However, it should be borne in mind that all the rights noted below (which are not exhaustive but can be regarded as the most significant) are subject to control and restriction by a court where this is judged to be in the best interests of the child.

Possessory features of parental responsibility

Possession of the child's person
At common law, a parent (or originally, the father of a legitimate child) had a right to possession of the child. In the modern law, the parent (or anyone else with parental responsibility) may determine where the child should be and where she should have her home. Removal of a child from a parent without lawful authority may amount to the criminal offence of child abduction.[22] This possessory right is now justified, not as an archaic relic of patriarchal domination over other family members, but as reflecting the liberal view that the family and the members who comprise it should be free from arbitrary state interference. On this thinking, it is not for the state, at least in the absence of special circumstances (such as a dispute between the parents, or abuse, or neglect) to determine where a child should live. Otherwise there would be nothing to stop a powerful state from redistributing children to 'better' parents than those to whom they were born. Such an approach would clearly infringe international human rights law as set out, for example, in Article 8 of the European Convention on Human Rights, and the European Court has upheld a mother's claim for breach of this provision where a local authority negligently investigated suspected abuse of her daughter with the result that mother and child were wrongly separated for a year.[23] The domestic law at first sight appears slightly at odds with this ruling, since it has been held that in such circumstances, the parents have no claim for negligence by the local authority (although the child may sue).[24] They could, however, bring proceedings under s 7 of the Human Rights Act 1998 for a

---

[22] Child Abduction Act 1984, s 2. Removal *by a parent* of the child out of the United Kingdom without the appropriate consent of others with parental responsibility may be an offence under s 1. Removal of the child without the *child's consent* may amount to the common law offence of kidnapping: *R v D* [1984] AC 778, HL.

[23] *TP and KM v United Kingdom* (2002) 34 EHRR 2.

[24] *JD v East Berkshire Community Health NHS Trust* [2003] EWCA Civ 1151, [2004] 2 WLR 58.

remedy, which, under s 8, could include compensation. By contrast, where a child has been looked after by a local authority because the parents are unable to do so, and it is subsequently decided that the child's interests prevent her return to the parents, there is no right of action for interference with the parents' rights over the child.[25]

Arranging for the child's future care
The corollary of possession is the relinquishment of the child. As the person with the right to possess the child, someone with parental responsibility may, under s 2(9) of the Children Act 1989, arrange for aspects of parental responsibility to be exercised by others acting on his behalf. This provision would cover matters such as hiring a nanny to look after the child or sending the child to be educated at school. The section does not permit the 'surrender or transfer' of parental responsibility. But a *parent* (except an unmarried father without parental responsibility), does have the right, under s 47 of the Adoption and Children Act 2002, to consent to the adoption of the child. This will result in the complete transfer of parental responsibility to the adopters.[26]

Similarly, a parent with parental responsibility can appoint, in writing, a person to be the child's guardian after his death and the guardian will then exercise parental responsibility. Under s 5(8) of the Children Act 1989, the appointment of a guardian does not take effect until the death of a surviving parent with parental responsibility, unless the parent making the appointment had a residence order in respect of the child at the time of his death. In this way, where parents were living together at the time of the death, the survivor can continue to raise the child free from interference by the guardian. But where they were separated and the deceased parent had the care of the child by virtue of the residence order, he can limit the absent parent's interference and ensure that the guardian he has chosen can take over the child's care.

Contact with the child
Where a parent cannot have the child living with him, usually because of the breakdown of the relationship with the other parent, the view of the courts in England and Wales has been that contact (by visits or other forms of communication), in so far as it can be described as a right, is one

---

[25] *F v Wirral Metropolitan Borough Council* [1991] Fam 69.
[26] Adoption and Children Act 2002, s 46. Pending implementation of the 2002 Act, the relevant provisions are contained in ss 16 and 12 of the Adoption Act 1976.

belonging to the child rather than the adult.[27] This reflects the importance now attached to the child's psychological well-being. It is regarded as preferable for a child's psychological health and development to know and continue to have contact with an absent parent (and other relatives). However, it is probably more accurate to view contact as reflecting a possessory view of the relationship between adult and child because, at heart, contact disputes concern how far the resident parent is to be left free to control the child's contact with others, and English law imposes no obligation on an absent parent to maintain contact with the child. As Thorpe LJ put it in *Re L (A Child) (Contact: Domestic Violence)*:[28]

The errant or selfish parent can not be ordered to spend time with his child against his will however much the child may yearn for his company and the mother desire respite.

It might be argued that this reflects a recognition that the law is impotent to control a person's feelings and ability to *love*. But this rationale is not extended to the child. The law may be used to enforce the parent's right to have contact by compelling the person with whom the child lives to allow the contact to take place (and thus, to coerce the child into accepting the contact), if necessary, by committal for contempt of court. Moreover, other jurisdictions are readier to view contact as a parental *duty* and not just a right. For example, s 1(1)(c) of the Children (Scotland) Act 1995 states that that parent has the responsibility 'to maintain personal relations and direct contact with the child on a regular basis'.

A similarly contradictory message emerges from international law. On the one hand, Article 9(3) of the UN Convention on the Rights of the Child makes clear that contact (with parents, but not other relatives) is a right of the child:

States Parties shall respect the right of a child who is separated from one or both parents to maintain personal relations and direct contact with both parents on a regular basis, except if it is contrary to the child's best interests.

By contrast, Article 8 of the European Convention on Human Rights grants the right to respect for family life to *all* family members. This requires a balance to be struck between the competing interests of both adults and children and places a greater emphasis in consequence upon the position of the adults concerned, although the European Court of Human Rights has consistently held that the child's welfare must take

[27] *M v M (Child: Access)* [1973] 2 All ER 81.
[28] [2001] Fam 260, 294G, CA.

priority over the parent's right.[29] It has yet to be determined, either domestically or by the Strasbourg Court, whether a failure *by an adult* to visit or have contact with a child constitutes a breach of the child's right under Article 8. Such a case would clarify whether contact should indeed be seen as a right vesting in the child, or in the adult.

The child's name
We saw above that English law is relaxed concerning the choice of surname taken by a married couple (or indeed any adult). But the position is different regarding the naming of a child. The courts have taken the view that the surname has a symbolic and psychological significance for the child, and have relied upon Articles 7 and 8 of the UN Convention on the Rights of the Child in support. Article 7 provides that a child has the right 'from birth to a name, the right to acquire a nationality and, as far as possible, the right to know and be cared for by his or her parents'. Article 8 states that the child has a right 'to preserve his or her identity, including nationality, name and family relations'. Neither of these was intended to address the issue of choice of surname, but rather was concerned with the problem of stateless children and those abducted from their families by dictatorial military regimes. It would be more honest of the courts to accept that the chief purpose of a surname is to link a child with a particular family group and that disputes over surnames are really concerned with determining the child's 'affiliation' with a particular parent. It is no surprise, therefore, that parents may hold very strong, conflicting views on the child's surname when their own relationship has ended and they are no longer seen to constitute an 'intact' family group.

There is no rule that a child born to married parents must have her father's surname, or that a child born to unmarried parents must take that of her mother. But if married parents cannot agree on the surname to give to the child, they must ask the court to resolve the issue. An unmarried mother, with sole parental responsibility, has the sole right to name the child, but the father may nonetheless challenge her in court. In either case, the court may make a 'specific issue order' under s 8 of the Children Act determining the name to be given. Once a surname has been registered, it should not be changed without the consent of the other parent with parental responsibility. Family breakdown and re-constitution can cause complications. In *Dawson v Wearmouth*,[30] a woman who had divorced had kept her married surname. She had a child outside marriage

[29] *Johansen v Norway* (1997) 23 EHRR 33; *Yousef v Netherlands* (2003) 36 EHRR 20.
[30] [1999] 2 AC 308, HL.

with the father, but left him a few days after the birth, and registered the child with her (former married) surname. The father asked the court to make a specific issue order requiring her to register the child with his surname. The House of Lords rejected the father's case, accepting that it was in the best interests of the child to keep his current surname. It has also been held that the fact that a child will have a different surname from that of others in his family unit is not decisive, even where the child wishes to have the same surname.[31]

Disputes may also arise concerning a child's forenames. The courts have regarded these as less significant than a surname, and have recognized that children are frequently known by names other than those registered on their birth certificate (as is this author). They have nonetheless made clear that choice of given name is a matter for parents—foster carers who wish to call a child in their care by a new name must obtain the parents' consent or the permission of the court, since forenames, like surnames, are matters going to the child's identity under Article 8.[32]

Determining the child's upbringing

Modern parenting may be viewed as an enterprise in which the aim is to produce a well-adjusted adult. This is also a variation on the common law and liberal belief that a parent has the right, subject to legitimate state interests, to try to shape how his child will turn out. There are several aspects of parental responsibility which facilitate this.

Religion

At one time, the right to determine the child's religion would have been regarded as perhaps the most important aspect of that child's upbringing.[33] In the secular society of modern times, religious adherence may sometimes appear extreme, but a person with parental responsibility retains this right, and may withdraw a child from religious assembly and religious education at school.[34] A local authority looking after a child may not change the child's religion. However, where they are unable to care for the child themselves, parents may not insist on the child being adopted by or placed with carers who share the same religion.[35]

---

[31] *Re B (Change of Surname)* [1996] 1 FLR 791, CA.
[32] *Re D, L and LA (Care: Change of Forename)* [2003] 1 FLR 339.
[33] See *Ward v Laverty* [1925] AC 101 for an example.
[34] School Standards and Framework Act 1998, s 71(1).
[35] *Re P (Section 91(14) Guidelines) (Residence and Religious Heritage)* [1999] 2 FLR 573, CA.

The courts are generally careful to avoid passing any judgment on the merits of a given religion or sect, and it is a breach of the European Convention on Human Rights to deny a parent the care of her child simply because of her religious beliefs.[36] But they may find it hard to empathize with a parent wishing to follow religious practices in respect of the child, such as circumcision, against the will of the other, less religious, parent. In *Re J (Specific Issue Orders: Child's Religious Upbringing and Circumcision)*[37] for example, the Court of Appeal declined to grant an order to a Turkish Muslim father that his child, who lived with his English, non-practising Christian, mother, be circumcised. The Court noted that the child lived in a secular household and his only contact with Islam was through his father, but whether their approach gave sufficient weight to the religious and cultural significance attached by Muslims (and Jews) to male circumcision is open to question.

Education

Determining how a child is to be educated is a right stemming from the common law, and is also recognized in Protocol 1, Article 2 of the European Convention on Human Rights. Indeed, the Convention sets as much, if not more, store upon the *parents'* right to have the child educated 'in conformity with their religious and philosophical convictions' as upon the *child's* right to be educated. This emphasis is understandable given the history of the Convention and its concern to protect individuals from interference and oppression by totalitarian states, although it can appear a little misplaced when applied to liberal democracies. In *Campbell and Cosans v United Kingdom*,[38] for example, the European Court held that exclusion of children from school because their parents refused to permit the school to use corporal punishment on their children infringed the parents' right, but not that of the children. By contrast, the Court of Appeal has held that s 548 of the Education Act 1996, which prohibits the use of corporal punishment in all schools (be they private or state schools), does not infringe the rights under the Convention, either to have their child educated in accordance with their wishes or to manifest their religious beliefs under Article 9, of parents who believe that such punishment is sanctioned by scripture, in part because they are still free to administer such punishment themselves (see below).[39]

[36] *Palau-Martinez v France* (app No 64927/01) judgment 16 December 2003.
[37] [2000] 1 FLR 571, CA.   [38] (1982) 4 EHRR 293.
[39] *R (Williamson) v Secretary of State for Education and Employment* [2002] EWCA Civ 1926, [2003] QB 1300.

Notwithstanding the importance of the ideology of non-interference with the family, the state's interest in producing an educated work-force compelled even the laissez faire Victorians to require parents to educate their children. Accordingly, under the Education Act 1996, ss 7 and 8 there is a statutory *duty* on those with parental responsibility (or the care) of a child to ensure that the child receives efficient full-time education, suitable to his age, ability, and aptitude and to any special educational needs he may have. However, this may be secured either by regular attendance at school or otherwise, so parents may choose to educate the child themselves (subject to their local education authority being satisfied as to the suitability of the education they are providing) rather than send her to school. The duty may be enforced by either civil or criminal proceedings against the parents.[40]

Discipline

A person with parental responsibility has the right to administer lawful correction to a child, including 'moderate and reasonable' physical punishment.[41] This power may be delegated to another person in loco parentis, such as a step-parent, but not a teacher.[42] In *A v United Kingdom*,[43] a child aged nine was beaten by his step-father with a cane, suffering bruising. The father was charged with assault occasioning actual bodily harm, but was acquitted. The European Court of Human Rights held that such treatment, having regard to its nature and content, its duration, its physical and mental effects, and the sex, age, and state of health of the victim, could amount to inhuman or degrading treatment under Article 3 of the Convention. On the particular facts of the case, the Court ruled that the child's right under the Article had been infringed. However, the Court did not rule that *all* physical punishment of a child is unlawful under the Convention and hence, given the political sensitivity of the issue, raising strong feelings on both sides of the argument and directly involving the ideology of the sanctity of the private sphere, the Government has felt able to leave it to the courts to determine, as cases arise, where the boundaries of reasonable and unreasonable punishment lie in line with the European Court's guidance.[44]

---

[40] Children Act 1989, s 36; Education Act 1996, s 444.
[41] Children and Young Persons Act 1933, s 1(7).
[42] Education Act 1996, s 548. See the *Williamson* case, above n 39.
[43] (1999) 27 EHRR 611.
[44] *R v H (Assault of Child: Reasonable Chastisement)* [2001] EWCA Crim 1024, [2002] 1 Cr App R 7. A backbench attempt to prohibit all, or more serious, physical punishment through an amendment to the Children Bill 2004 may affect the above discussion.

Protection of the Child

Most of the aspects of parental responsibility so far considered have concerned rights, or powers. The remaining two aspects discussed here may be primarily categorized as duties toward the child.

Consent to medical treatment

It was noted above that a person with parental responsibility has the right to consent to medical treatment for a child, if need be overriding the child's own refusal. There is also a duty, laid down by s 1(2) of the Children and Young Persons Act 1933, to provide adequate medical aid for a child and failure to do so may be a criminal offence. Where there is disagreement over whether treatment should take place, either between those with parental responsibility, or between the adults and the child, or between the adults and the doctor, the matter may be resolved by the court. The court will determine the issue according to the best interests of the child, and it has powers to sanction treatment—or non-treatment—beyond those encompassed within parental responsibility. For example, the court, but probably not others, may authorize the sterilization of a child with learning difficulties to avoid her running the risk of pregnancy and childbirth.[45] Furthermore, the court may sanction treatment that will shorten the life of a terminally ill child, in order to relieve suffering.[46]

Indeed, in *Re A (Children) (Conjoined Twins: Surgical Separation)*,[47] which concerned conjoined or 'Siamese' twins, 'Jodie' and 'Mary', it was held that the High Court had power to sanction treatment, against the parents' wishes, even though this would result in the death of one child, in order to save the life of another, and even though there were many respectable bodies of opinion morally opposed to such action. Failure to perform the surgery would inevitably lead to the death of both twins some time during their infancy. Their parents refused to consent to the operation, holding the religious belief that it was God's will that the two twins should die and that it would be immoral to cause the death of the weaker twin to save the life of her sister. The Court of Appeal unanimously gave approval for the operation to be carried out, considering that this would be in the best interests of the stronger twin, Jodie.

---

[45] *Re B (A Minor) (Wardship: Sterilisation)* [1988] AC 199. It is generally accepted that where the purpose of the sterilization is contraceptive rather than therapeutic, the court's sanction is required.
[46] *Re C (A Minor) (Wardship: Medical Treatment)* [1990] Fam 26, CA.
[47] [2001] Fam 147, CA.

Usually, as in *Re A*, the Court upholds the opinion of the doctors against that of the parents. However, in *Re T (A Minor) (Wardship: Medical Treatment)*[48] the Court of Appeal upheld the parents' refusal of a liver transplant for their child because they preferred him to spend the rest of his short life free from medical intervention rather than undergo further invasive surgery which might fail. Moreover, in *Glass v United Kingdom*[49] the European Court of Human Rights found a breach of the Article 8 right of both a parent and her severely physically and mentally handicapped child, when hospital staff failed to obtain court authorization to administer diamorphine to relieve the child's suffering, against the parent's wishes. The mother wished the hospital to take all possible measures to prolong her son's life, whilst the hospital considered that no more could be done for him. In fact, the child's condition eventually improved sufficiently to enable the mother to care for him at home. All such cases demonstrate the difficulty of determining whether it is right to override parental wishes in situations of tragedy and moral uncertainty. *Re A* showed that there is a strong belief among large sections of the public that it is best to leave the parents to decide the outcome. Indeed, in so far as Ward LJ considered that, if the doctors and parents had been in agreement with each other that the operation should not be performed, it would not have been necessary to seek the Court's ruling, he seems to have shared this opinion.[50] *Glass v United Kingdom* shows too that parents may legitimately disagree with medical experts on the prognosis for the patient. But it might be thought that it cannot be right to allow the fate of a child to turn on whether the adults responsible for her care happen to agree with each other, and on whether they choose to bring the case to the courts' attention or not.

Maintenance of the child
There is an obligation upon a parent—but, oddly enough, not upon others with parental responsibility—to maintain his child. At common law, the duty applied only to the father of a legitimate child and, like the duty to maintain a wife, it was not directly enforceable against the father. However, as we have noted, the Poor Law imposed a duty upon all parents to support their children, born inside or outside marriage, and parishes could take proceedings against a father to meet the costs of parish relief. The modern legacy of this system is that the obligation to maintain is more accurately understood as a liability of parenthood,

---

[48] [1997] 1 All ER 906, CA.   [49] [2004] 1 FCR 553.
[50] [2001] Fam 147, 173.

rather than a duty contained within the concept of parental responsibility. An unmarried father without parental responsibility is nonetheless required to support his child, even where he is prevented (lawfully or unlawfully) from having contact with the child, and this 'taxation without representation' has been used as a major argument in the campaign of such fathers to be granted automatic parental responsibility.

With increased family breakdown, and consequential high numbers of lone parents dependent upon social security benefits, a concern to recoup the costs of child maintenance from absent parents became a political priority in the 1990s. Although there remains jurisdiction in the courts to order financial provision for a child, against a parent (or step-parent who has treated the child as a 'child of the family'),[51] the main mechanism for enforcing the liability to maintain is now contained within the Child Support Act 1991. This limits the obligation to maintain to the legal parents of a child, thus excluding step-parents from liability under the Act. It also applies only where the parent is living apart from the child.[52] As is the norm, therefore, the state provides no direct help to a child whose parent might be able, but is unwilling, to give her a decent standard of living, so long as they live under the same roof. In this way, the privacy of the family is upheld. It is only where the child is actually deprived to the point of being neglected, that the state will be able to intervene, under child protection legislation.

CONCLUSION

There is a certain irony in the fact that the two key relationships recognized in family law—that of marriage and that of parent and child—are governed by concepts which have no precise definition or content. The Government considered that spelling out the rights and responsibilities of marriage (and possibly cohabitation) in a readily available guide would be a valuable means of bringing home to people the implications of entering into such relationships (Home Office, 1998, para 4.13). However, as this Chapter has shown, it is not easy to elucidate precisely what these rights and responsibilities are.

---

[51] See Chapter 2 for explanation of this term. Matrimonial Causes Act 1973, s 27 and s 21; Domestic Proceedings and Magistrates' Courts Act 1978, s 2; Children Act 1989, Sch 1. Such a step-parent may well lack parental responsibility, but may nonetheless be obliged under these Acts to support the child.
[52] Child Support Act 1991, ss 1, 3.

Given this uncertainty, it has been mooted that couples should be free, and encouraged, to enter into pre-nuptial agreements and cohabitation contracts that would set out their rights in the event of the relationship ending. Such agreements are common in other jurisdictions, especially community property systems, no doubt reflecting a dissatisfaction with the equal split approach to property division. We have seen that the courts have been reluctant to recognize contracts made by spouses *during* the marriage. There might be less objection to upholding agreements reached before the wedding, when the parties are still at arm's length, at least if they could show they had each received independent legal advice. There is now some Government support for such agreements, but this is motivated by a wish to reduce conflict (and legal costs) on divorce. Whether legal recognition would be given to agreements purporting to set out the ongoing rights and responsibilities of the parties during their relationship is another matter. Would, for example, a court uphold a contract allowing for the spouses to have multiple sexual partners, or requiring the wife to remain at home with the children and sacrificing her career? To do so would mark a fundamental change in the legal conception of marriage, by viewing it as a contract whose terms are shaped by the parties themselves, rather than by the state. If this were permitted, it would be difficult to see why a court should not uphold a similar arrangement between cohabitants, or same sex partners—or more than two people. At this point, marriage would effectively cease to exist as a separate legal concept.

Interestingly, the parent/child relationship is in some ways closer to this point of flexibility. Parental responsibility is a bundle of rights and obligations which, as was explained in Chapter 2, can be held by non-parents as well as parents, and by more than two people at a time, regardless of their legal relationship with each other, and regardless of their sexual orientation. The basic content of parental responsibility remains firmly a matter for the public sphere to determine, but its application in fact allows for a reasonable degree of individual (parental) choice and autonomy in determining how the child is to be brought up. It is hard to see why this liberalism should be conceded where children's interests are at stake, yet not in the case of adults.

4

The Family Home

INTRODUCTION

The family home has a significant symbolic role in family life as well as important practical functions. Contrary to other cultures where extended family generations may live under the same roof, it has long been assumed in England and Wales that married couples should form their own independent household. A bride's 'bottom drawer' would hold items such as linens made and collected over time which she would use to begin to furnish her marital home, and modern-day 'wedding lists' generally consist of more or less essential household items. In the past, an engaged couple might have to delay their marriage for several years until they could afford to set up home together, and living with the in-laws has not been regarded as a satisfactory long-term way of establishing a married relationship. For couples who reject marriage, commencing cohabitation—the very essence of which means living together in the same household—may come to mark a rite of passage equivalent to marriage in former times. Many people will have had their own homes before marrying or cohabiting, and in either case, 'moving in together' is a representation of their commitment to their relationship. Creating a family home, decorating, and furnishing it, has become an embodiment of the conception of marriage—and cohabitation—as a joint enterprise (see Chapter 1).

The family home is also, for most people, the most valuable capital asset they will acquire during their lifetimes and there is a strong desire to pass this (or its cash value) on to the next generation. The preservation of family wealth, usually in the form of land, and its orderly inheritance, were the driving forces behind the development of the rules of real property and trusts before the advent of industrial capitalism. Today, resistance to paying inheritance tax and to the requirement to realize capital in order to pay for long-term care in old age reflects the same determination to see, in the words of the former Prime Minister, John Major, one's 'wealth cascading down the generations'.

In the liberal conception of private and public spheres, the home represented a haven to which the male head could withdraw from the demands of the public world of affairs. At home, he would find a welcoming and loving reception from his wife and children at the end of a hard day and there, regardless of his standing in the outside world, he would reign supreme. 'The Englishman's home is his castle' is a saying that therefore encapsulates not just the right of a freeborn Englishman to privacy and freedom from state interference but also his status within the family. The problem with this arcadian image is that it ignores the position of the other family members, for whom the home might embody not so much a haven as a constricting prison in which they might appear to have no rights and no interests. Far from being a place of harmonious security and stability, for some family members the home might be a truly dangerous place. After all, women and children are most at risk of suffering violence when they are at home.

The privacy of the home is also recognized in modern human rights law. Article 8 of the European Convention on Human Rights, for example, links the right to respect for one's private and family life with a right to respect for one's home and correspondence, safeguarding the integrity of an individual's private space, within which he or she can behave free from scrutiny. As Lord Millett put it in *Harrow LBC v Qazi*:[1]

A person's 'home' is. . .the place where he and his family are entitled to be left in peace free from interference by the state or agents of the state. It is an important aspect of his dignity as a human being, and it is protected as such and not as an item of property.

This appears to run the risk of endangering the position of more vulnerable family members within the home and of creating a tension between privacy and protection. However, it should be recalled that Article 8 contains a proviso, which may require that the right being asserted be balanced against those of the other family members. This Chapter explores how far domestic law strikes the appropriate balance between preserving the unity and autonomy of the family on the one hand, and upholding the interests of individual family members on the other.

---

[1] [2003] UKHL 43, [2003] 3 WLR 792.

OWNERSHIP OF THE FAMILY HOME

England and Wales have very high rates of home ownership as compared with other countries, with 69 per cent of homes being owner-occupied (ONS 2004*b*: 30). For owner-occupiers, the home fulfils two practical functions—first, as the place in which they live, and secondly, as an item of property that may grow in monetary value. Not only will keeping up the payments for the home take the largest slice of the family income, but the capital value may be utilized to advance the standard of living of the family in various ways. The home may be used as security for a loan, taken out either for business or for personal spending and lifestyle purposes. At times of strong house price inflation, the growing equity value of the home may provide a windfall at the end of a marriage, enabling a divorcing couple to move into separate homes. An elderly couple may sell the home and move into a smaller property, using the surplus balance for income purposes. Equally, when prices crash, negative equity may tie a couple to a home which cannot be sold without a loss, building up further debts and opening up the possibility of loss of possession.

The ownership of land, as opposed to personal property, is subject to particular rules. Whoever is named on the title is the legal owner of the land; if the title also declares the beneficial ownership of the property, then this is conclusive in the absence of fraud or mistake.[2] However, notwithstanding the clear urging of the courts since at least 1970, instances still arise where the conveyance fails to spell out the parties' intentions regarding the beneficial interest in the property. This will particularly be the case where one partner moves into a home first acquired by the other.

THE RESIDUAL SIGNIFICANCE OF MARRIAGE

On divorce (discussed in Chapter 6), the courts have broad powers and a wide discretion to distribute the spouses' property between them regardless of which spouse is the legal or equitable owner. But in other situations, the law governing ownership of the family home has developed largely regardless of the marital status of the parties. At one time, the courts did occasionally rely on an old equitable doctrine, the 'presumption of advancement', which gave some recognition to the economic dependency of wives and which stemmed from the husband's duty to

---

[2] *Goodman v Gallant* [1986] Fam 106, CA.

maintain his wife. Under the presumption, where a husband transferred property to his wife, the transfer was regarded as an outright gift rather than, as would otherwise be presumed the case, giving rise to a resulting trust whereby the recipient holds the property on trust for the transferor. In *Pettitt v Pettitt*,[3] the House of Lords considered the presumption to be outmoded and to be relevant, if at all, only where no evidence was available to show what the parties had actually intended.

The courts' reluctance to regard marriage as giving rise to any special property relationship between the parties is also apparent in two further examples, both influenced by a fear of allowing the spouses to put their property beyond the reach of creditors. First, not only have the courts largely rejected the presumption of advancement, but they have also been wary of finding on the facts that a spouse has made a gift of property to the other. In *Re Cole*,[4] a husband furnished a new house and then took his wife into it saying 'It's all yours'. But the property remained insured in his name, and when he was subsequently made bankrupt it was held that there had been no effective delivery to the wife of the contents of the house, which therefore vested in the trustee in bankruptcy.

The second example has been more important in recent years. With the rise of home ownership in the post-war era and the drive since the 1980s to start up small businesses and raise credit for spending, more people have taken the opportunity to raise loans on the security of their house. The majority of matrimonial homes are now co-owned and the agreement of both spouses is therefore required before the home can be used in this way. Where loans cannot be repaid and the creditors seek possession of the property, the question arises whether the wife (in most cases) has given a true agreement for if not, the transaction may be liable to be set aside. In *Barclays Bank plc v O'Brien*,[5] the House of Lords rejected the argument that the spousal relationship *of itself* gives rise to a presumption of undue influence by the husband over his wife. Indeed, the House later accepted[6] a joint enterprise view of marriage whereby it recognized that the fortunes of husband and wife are bound up with each other and that there will usually be reciprocal trust and confidence between them. The fact that a wife lends her support to the husband's financial or business decisions is therefore entirely to be expected and should not, of itself, suggest that undue influence has occurred. Rather, to establish such undue influence, a wife has to show that as a matter of fact,

---

[3] [1970] AC 777.   [4] [1964] Ch 175, CA.   [5] [1994] 1 AC 180, HL.
[6] *Royal Bank of Scotland v Etridge (No 2)* [2001] UKHL 44, [2002] 2 AC 773.

not only had she reposed trust and confidence in her husband when it came to financial matters but that the transaction to which she agreed was not readily explicable by their relationship. An evidential presumption of undue influence will then arise and the onus then shifts to the other party to provide evidence to explain how the transaction was not procured by such influence. But it is not the fact of being a wife or in a marriage that is important here. Any other person in an emotional relationship with the debtor may also be able to establish that she—or he—reposed such 'trust and confidence' in the other to handle financial matters. As was discussed in relation to the formation of relationships in Chapter 2, what is relevant is the nature of the relationship, not its status.

A TRUST OF THE FAMILY HOME

Where the beneficial ownership of property is in dispute, the party excluded from the title may seek to argue that the legal owner holds the property on trust. Usually, a trust of land will fail unless it is evidenced in writing. However, this is not the case in respect of 'resulting, implied or constructive trusts'.[7] It is at this point that the idea of a joint enterprise, be it marital or based on cohabitation, becomes crucial. In this area of the law, joint enterprise may become translated into the concept of a 'common intention' between the legal owner and the other party that they will share the beneficial interest in the property. The problem with this is that couples may not be able to show clear evidence of their intention. However, in *Gissing v Gissing*,[8] the House of Lords held that while a court cannot ascribe to the parties an intention they never had, it may infer their intention from their conduct.

A constructive trust based on *express* agreement

In the later House of Lords decision of *Lloyds Bank plc v Rosset*,[9] Lord Bridge clarified the test for establishing a trust in such cases. He elucidated two rather different situations. In the first, there is evidence of *express discussion* 'however imperfectly remembered and however imprecise their terms must have been' of an agreement, arrangement, or understanding reached between the parties that they are to share the property. If such an agreement is established, then the party asserting the claim must show that she has acted to her detriment, or altered her position in reliance on the agreement, to give rise to a constructive trust.

---

[7] Law of Property Act 1925, s 53(1)(b), (2).   [8] [1971] AC 886.
[9] [1991] 1 AC 107.

In fact, in a case of this type, the reality may be that the parties never had a *common* intention in the sense of a mutual agreement. Rather, the person seeking to rely on the trust may have been misled into believing that the owner intended to share. For example, in *Grant v Edwards*,[10] the man told his cohabiting partner that her name should not be put on the title to their home as this might prejudice her position in divorce proceedings with her husband. The woman contributed to meeting the household budget through her earnings, thus enabling the mortgage payments to be met, although she did not pay these herself. It was held that she was entitled to a half share of the equity.

If there is no sufficient discussion of what the parties' shares are to be, then the court may conclude there was no common intention as to ownership, even if the parties did assume joint *use* of the property. In *Lloyds Bank plc v Rosset* itself, it was said that the expectation of the spouses in a happy marriage is that they will share the 'practical benefits of occupying the matrimonial home whoever owns it. But this is something quite distinct from sharing the beneficial interest in the property asset which the matrimonial home represents'.[11] Here, marriage appears to be seen as a joint enterprise in terms of sharing a life together, but with no necessary assumption that the parties will be jointly entitled to the fruits of that shared life.

Assuming there is evidence of a sufficiently precise common intention to share the beneficial interest, the claimant must then establish 'detrimental reliance'. Here, assumptions about the altruistic nature of family life, and the gendered division of labour within the household, come to the fore. 'Normal' activities for a wife and mother, such as looking after the home and children, have not usually sufficed, for two reasons. First, they are not conceived in financial terms and therefore they are regarded as having no 'value' even though housekeeping and child-care services can be expensive when provided on a commercial basis. Mrs Rosset's supervision of builders, and her undertaking of some redecoration of the property, were dismissed as 'so trifling [in financial terms in comparison with the value of the house] as to be de minimis'.[12] Secondly, it is assumed that the woman would perform these tasks anyway, with no expectation of financial reward. 'The wife does not get a share in the house simply because she cleans the walls or works in the garden or helps her husband with the painting and decorating. Those are the sort of things which a

---

[10] [1986] Ch 638, CA.   [11] [1991] 1 AC 107, 127–8.
[12] Per Lord Bridge at 131.

102 *An Introduction to Family Law*

wife does for the benefit of the family without altering the title to, or interests in, the property'.[13] Gender stereotyping will equally disadvantage men. In *Pettitt v Pettitt*, for example, the man, who did DIY jobs round the house, did not qualify thereby for a share in the beneficial interest, since he had done no more than 'a reasonable husband might be expected to do'.[14]

Accordingly, where the conduct takes a form other than that of payments toward the acquisition of the home (which, as we saw in *Grant v Edwards*, will suffice), then only if it is out of the ordinary will it be regarded as 'detrimental'. In *Eves v Eves*,[15] for example, the woman broke up the concrete in the front garden wielding a sledge-hammer, rebuilt a shed, stripped off wallpaper, and painted woodwork. These activities were regarded as going beyond what might be expected of a woman, and she was rewarded with a quarter share in the equity.

It is possible that these attitudes would now be regarded as outmoded. Certainly, in divorce law, the courts have moved closer to recognizing the differing contributions of each spouse as having equal weight when determining the allocation of property to them on the termination of their marriage[16] (see Chapter 6). Similarly, in *Hammond v Mitchell*, Waite J took account of the woman's contribution as 'mother/helper/unpaid assistant and at times financial supporter to the family prosperity' in reaching his conclusion that she was entitled to a half share in the property.[17] However, there was also clear evidence of a contribution (in the form of postponing her interest in the property to secure a bank loan for the man's business) which could be regarded in financial terms, so the position remains unclear.

A trust based on direct financial contributions

The second situation Lord Bridge identified in *Lloyds Bank plc v Rosset* is where there is no evidence of an express agreement to share, and the court relies entirely on the parties' conduct both to infer their common intention and to find that a constructive trust has arisen thereby. He concluded that in this type of case, only 'direct contributions to the purchase price' would suffice to give a share. It is hard to see how this differs from a standard resulting trust which is presumed to arise whenever one person pays money for property that is put in another's name.

---

[13] Per Lord Denning in *Button v Button* [1968] 1 WLR 457, 461.
[14] [1970] AC 777, 806C per Lord Morris of Borth-y-Gest.
[15] [1975] 3 All ER 768, CA.   [16] *White v White* [2001] 1 AC 596, HL.
[17] [1991] 1 WLR 1127, 1137G.

Further, by limiting qualifying contributions to those which are direct (such as payment of the initial deposit on the property, or of mortgage instalments), Lord Bridge appears to have cut down the scope of previous case law, which had recognized that 'indirect' contributions might suffice. For example, in *Gissing v Gissing*, Lord Pearson and Lord Diplock seemed to suggest that payment by the wife of household expenses, without which help the husband could not meet the costs of the mortgage, should be regarded as sufficient, and this approach has been followed in one subsequent reported decision.[18] It certainly seems quite arbitrary to allow a small direct contribution to entitle the claimant to a share but to ignore very substantial indirect contributions. The most striking generosity in respect of finding a direct contribution is perhaps to be found in *Midland Bank v Cooke*.[19] There, the groom's parents gave the couple a cash wedding present of just over £1,000. This was regarded as belonging to the couple jointly. The money was put towards the deposit on the matrimonial home. On the strength of this 'contribution' together with payments for improvements and household expenses, the wife was credited with a half share in the property.

By contrast, the harshness of requiring a contribution that can be quantified in financial terms is best illustrated by *Burns v Burns*.[20] The couple were unmarried and lived together for nineteen years. The woman gave up work for a time to care for the couple's children and the home and later used her earnings to pay for household expenses, clothes, and furnishings for the house. None of this was deemed sufficient to give her a share in the equity. The unfairness to Mrs Burns is all the more striking if one bears in mind that, had the couple been married, a divorce settlement could have resulted in the court awarding her the entire equity (see Chapter 6).

Proprietary estoppel

An alternative approach to ensuring that the owner of property is not allowed to act unconscionably is to apply the doctrine of equitable estoppel. This is very similar to the test of detrimental reliance discussed above. The essence of the doctrine is that, where one person acts to her detriment on the faith of a belief, known and encouraged by the other, that she has, or will be given, a right to the other's property, that other cannot insist on his strict legal entitlement. It can be seen that this is

---

[18] *Le Foe v Le Foe and Woolwich plc* [2001] 2 FLR 970.
[19] [1995] 4 All ER 562, CA.   [20] [1984] Ch 317, CA.

effectively the same as the situation above where the owner leads the claimant to believe that he will share the property with her. The only difference is that there is no need to establish a 'common intention' to share, and in this regard, estoppel is a rather more honest interpretation of the situation than the constructive trust set out in *Lloyds Bank v Rosset*. It may also operate extremely generously towards the claimant. In *Pascoe v Turner*,[21] a woman remained in the house she had shared with her former lover, he having told her that it was hers. On the strength of this assurance, she spent money on the property, though did nothing 'out of the ordinary'. The man tried to regain possession of the property. The Court of Appeal held that by standing by and encouraging the woman to believe the house was now hers, he was estopped from denying that this was the case.

QUANTIFYING THE SHARE IN THE BENEFICIAL INTEREST

The size of the share that a court may award to a person who has established an entitlement depends upon how the case is categorized. If there is an express declaration of trust in writing setting out the respective shares, then this will generally determine the matter.[22] If the case is regarded as one of a *resulting* trust arising from the claimant having paid money for property that is put into the other's name, then the share will be proportionate to the contribution made by the claimant. If the court finds a *constructive* trust, however, which is generally the position following Lord Bridge's categorization in *Lloyds Bank plc v Rosset*, then the court must establish the size of share either from what the parties said and did at the time of acquisition, or by taking into account the whole course of dealing between them, including the arrangements they made to meet the various outgoings on the property, over what may be a substantial period of time while they lived together. This may, but need not, result in a half share—the courts take a broad view of what will be 'fair' or 'right' in the circumstances.[23] The claimant's share ultimately depends on her financial contribution and the court's view of how much she deserves to take with her from the partnership. The position has been even more vague where the court finds a proprietary estoppel. In such a case, the claimant's share depends entirely on what the court thinks is necessary to

---

[21] [1979] 1 WLR 431, CA.
[22] The Land Registration Rules 1925, rr 19(1), 98, Sch 1, as amended, require that where land is to vest in persons as joint proprietors, they must state whether they hold on trust for themselves beneficially as joint tenants, as tenants in common or on any other trusts.
[23] *Oxley v Hiscock* [2004] EWCA Civ 546, 6 May 2004.

satisfy the equity. In *Pascoe v Turner*, as noted above, the Court of Appeal held that the only way to do justice between the parties was to transfer the house to the claimant. However, in *Oxley v Hiscock* (above) the Court considered that there should be no difference in outcome, in the standard case, whether it is analysed as one of constructive trust or of estoppel. In either case, the outcome must be one that is *fair*.

This approach, whilst emphasizing fairness, nonetheless reinforces the partnership (though not necessarily an 'equal' one) rather than joint enterprise model of the parties' relationship (be it marriage or cohabitation). The parties are regarded as separate individuals with separate entitlements; the fact that they have lived together does not, of itself, imply that they should be treated as having been engaged in a joint enterprise which should produce an outcome of substantive equality. This may be compared with the approach taken to a 'fair outcome' in financial provision cases following a divorce where more emphasis is now placed upon equal valuation of the parties' contributions to the relationship (see Chapter 6).

Improvements to property

Rather than claim a share in the value of the property because of a contribution to its *acquisition*, a party to a relationship may argue that he or she has made a financial contribution to its *improvement*. It was established in *Pettitt v Pettitt* that payments or work carried out to improve the property do not 'count' as establishing a share because they are not referable to its *purchase*. This particular issue is now covered by s 37 of the Matrimonial Proceedings and Property Act 1970, at least as far as spouses (and in future, civil partners) or fiancés are concerned. They may acquire a share in the beneficial interest in the property (which is not limited to the matrimonial home and extends to personal property as well), provided they can show that they made a substantial contribution, in money or money's worth, to its improvement. The share will either reflect any agreement of the parties, or will be what is just in all the circumstances. This has usually been taken to mean that the share should be proportionate to the increase in the value of the property produced by the improvement, but this must be too narrow. Some 'improvements' such as double-glazing cost substantial amounts of money but make little difference to the selling price of a house. In times of declining house prices, improvements may not prevent a fall in the value of the property. In such circumstances, it is submitted that a court should give a share reflecting the proportion of the value of the property represented by the costs incurred.

A £10,000 conservatory built onto a house worth £100,000 should give a 10 per cent share, even if the selling-price does not increase.

COHABITATION CONTRACTS

One way of clarifying rights in the home for an unmarried couple would be for them to enter into a written 'cohabitation contract'. It used to be thought that such contracts would be regarded as immoral and contrary to public policy but this was rejected in *Sutton v Mishcon de Reya and Gawor & Co.*[24] The case involved a 'master-slave' sado-masochistic relationship between two men, in which the wealthier 'slave' contracted to buy a flat for the 'master' and provide him with a substantial income during their relationship. Hart J distinguished between a contract for sexual relations, which he found to have existed here, which is void, and a contract determining the property consequences arising from a sexual relationship, which may be valid. On the strength of this authority one might expect that cohabitation contracts will become more common. But they are unlikely to provide a general solution to the problem of resolving disputes between former cohabitants, since many couples will fail to enter into them, either because of ignorance or apathy.

REFORMING THE PROPERTY RULES

The unsatisfactory state of the rules governing ownership and use of family property exercised the minds of the Law Commission for thirty years. In the 1970s, their focus was upon *matrimonial* property and they recommended that statute should extend the principle of co-ownership automatically to the matrimonial home, unless the spouses otherwise agreed, or the property had been given or inherited and the donor stipulated otherwise (Law Commission, 1978). This proposal implies a joint enterprise view of marriage, with the spouses sharing the benefits of the relationship—subject to their own prior agreement otherwise—and entitled by virtue of their status to continue to enjoy these regardless of marital difficulties. However, it was complicated and politically unpopular and no legislation resulted. To some extent, the problem of co-ownership of the matrimonial home has been resolved by changing social practice. Most such homes are co-owned, and those that are not would most probably have fallen within the exceptions provided for by the Law Commission.

---

[24] [2003] EWHC 3166, Ch, [2004] 1 FLR 837.

By the 1990s, the focus had changed. The growth in cohabitation, both
heterosexual and homosexual, suggested that reforms directed only at
marriage would leave a significant gap in protection for people such as
Mrs (sic) Burns, whose failure to acquire a share in the family home after
19 years of cohabitation was noted above. The Law Commission therefore began a re-examination of the law and widened the scope of their
inquiry to consider *all* forms of home sharing, including but not limited
to marital and non-marital cohabitation. The difficulties in arriving at
proposals which would meet the needs of all home-sharers and which
might be fair, workable, and predictable ultimately defeated the Law
Commission, however. They attempted to develop a scheme which would
base a party's entitlement to a share in the home on his or her contributions (including those of a non-financial kind) rather than intentions,
regardless of the nature of the parties' relationship. But they concluded
(Law Commission, 2002) that this was impossible to achieve. They found
that they could not produce a scheme of sufficient flexibility when evaluating a party's contributions to enable them to distinguish between
deserving and undeserving cases. This appears to have been because of
their insistence on having to produce a model which would fit all kinds of
home-sharers rather than concentrating upon particular relationships,
such as those of spouses and cohabitants. They recognized that both of
these might deserve particular recognition and consideration but
regarded the issue of relationship status as a matter of social policy outside their remit. They therefore threw the problem back to government
and the courts to resolve, with the rather timid exhortation that couples
living together should be encouraged to explore the legal consequences of
their relationships and with a plea to the courts to adopt a broader
approach to the kinds of contributions that would give rise to a share
under trusts doctrine, and in how they quantify the value of such shares.

One might deprecate this apparent loss of courage by the body specifically entrusted to unravel the legal complexities which have sprung up as
the result of piece-meal case and statutory development over the years,
but the Law Commission's withdrawal from the fray is understandable.
Part of the problem in attempting to produce a coherent reform is
in arriving at a view of which types of relationship (based on their nature
and duration) are deserving of protection, as was discussed in
Chapter 2—the Law Commission could not find a principled way of
distinguishing these and hence, as we have seen, attempted to include
everyone only to find that this was not workable. Then there is the matter
of arriving at a mechanism for reaching a resolution. Should the law lay

down clear entitlements at the outset that will govern the duration and aftermath of a relationship? If so, should parties be able to opt out of these if they choose? Or should there be an element (and how large?) of discretion and adjustment available to take account of individual circumstances at the time the issue has to be decided? And what ideological message will be sent out if all relationships are regarded in law as the same? The political sensitivity of this issue makes it very difficult to enact a law which is seen to downgrade marriage any further, which is why the Government's proposals for civil partnerships, noted in Chapters 2 and 3, have so far excluded heterosexual cohabitants. How ironical that it was the concept of separate property enshrined in law by the Victorians, those guardians of traditional family values, which in fact originally undermined the concept of marriage.

SAFETY AND SECURITY WITHIN THE HOME

As a refuge from the public sphere, and the physical location in which a couple can create a family and bring up children, the home represents a place of safety and security. In translating this representation into reality, the right to occupy the family home may be as important as the question of who owns it. There are two dimensions here. On the one hand there is the question of ensuring security against third parties, such as purchasers, creditors, mortgagees, and landlords who may seek to take possession of the property. On the other hand, there is the problem of protecting family members from each other's violence or intolerable behaviour. In the former instance, the bastion of the home is invaded by third parties invoking the support of the state to enforce a debt incurred by the family members. Since the market is involved here, liberal philosophy appears not to have conceived any difficulty about interfering in the private sphere of the family, for all that is happening is that a commercial transaction is being enforced. Indeed, the demands of the market have generally been regarded as taking priority over the needs of the family members and it is only recently that some recognition of these needs has been conceded.

But in the latter situation, family members themselves may call on the state for assistance. This has been much more problematical for liberal societies to deal with, because it requires them to acknowledge a rupture in the fabric of the family's unity and to pass judgment on relations between the family members. Recognition of intra-family abuse requires a refusal to respect the sanctity of the private sphere and represents a rejection of classical liberal philosophy. It also entails an acknowledgement that the relationship between the adults may not be based on an equal partnership, but rather on an imbalance of power. The grant of protective remedies to family members in this situation has therefore historically been just as reluctantly given as in the case of repossession by creditors, but the reason for the reluctance has been a concern to preserve 'family unity' rather than the needs of commerce.

PROTECTION AGAINST THIRD PARTIES

RELIANCE ON THE BENEFICIAL INTEREST

The best protection for a family member seeking to preserve her occupation of the family home is to be on the legal title so that no dispositions can be made without her consent. Where this is not the case, and there is a sole legal owner, perhaps these days more commonly in the case of a cohabiting couple, he may agree to sell (or mortgage) the home without telling his partner. If she is found to have a beneficial interest in the property, for example by way of constructive trust, as explained above, the question arises whether her interest is binding on the new purchaser or mortgagee. The basic rule is that the third party is not bound provided that he pays over the money he has agreed to pay or advance to at least two trustees.[25] So if the man and his brother were joint legal owners, they could sell the property over the head of the man's cohabitant. But where there is no second legal owner, any protection of the beneficial interest currently depends upon whether the property is registered land or not. In the case of registered land, the beneficiary may, if she finds out about the proposed transaction in advance, enter a restriction against the property under the Land Registration Act 2002, s 42, which will then ensure that the third party is aware of her interest. However, as with matrimonial home rights (see Chapter 3) this is likely to be done only where the relationship has been in difficulties and she has been given the appropriate legal advice. Much more usefully, if she is 'in actual occupation' of the property, that is, in physical possession, she can claim an 'interest that overrides', which takes priority,[26] unless either she fails to disclose her

---

[25] Law of Property Act 1925, s 27, as amended by the Trusts of Land and Appointment of Trustees Act 1996, Sch 3, para 4(8).

[26] *Williams & Glyn's Bank v Boland* [1981] AC 487, HL. Land Registration Act 2002 Sch 1, para 2 and Sch 3, para 2. Note that a person who happens to be in actual occupation is only protected if she has a beneficial interest—the legislation does not protect occupation per se.

interest on inquiry before the disposition when she could reasonably have been expected to do so, or her occupation would not have been obvious on a reasonably careful inspection of the land at the time of the disposition and the buyer does not have actual knowledge of it at that time. In the case of unregistered land, a beneficial interest cannot be registered as a land charge but the doctrine of notice may apply where the third party is aware (or should be aware) of the occupation of the property by a person other than the legal owner, so as to be put on enquiry as to her interest.[27]

Williams & Glyn's Bank v Boland and the cases following it represented a significant shift in approach by the courts towards giving greater protection to the interests of family members rather than those of commercial organizations. As Lord Scarman put it:[28]

> The courts may not. . .put aside, as irrelevant, the undoubted fact that, if the two wives succeed, the protection of the beneficial interest which English law now recognises that a married woman has in the matrimonial home will be strengthened whereas, if they lose, this interest can be weakened, and even destroyed, by an unscrupulous husband. Nor must the courts flinch when assailed by arguments to the effect that the protection of her interest will create difficulties in banking or conveyancing practice. . .bankers, and solicitors, exist to provide the service which the public needs. They can—as they have successfully done in the past—adjust their practice, if it be socially required.

Indeed, the effect of the decision was primarily to alter conveyancing and lending practice so as to ensure that potential beneficiaries consent to transactions affecting their interests and agree to postpone these to the third party.[29] In the same way, a stream of cases following *Barclays Bank plc v O'Brien*[30] and culminating in *Royal Bank of Scotland v Etridge (No 2)*[31] (discussed above) further altered commercial practice in an attempt to ensure that such consent, by either a legal or equitable owner, should not be procured by undue influence.

RESISTING SALE IN CASES OF INSOLVENCY AND DEBT

A similar greater sympathy for the interests of other family members emerged in legislation relating to insolvency. The Insolvency Act 1986 was enacted during a decade of increasingly high levels of house repossession, brought about by an unstable economic cycle, coupled with

---

[27] *Kingsnorth Finance Co Ltd v Tizard* [1986] AC 54, CA.
[28] [1981] AC 487, 510A–C.
[29] A court may be able to infer consent from the circumstances: *Abbey National Building Society v Cann and another* [1991] AC 56, HL.
[30] [1994] 1 AC 180, HL.   [31] [2001] UKHL 44, [2002] 2 AC 773.

increasing ideological emphasis on home ownership and a credit boom resulting in greater use of the home as security for business and lifestyle debt. On bankruptcy, the assets of the bankrupt vest in his 'trustee in bankruptcy' whose duty is to realize these so far as possible to meet his debts. It can be seen how important it is for a spouse or partner to seek to establish a beneficial interest in the home, since this remains her property and cannot be used to discharge the debts owed by the bankrupt. However, even if a share of the cash value of the equity is thus protected, this does not prevent the creditors from demanding that the home be sold so that the remaining share can be realized to go towards satisfying the debt. The traditional view of the courts was that the need of the family for a roof over their heads should not generally take priority over the interests of the creditors. As Nourse LJ put it in *Re Citro (a Bankrupt) and another*,[32] the plight of a 'wife with young children' being evicted from the home in such circumstances 'while engendering a natural sympathy in all who hear of them, cannot be described as exceptional. They are the melancholy consequences of debt and improvidence with which every civilised society has been familiar'.

This rather Victorian-sounding attitude was later softened. Section 335A of the Insolvency Act provides that when an order for sale of the home[33] is sought by the trustee in bankruptcy, the court must have regard to a number of factors in deciding whether to grant the order. The interests of the creditors, the conduct of the spouse or former spouse of the bankrupt, so far as this may have contributed to the bankruptcy, the needs and financial resources of the spouse or former spouse, the needs of any children, and all the circumstances of the case, other than the needs of the bankrupt, must be taken into account. The conduct and needs of a *cohabiting* partner are not expressly mentioned, although these would form part of the circumstances of the case. The express inclusion of the needs of the spouse and children is intended to encourage the court to weigh these in the balance rather than, as in the past, relegate them to an inferior position. Effectively, the family can be given a year's grace before the court grants possession. However, s 335A(3) provides that where the application is made after the end of one year following the beginning of the bankruptcy, it 'shall assume, unless the circumstances of the case are exceptional, that the interests of the bankrupt's creditors outweigh all other considerations'. Since *Re Citro* shows that the family becoming

---

[32] [1991] 1 FLR 71, 78, CA.
[33] Under s 14 of the Trusts of Land and Appointment of Trustees Act 1996.

homeless as a result of the bankruptcy is not 'exceptional', it is clear that more than this will be required to satisfy the court. An example can be found in *Judd v Brown*.[34] There, the wife had cancer and the court considered that her chances of recovery would be adversely affected by the trauma of losing her home.

A potentially more generous approach has also been indicated where sale is being sought although the defendant has not been made bankrupt. In *Bank of Ireland Home Mortgages Ltd v Bell*[35] the Court of Appeal, whilst over-ruling the trial judge's decision to refuse to order a sale at all, did consider that changes to the law governing the sale of jointly owned property, enacted in s 15 of the Trusts of Land and Appointment of Trustees Act 1996, give some scope for change in the courts' previous practice of giving priority to creditors unless exceptional circumstances apply. The merits of the case did not lie with the family members, however. Although the wife was in ill-health, her signature to the mortgage was found to have been forged and the fraudulent husband had disappeared from the scene, the debt was very large, the bank had been kept out of its money for several years, and the dependent child was nearly 18. The Court therefore ordered a sale, although its timing was to be subject to considering the wife's health needs.

The approach taken to the question whether to repossess the home can be regarded as reflecting the joint enterprise model of the marriage or relationship, extended to all the family members. All are expected to share in both the good and bad times—if the financial arrangements made prove disastrous, then all the family must take the consequences. But at least the needs of the family members are now expressly to be considered, and the delay of one year in giving possession in insolvency cases grants a reasonable breathing space to the family to seek alternative living arrangements.

PROTECTION FROM ANOTHER FAMILY MEMBER

Where a family member's continued safety and security within the home are jeopardized, not by the clinical operation of market forces, but by the behaviour of another member, the mythology of family unity and love is destroyed. Instead of the home being seen as a haven of peace and tranquility, it is revealed as a place of disharmony and potential danger. Where, as is the norm, the source of this disruption is the male 'head of

[34] [1998] 2 FLR 360.   [35] [2001] 2 FLR 809.

the household', the image of the benign patriarch presiding over and protecting his family is also shattered. How far the law can be used to protect individual family members from the undesirable behaviour of the dominant figure in the household is a direct reflection of how women and children's social and cultural status are viewed. While physical punishment of wives by their husbands was regarded as acceptable (as 'moderate' punishment of children is still so regarded), women could have no recourse to law for protection. It was only when middle-class distaste for brutal physical violence led to a campaign for reform in the nineteenth century that laws were enacted to offer such protection. In 1878, magistrates' courts were given the power, where they had convicted a man of aggravated assault on his wife, to make a 'separation order' relieving the victim of the duty to live with her husband. The blending of criminal and civil sanctions, and the view that protection may ultimately be best afforded by separating the parties—and hence breaking up the home—remain characteristic of the modern law.

THE DEVELOPMENT OF THE MODERN LAW

The problem of domestic violence within the family did not emerge again as a social issue until the 1970s with the rediscovery of 'battered wives' and the establishment of the first women's refuges. The use of the term 'battered wives' still reflected a rather narrow view of unacceptable behaviour within the family, focusing on clear physical violence and limited by a perception of the family as involving a married couple. But as cohabitation grew more common and socially acceptable, it became clear that cohabitants were just as much at risk from abuse as spouses. The Domestic Violence and Matrimonial Proceedings Act 1976 was one of the first statutes to give legal recognition to cohabitation as such (and produced the now standard definition of cohabitation as living together in the same household as husband and wife). Today, it is recognized that homosexual couples and others sharing households, or having had intimate relationships, may also be vulnerable to abuse. It has also become apparent that abuse may take many forms other than direct physical violence. One all-encompassing definition, adopted by the Home Office (2003: 8) is

Any violence between current and former partners in an intimate relationship, wherever and whenever the violence occurs. The violence may include physical, sexual, emotional and financial abuse.

However, different policy considerations may apply where a party needs protection from direct physical violence, compared with the situation where a relationship has broken down and the atmosphere between the couple has become intolerable. The latter may not require the same degree of urgency as the former, although it may require an equally robust response from the law.

Using the criminal law

A victim of abusive behaviour will primarily wish it to stop, or at least, she[36] will wish to stop suffering its effects. She may invoke both the criminal and the civil law to achieve this objective, although until recently, it has generally been assumed that the civil law is preferable. This is for both ideological and practical reasons. Resort to the criminal law directly invokes the coercive power of the state and characterizes 'private' behaviour as something that deserves public sanction. It thus invades the private sphere and opens up the family unit to outside scrutiny. Until recent years, unless the scale of violence was serious, or there was a risk of public disorder, there was considerable reluctance on the part of the police to see the criminal law used as a means of handling what were regarded as domestic and private disputes between partners. This unwillingness to 'interfere' was reinforced by a perception, perhaps as a result of sexist attitudes, of such behaviour as 'trivial' or even justified, which was in turn reflected in judicial sentencing practice where relative leniency might be shown in the case of 'family' rather than 'stranger' violence.

Whilst police and prosecution policy was officially changed in the 1990s to encourage victims to come forward, a study published in 2004 found that there was still patchy implementation at local level, with different services attaching different priority to domestic violence, few officers or crown prosecutors receiving specialist training, and substantial variation in arrest rates (HM Inspectorate of Constabularies and HM Inspectorate of the Crown Prosecution Service, 2004). The researchers found that, from crime report to conviction, there was roughly a 50 per cent dropout rate at every stage in the criminal process, so that only 11 per cent of matters recorded as crimes resulted in a conviction. The Inspectors called for strategic reforms to ensure more uniform implementation of policy, better sharing of information between the various agencies, and clearer guidance on evidence gathering and support for

---

[36] The adult victim will be referred to as the female in the relationship, since this is most commonly the case. It will also be assumed in this section that the victim is an adult partner—the position where children are abuse victims is discussed in Chapter 5.

vulnerable witnesses. Nonetheless, this low rate of conviction mirrors that found in relation to sexual offences and prompts the question whether there is not continuing gender bias in the system.

Even if such bias no longer exists, there may be valid practical objections to using the criminal justice system. A victim may be uncertain whether the relationship can be salvaged and anxious not to make things worse by having the abuser declared a criminal. Research into the use of the criminal law to handle domestic violence found that the 'main problem facing police and prosecutors in domestic violence cases is that of the fearful witness' (Edwards, 2000). The 2004 study found that victims sought to withdraw their complaints in 44 per cent of the cases received by the Crown Prosecution Service. This may make the collection of other evidence, such as forensic evidence or statements under caution, more important so that prosecutions can continue without the victim's participation, but even this would not address the victim's fear of retaliation should the perpetrator receive a non-custodial sentence, or on his release from prison.

Notwithstanding these objections, the thrust of recent Government policy (Home Office, 2003) has been primarily to emphasize the criminal nature of domestic violence by seeking changes to the criminal law and criminal justice system in order to increase the rate of convictions. For example, common assault will be made an arrestable offence under the Domestic Violence, Crime and Victims Bill, a change supported by the Inspectorates as a means of providing a clearer basis for officers to arrest perpetrators at the scene of an incident. The fact that two women each week are killed at the hands of a partner or former partner has led to the proposal that multi-agency 'domestic homicide reviews' be held to identify the lessons to be learnt from the death. The aim is to encourage inter-agency working, sharing of information, and better liaison in the provision of support for other victims and the process is similar to the reviews already conducted after the suspicious death of a child (see Chapter 5). Other measures which will utilize criminal sanctions for breach of civil orders, again in order to emphasize the criminal nature of domestic violence, are explained below, after an outline of the civil legal response to the issue.

Using the civil law

Contrary to this criminal focus, the option preferred by policy makers in the 1970s was to widen the scope of the civil law to respond to the needs of victims. An injunction is a civil order prohibiting the respondent from acting in a particular way. The Domestic Violence and Matrimonial Proceedings Act 1976 provided that a victim could obtain two types of injunction against the perpetrator, without having to seek any other remedy at the same time (usually, damages must be sought alongside an injunction, but victims may neither want nor need compensation). The first type of injunction was a 'non-molestation' injunction. By using the term 'molestation', the law made clear that direct physical violence need not be proved before an injunction could be granted. Indeed, the legislation did not define what 'molestation' means. Instead, it has been extra-judicially defined in very broad terms as 'deliberate conduct which substantially interferes with the applicant or child, whether by violence, intimidation, harassment, pestering or interference sufficiently serious to warrant intervention by a court'.[37] A victim of abuse may leave the home in order to seek safety, and refuges were set up to provide temporary shelter in such cases. But a better solution will be to evict the abuser and permit the victim (often with children) to return to the home in safety. The second type of injunction was therefore an exclusion injunction, which excluded the respondent from part or all of the matrimonial home (or the area where it is situated), or required him to permit the applicant to return to it.

A drawback of using the civil law is the difficulty of enforcing civil orders. Waving a piece of paper ordering a person not to do something may be an ineffectual shield against an abuser who threatens violence or refuses to stay away from the home. The 1976 Act accordingly provided that the court could attach a police power of arrest to its injunction, provided that there was proof that the respondent had caused harm to the applicant or a child and was likely to do so again. This enabled the police to arrest for breach of the injunction and to detain the respondent for up to twenty-four hours before bringing him before the court to be punished for the breach.

However, the case law on the use of injunctions became complicated (in part because the 1976 Act was not the only basis of jurisdiction on which they could be granted), and the Law Commission (1992) identified gaps and difficulties in its coverage, not least a strong judicial reluctance to grant exclusion orders which had the (intentional) effect of excluding an owner from his own home, even at the behest of a cohabitant to whom he owed no duty, as he would on marriage, to provide accommodation.

[37] HH Judge Fricker, 'Molestation and Harassment after *Patel v Patel*' [1988] Fam Law 395, 399.

Courts' attachment of the power of arrest was also inconsistent and often grudging, the power being seen as an infringement of the perpetrator's civil liberties. New legislation, using the same remedies of injunctive relief and police enforcement, but wider in scope and intended to be more focused on the needs of the victim, was eventually enacted in Part IV of the Family Law Act 1996.

PART IV OF THE FAMILY LAW ACT 1996

This legislation provides, as before, for two types of order to be made—a non-molestation order and what is now called an occupation order. Orders may be granted by a family proceedings court, a county court, or the High Court.

Non-molestation orders

Under s 42(2)(a) of the Act, the court may make a non-molestation order on the application of a person 'who is associated with the respondent'. By s 62(3), a person is defined as associated with another if they are or have been married to each other; they are cohabitants or former cohabitants (including, under a proposed amendment in the Domestic Violence, Crime and Victims Bill, same-sex cohabitants); 'they live or have lived in the same household, otherwise than merely by reason of one of them being the other's employee, tenant, lodger or boarder; they are relatives'; they have agreed to marry one another (whether or not that agreement has been terminated); they are the parents of, or have or had parental responsibility for, a child; and they are parties to the same family proceedings. This expansive range of categories goes much further than the 1976 Act, which was limited to people who were currently spouses or cohabiting. The aim was to ensure that those who have or had an intimate, family, or quasi-family relationship, should be able to obtain protection. But the focus of the categories remained primarily on blood or marriage ties or on relationships where a home has been shared. Contrary to the recommendation of the Law Commission, the 1996 Act excluded couples who had never lived together and did not agree to marry each other from the list of 'associated persons'. Fresh recognition that those who have had a close relationship but have not lived together may also require protection led to a provision in the Domestic Violence, Crime and Victims Bill to include those 'who have or have had an intimate personal relationship with each other which is or was of significant duration'. The meaning of 'significant' duration will no doubt be illuminated by case law.

Before the enactment of s 42, no criteria were laid down determining when a non-molestation injunction should be granted. Section 42(5) focuses attention upon the needs of the victim, by providing that the court may grant the order having regard to all the circumstances, 'including the need to secure the health, safety and well-being' of the applicant or a relevant child. The court has flexible powers to determine the terms of the order. It may specify the conduct to be prohibited (such as ordering the respondent not to contact the applicant by telephone) or prohibit molestation in general. It may also grant the order for either a fixed period or until further order. The rationale for making a fixed term order is to provide the parties with a time-limited breathing space during which they can seek to resolve the problems in the relationship. An open-ended order may be granted where it is considered appropriate for the respondent to have to justify why the order should be lifted.

Occupation orders

Where the victim of abuse considers that her safety in the family home can only be secured by excluding the respondent, or she has herself fled the home but has nowhere suitable to stay, she may seek an occupation order. However, such an order may only be sought by an applicant who either has a legal right to occupy the home or who is a former spouse or current or former cohabitant.[38]

The Law Commission's proposals for occupation orders were originally regarded as uncontroversial and non-party political. However, when they were introduced into Parliament, some members of both Houses were concerned that the law would be seen to be 'undermining marriage' if cohabitants were given the same protection as applicants who had been married. (They appear to have been quite ignorant of the protection they had already granted to cohabitants when enacting the 1976 Act.) They accordingly sought to make it harder for cohabitants to obtain an order and limit the protection to be granted, as is explained below. However, the major distinction between applicants for an order lies in whether they have property rights rather than in their marital status. Parliament, reflecting the attitude of the courts under the old law, and echoing the long-standing approach to determining the ownership of family property, appears ultimately to have been concerned to place strict property rights before the need for protection. The legislation therefore distinguishes

---

[38] In future, civil partners and same-sex cohabitants will be included.

between applicants who are 'entitled' by virtue of some legal right to occupy the property, and applicants who are 'non-entitled'.

Entitled applicants

Under s 33, an 'entitled applicant' is a person who is entitled to occupy a dwelling-house by virtue of a beneficial estate or interest or contract or by virtue of matrimonial home rights. This definition therefore includes a joint owner or tenant of the home, a partner who has a beneficial interest by way of a trust, as discussed above, a person who occupies under a contract, or a spouse with matrimonial home rights. Such an applicant may obtain an occupation order against any associated person with whom she shared, or it was intended that she share, the home. The order may declare the parties' respective rights in the home, and/or regulate their exercise, in particular by making the usual order requiring the respondent to leave the home (or part of it), and may last for a fixed term or until further order.

The Law Commission was anxious to ensure that, in deciding whether to grant an occupation order, the courts would take greater account than hitherto of the needs of the victim. Section 33(7) accordingly provides that, if it appears to the court that the applicant or a relevant child 'is likely to suffer significant harm attributable to conduct of the respondent' if an order is *not* made, then it 'shall' make the order, unless it appears that the respondent or a relevant child would suffer greater harm if the order *were* made. This 'balance of harm' test is intended to encourage the court to weigh the competing effects of its decision on the two parties. This will not always work in the applicant's favour. In *B v B (Occupation Order)*,[39] the two parties each had a child living with them from an earlier relationship. The mother, having left the home because of the father's violence, was regarded as unintentionally homeless and was given temporary accommodation by the local authority. However, the father, as the respondent to the order excluding him from the home, would be regarded as having made himself intentionally homeless and therefore not entitled to such help for him and his child. The Court of Appeal held that an order should therefore not have been made because the respondent father and his child would suffer greater harm if it were made, than the applicant mother and *her* child would suffer if no order were made.

Even if the balance of harm test is not satisfied, so that there is no *presumption* in favour of making an order, it is still possible for an

---

[39] [1999] 1 FLR 715, CA.

application to succeed because the court must also consider whether it should make an order in light of the criteria set out in s 33(6). These require the court to have regard to all the circumstances, including the parties' housing needs and resources, and those of any relevant child; the parties' financial resources; the likely effect of any order, or decision not to make an order, on the health, safety, or well-being of the parties and of any relevant child; and the conduct of the parties in relation to each other and otherwise. The intention is to balance the competing positions of the parties, and, while their conduct towards each other is a relevant factor as under the old law, the ability of each to respond to the making, or non-making, of the order, is equally important. The court will examine how easy it will be for either party to obtain alternative accommodation given their financial resources and needs. Generally, it is easier for men to re-house themselves than women, because they are less likely to have the children living with them, but this is not always the case, as was shown in *B v B*. Equally, the court might consider that the misconduct complained of by the applicant is trivial, or the tensions between the parties will be relieved shortly (perhaps where divorce proceedings are pending). Thus, in *G v G (Occupation Order: Conduct)*[40] the Court of Appeal rejected the wife's appeal against the judge's refusal to exclude her husband from the home when the final proceedings concerning the divorce were only a few weeks away, there had been no violence and the husband was often away from home anyway. In so doing, the Court maintained the judicial stance taken under the previous legislation that occupation orders are 'Draconian' and to be made only in exceptional circumstances. It is therefore likely to remain difficult for an applicant, in the absence of violence, to persuade a court to exclude a spouse or partner.

Non-entitled applicants
Where the applicant is not entitled to occupy the home, her position is more limited and the law is more complex. In line with Parliament's wish to 'uphold the institution of marriage' it has distinguished between a former spouse on the one hand, and a cohabitant or former cohabitant on the other.[41] A former spouse may seek an order according to the same criteria, and balance of harm presumption, as apply to entitled applicants. However, in addition, under s 35(6), the court must consider the length of time that has passed since the parties' separation and divorce, and whether there are proceedings in train relating to the future disposition of

---

[40] [2000] 2 FLR 36, CA.
[41] In future, it will uphold the 'institution' of civil partnership via these provisions too.

their home. It may, for example, be unfair to the respondent to grant an order in relation to a property the parties have not lived in together for a number of years. A former spouse cannot obtain an order lasting longer than six months in the first instance, although such an order can be renewed on more than one occasion.

A cohabitant or former cohabitant who is also non-entitled faces further hurdles to obtaining a remedy, but it is arguable how much of an obstacle they are in practice. First, under s 36(6)(e), in addition to the kinds of factors relevant to entitled applicants and non-entitled former spouses, noted above, the court must also consider the 'nature of the parties' relationship'. In the original enactment, s 41 of the Family Law Act explained that this meant that the court 'is to have regard to the fact that they have not given each other the commitment involved in marriage'. It is hard to see how this adds to the other factors the court would already take into account, such as the duration of the parties' relationship, their respective needs and resources, and so on. If Mrs Burns, instead of seeking to establish a beneficial interest in the family home (see above), were applying for an occupation order, it is doubtful that a court would regard her 19 years of cohabitation as less deserving of protection simply because she had lacked the 'commitment' to get married. The Domestic Violence, Crime and Victims Bill would repeal this provision, requiring the court instead to consider 'in particular the level of commitment involved' in the relationship. This is a more sensible and less offensive requirement, which removes the value judgment implicit in the original version and instead enables the court to focus upon assessing the substance of the parties' relationship rather than its label.

The balance of harm *presumption* does not apply where the applicant is a cohabitant or former cohabitant. However, under s 36(8), the court is still required, in the exercise of its discretion, to weigh the likelihood of harm resulting to either party if an order is made or not made. It is doubtful that this would make much difference in practice; if the applicant shows that the harm she would suffer if the order were not made outweighs that which the respondent would suffer if it were, then the court should grant the order in any case.

Potentially of greater impact on a cohabitant is the requirement under s 36(10) that an occupation order may only be granted for a maximum of six months in the first instance and then may only be renewed once for a further maximum six-month period. This contrasts with the ability of an entitled applicant to obtain an order of unlimited length and of a former spouse to obtain repeated renewals. However, a year's breathing space is

the same length of time offered to families facing repossession after bankruptcy, as has been discussed above, and is probably long enough, in most
cases, to enable the applicant to make permanent alternative arrangements.

While the legislation therefore appears to discriminate against cohabitants, the impact of this discrimination is probably minimal. As in the case
of ownership of family property, the most important question is whether
the applicant can establish a proprietary right in the home and the status
of her relationship with the respondent is a secondary factor.

PROCESS

There is continuing uncertainty about how the family crises underlying
applications for these kinds of orders are best handled. How far should
the protection of the individual take priority over the continuing preservation of the family as a unit? Should the focus of attention be on the
immediate problem of violence or the antagonistic atmosphere, making it
impossible for the parties to go on living together, or on a longer-term
assessment of the state of the relationship and its scope for salvage? As
was discussed in Chapter 1, the family justice system holds strongly to
the view that family disputes should be settled wherever possible without
recourse to adversarial litigation. But where one member of the family
unit is complaining about the potentially criminal behaviour of another,
there appears to be less room for a low-key approach to resolving the
issue. Indeed, to ensure that orders are properly enforced, s 47(2) of the
1996 Act requires that a police power of arrest *must* be attached where it
appears to the court that the respondent has used or threatened violence
against the applicant or a relevant child, unless the court is satisfied that
they will be adequately protected without it.[42] Amendments to this
section under the Domestic Violence, Crime and Victims Bill add to this
dilemma. The legislation provides that breach of a non-molestation order
('without reasonable excuse') would amount to a criminal offence, punishable by up to five years' imprisonment, and hence arrestable without
warrant. This means that all non-molestation orders will be automatically
enforceable by the police and bring the perpetrator within the reach of
the criminal process. A court considering whether to make an occupation
order (breach of which will *not* be a criminal offence) will also have to
consider whether to make a non-molestation order as well, in order to
bring the potential abuser within the scope of the criminal law. Such

---

[42] Section 47(2). However, in the case of applications made without notice, the court
retains the discretion whether to attach the power or not: s 47(3).

measures appear to recognize that the victim's vulnerability may demand the support of the formal legal process to redress the imbalance of power between the two parties. It is therefore questionable whether there is much scope for mediation or compromise where complaints of violence or abusive behaviour are concerned.

Nonetheless, the wish to avoid making things worse, which under-pinned the traditional preference for using the civil process rather than the criminal justice system in the first place, was reinforced by the prac-tice of accepting an undertaking[43] from the respondent rather than mak-ing an order. An undertaking is a promise to the court that the respondent will refrain from the undesirable behaviour, or will leave the home. The advantage of it is that the court does not make any findings of fact against the respondent, so that the applicant need not give evidence against him, and no recording of misconduct is made. The process also saves court time. However, no power of arrest can be attached to an undertaking, so it cannot be enforced by the police. The Domestic Violence, Crimes and Victims Bill provides that a court should not accept an undertaking instead of making an order where it appears that violence has been used or threatened by the respondent and a non-molestation order is necessary to protect the applicant or child so that breach may be punishable as a crime. This measure appears to reject, or minimize further, the scope for the traditional family law, consensual approach to handling these cases.

UTILIZING THE PROTECTION FROM HARASSMENT ACT

Taking a different approach to intra-family abuse may be justified if this is necessary to preserve family relationships. For example, it might be the case that the majority of those families in which proceedings for non-molestation or occupation orders are taken remain intact afterwards and that the problem in the parties' relationship is usually resolved harmoni-ously. However, there is no evidence to indicate that this is the case. Alternatively, it might be necessary to have particular laws pertaining to the family in this context, because the behaviour complained of is not amenable to control through other laws. This was certainly the case in the past in relation to 'pestering' or harassment, which were regarded as amounting neither to a crime nor a tort[44] and hence were only controllable in the family jurisdiction as forms of 'molestation'.

---

[43] Section 46.
[44] Held to be a criminal assault only in 1998, in *R v Ireland, R v Burstow* [1998] AC 147, HL; held not to be a tort in *Patel v Patel* [1988] 2 FLR 179, CA.

However, the Protection from Harassment Act 1997 now provides that such conduct may be dealt with either as a criminal offence or as a tort, and may be punished with criminal sanctions or restrained by an injunction. The Act was passed primarily to deal with the phenomenon of 'stalking' whereby an obsessive person persistently follows, harasses, or threatens a victim. This kind of behaviour may occur where the victim and stalker have never met, but it may also occur after a relationship has ended badly. Section 1 of the Act states that a person must not pursue a course of conduct which amounts to harassment of another, and which he knows or ought to know amounts to harassment. Breach of s 1 may amount to an offence under s 2. The Act does not define harassment (just as the 1996 Act does not define molestation), but s 7(2) provides that harassing a person includes 'alarming a person or causing the person distress' and that a course of conduct must involve conduct on at least two occasions. The Court of Appeal held in *R v Hills*[45] that there must be a linkage between the events complained of to justify the description that they form a 'course of conduct'. The offence is defined in broad terms and it can be seen that it overlaps to a great extent with many instances of 'molestation' which might also be handled under the Family Law Act. However, in *R v Hills* the Court of Appeal thought that where a couple have a turbulent relationship involving violence, but with frequent reconciliations and partings, the 1997 Act might be an inappropriate means of handling the situation. The offence is punishable on summary conviction by imprisonment for up to six months and is an arrestable offence enabling the police to arrest without a warrant. A more serious offence, of putting a person in fear of violence, is also created by s 4 of the Act.

Just as the family jurisdiction has had to invoke police and criminal justice powers to enforce non-molestation and occupation orders effectively, thus blurring the distinction between the civil and criminal process, so the 1997 Act merges the two, but much more comprehensively. First, it provides, in s 3, that an actual or apprehended breach of s 1 may be the subject of a claim by the victim, in the High Court or county court, for damages or an injunction. Unlike under the Family Law Act, a power of arrest cannot be attached to the injunction at the time that it is granted, but a warrant for arrest may subsequently be issued where the court has reasonable grounds for believing that the defendant has broken the terms of the injunction. Breach of such an injunction without reasonable excuse is a criminal offence punishable by up to five years' imprisonment.

[45] *R v Hills* [2001] 1 FLR 580, CA.

Secondly, s 5 introduced the possibility of making a 'restraining order', prohibiting the defendant from further conduct which amounts to harassment or will cause a fear of violence, on conviction of an offence. Breach of this order is again itself a criminal offence. The Domestic Violence, Crimes and Victims Bill widens the scope of this sanction to conviction of any offence, and not just, as originally drafted, those under ss 2 and 4. Moreover, and controversially, it also empowers a court to make a restraining order even where the perpetrator has been acquitted, provided that the court considers it necessary to do so protect the victim from harassment by the defendant. The Bill therefore provides a graphic illustration of the blending of civil and criminal remedies—not only may the perpetrator be subject to criminal proceedings for assault, harassment, or any other crime against the victim, but the court may now attempt to provide a more effective means of protecting the victim by subjecting him to a continuing prohibition on further violence. This is clearly intended to reassure victims that they need not fear retaliation from the offender, but whether a restraining order has this positive effect on perpetrators' behaviour and hence on victims' willingness to support a prosecution, is yet to be proven.

A PUBLIC OR PRIVATE PROBLEM?

The broad scope of the 1997 Act stands in stark contrast to the complex provisions contained in the Family Law Act. It is also noteworthy that the 1997 legislation passed through Parliament extremely quickly once the 'problem' of stalking had been highlighted by the media and identified by politicians as a matter which must be addressed urgently. By contrast, the provisions regarding protection contained in the Family Law Act were the subject of several years' consideration and consultation by the Law Commission, and endured a difficult passage through Parliament, including being lost in a failed bill, before their final enactment in 1996. The reason for this difference of treatment appears to lie in the political and social perception of the problem in issue. Stalking is seen as a criminal act that is a risk to public order. The stereotyped image of stalking involves a person with an obsession (usually sexual or romantic) for another, who has done nothing to arouse this interest or who has ended a relationship and wishes to move on. The stalker is assumed to be mentally disturbed, both because of the actions engaged in and their constant repetition, and because of the refusal to accept that the victim does not return his or her interest or affection. The stalker is seen as dangerous and likely to inflict serious harm on the victim if action is not taken. By contrast, domestic violence continues to be seen as a family matter, an undesirable but often understandable response to the pressures within an ongoing, mutual, and intimate relationship, still assumed to be based on a partnership of equals. The victim is often seen to forgive the perpetrator and to be prepared to give him another chance and there is an assumption, or at least a hope, that the parties may be able to 'work through' their difficulties and preserve the family unit. It is accordingly regarded as important that any legal response to the victim's call for help is tailored in such a way as to leave scope for reconciliation. A 'heavy-handed' response may do more harm than good. The irony is that the carefully worked out balance that has accordingly been struck by the provisions in the Family Law Act may simply be side-stepped, in an appropriate case, by recourse to the harassment legislation. Furthermore, while the onus is on a victim to take action under the 1996 Act, the police can shoulder the burden if criminal proceedings are taken under the 1997 legislation. The reality of the victim's vulnerability can thus be acknowledged rather than denied by the system. The Government's renewed emphasis upon criminal measures demonstrates an attempt further to influence the perception of domestic violence, to reframe it as indeed a criminal matter deserving public scrutiny and control. Accompanying this approach is the establishment of specialist domestic violence courts, support units and inter-agency co-operative working to strengthen the overall public response to domestic violence complaints (Home Office, 2003). The Protection from Harassment Act can thus be seen as the harbinger of a major policy shift seeking to turn family violence from a private into a public matter. The logical conclusion of this process should be the integration of civil and criminal remedies within the same court, alongside the provision of appropriate advice, support and assistance, as has been tried in some other jurisdictions, including Spain and the United States.

CONCLUSION

In this Chapter, it has been seen that the rules governing the ownership of family property, far from upholding the unity of the family, have ignored the *economic* inequality of women and have wrongly assumed an equality of opportunity to acquire property. This has resulted in a refusal to view the parties' relationship as a joint enterprise and, for example, to contemplate statutory co-ownership of the home. By contrast, where the continued occupation of the home is at risk because of commercial failure, the policy has been to view the family as a unit that must suffer the burdens as well as the benefits of their shared family life.

Family violence illustrates even more sharply the extent to which individual family members may need separate protection of their interests and recognition of their inequality in the family unit. In the last Chapter, it was noted that a contractual approach to the terms of family relationships has been advocated as offering a means of enabling couples to shape their relationship to meet their own wishes and interests. The present Chapter has illustrated that such a model may be of limited utility where the parties to the contract are not in fact economically, culturally, physically, or psychologically equal. Although family violence has traditionally been conceived as a private trouble, its existence highlights how, in the end, in order to ensure the safety of all family members, their relationships have to command the attention of the state. The next Chapter explores how this is done where the interests of children, who *are* clearly seen as unequal members of the family unit, are at stake.

5

Safeguarding Children's Welfare

INTRODUCTION

Chapter 3 outlined how the law relating to rights and responsibilities regarding children within the family has moved from a focus on the possessory right of the father over his legitimate children toward an emphasis on the interests of the child as an individual person. It also noted however, that aspects of parental responsibility continue to reflect a conception of the child as being (in) the possession of her parents. This Chapter explores how the law can be used to protect children's interests, if need be against the competing interests of their parents.

Courts exercising jurisdiction in family matters (see Chapter 1) have a range of orders at their disposal to deal with issues concerning children's welfare. These orders fall into two main categories. First, there are orders primarily designed to regulate the exercise of aspects of parental responsibility. These may be described as the 'private law' orders, and they are usually granted to resolve disputes between different family members, most often between the child's parents, over what is to happen to a child. Such orders are primarily made under s 8 of the Children Act 1989. Secondly, there are orders engaging the direct involvement of the state, which may be described as 'public law' orders, made under Parts IV and V of the Children Act 1989. These are intended to provide a degree of state scrutiny or control over the exercise of parental responsibility. The avenue for such control is the local authority, which is responsible for personal and social services on a local basis. For example, a 'care order' may authorize the removal of the child from the family and vests parental responsibility in the local authority, who then share this with the parents.

There are also two 'hybrid' jurisdictions where the courts exercise powers over matters concerning children that straddle the private/public law divide. First, there is the 'inherent jurisdiction' of the High Court, which is an ancient jurisdiction providing for the protection of minors and others unable to look after their own interests. This jurisdiction includes within it the power to make a child a 'ward of court'. It deals with issues arising both between private individuals (such as disputes between parents, or between parents and their own child) and between the state and families (such as disagreements between local authorities or health trusts and parents over the fate of their sick children). Secondly, there is the power to make adoption orders, exercised by all three tiers of courts with family jurisdiction. Adoption constitutes a hybrid jurisdiction because it establishes a new legal family of private individuals where the state has both an indirect interest in ensuring that this is in the child's interests, and a direct involvement where the child being adopted has been in the public care system.

FAMILY DISPUTES AS 'PRIVATE MATTERS'

Most proceedings regarding children's welfare concern 'private law' disputes, that is, disagreements between private individuals (usually parents) over how a child is to be brought up (usually where the parents' relationship has ended and they are in dispute over the future care of, and contact with, the child). Over four times as many applications in 2002 (some 111,000) were made in respect of such cases as were brought under the 'public law' jurisdiction by local authorities (where some 23,000 were initiated) (Lord Chancellor's Department, 2003: Table 5.1). But resort to the courts to resolve such disputes is discouraged, in both the private and public jurisdictions. The 'private ordering' approach is particularly strong in cases involving children because of the belief that continuing conflict is damaging to family relationships and especially to children's psychological well-being (discussed later in this Chapter). This is reinforced by the view of family life as a private matter that should be beyond the reach of the state. This, in turn, is underpinned by the ideological assumption that the family (or certain family members) has the presumptive right to determine the child's care and upbringing, because the child is regarded as 'belonging' to that family. Families are usually trusted—and expected—to determine a child's future without the imprimatur of a court order. Indeed, even where there is concern that a child may be at risk of abuse or neglect if left in the parents' care, social workers are encouraged to engage in social work 'in partnership' with parents and sometimes the wider family. This voluntary approach is regarded as preferable to initiating 'coercive' proceedings that may result in removal of the child from the home. It may come into sharp conflict with countervailing pressures on social workers to 'do something' when a child is perceived to be in danger.

Where a person wishes to invoke the court's jurisdiction to resolve a matter concerning a child, the ease with which they may do so generally depends on the extent to which they can be regarded as having standing to do so. Only those with a recognized claim to determine the child's future, by virtue of a prior legal or social relationship to the child, are usually viewed as having standing to invoke the court's assistance in the event that they find themselves in disagreement. In human rights terms, they satisfy the requirement to show that they share a 'family life' with the child, which the state must respect under Article 8 of the European Convention on Human Rights (see Chapter 2). The state, in the guise of a local authority, may seek to 'interfere' in the child's upbringing, but, in order to ensure compliance with human rights law, must go even further than private individuals to satisfy the court that there are sufficient grounds to warrant its doing so.

PRIVATE LAW PROCEEDINGS UNDER THE CHILDREN ACT 1989

THOSE WITH THE RIGHT TO APPLY TO THE COURT

The Children Act 1989, ss 9 and 10 distinguish between those applicants who have the *right* to take proceedings in respect of a child, and those who must seek the court's leave to do so. Parents (including unmarried fathers without parental responsibility), guardians, special guardians, step-parents who have acquired parental responsibility[1] and anyone who already has a residence order in respect of the child, may seek any s 8 order as of right.[2] They are regarded, by virtue of their legal relationship with the child, as having the strongest claim to determine the child's welfare. Under s 10(5), a category of applicants viewed as having a less extensive right to become involved may seek a residence or contact order only. These are parties to a marriage in relation to whom the child is a child of the family (see Chapter 2), any person with whom the child has lived for at least three years,[3] and any person who has the consent of those with a residence order or parental responsibility for the child, or of the local authority where a care order is in force. The applicants in this category are recognized as having a meaningful social relationship with

---

[1] Under s 10(4) as amended by Sched 3, para 56 to the Adoption and Children Act 2002.
[2] Unless they seek a residence order in relation to a child who is subject to a special guardianship order, in which case the leave of the court is required: ibid.
[3] Or, in the case of a local authority foster parent seeking a residence order, one year: ibid.

the child by virtue of having lived with her. They might include, for example, a lesbian seeking to share parental responsibility with her partner by means of a joint residence order over the partner's child.

APPLICANTS WHO MUST HAVE THE LEAVE OF THE COURT

Adult applicants

Anyone falling outside these two groups must obtain the leave of the court to apply for a s 8 order.[4] In deciding whether to grant such leave, s 10(9) provides that the court must have particular regard to

(a) the nature of the proposed application for the section 8 order;
(b) the applicant's connection with the child;
(c) any risk there might be of that proposed application disrupting the child's life to such an extent that he would be harmed by it; and
(d) where the child is being looked after by a local authority, the authority's plans for the child's future and the wishes and feelings of the child's parents.

These criteria enable the court to weigh the risk of disrupting the child's current family arrangements alongside the strength of the applicant's claim to have an interest in her well-being. A classic example might be in the case of paternal grandparents seeking contact with a grandchild where the resident mother is refusing to let them see her. At one time, grandparents had a specific *right* to seek contact after the divorce of their grandchildren's parents, but this was removed by the Children Act and they were placed in the broad category of those requiring leave, so as to minimize the risk of their unwarranted 'interference' in the nuclear family. However, courts will generally readily grant them leave to apply, recognizing that the social status of grandparent gives them standing and a legitimate interest in the child.[5]

Child applicants

Consistent with international human rights obligations, in particular Article 6 of the European Convention on Human Rights, and Article 12 of the United Nations Convention on the Rights of the Child, English

---

[4] A local authority foster parent must also have the consent of the local authority, or be a relative of the child, or the child must have lived with the foster parent for at least one year preceding the application: s 9(3) as amended.
[5] *Re J (Leave to Issue Application for Residence Order)* [2002] EWCA Civ 1346, [2003] 1 FLR 114.

law permits children themselves to seek court leave to apply for s 8 orders. Under s 10(8), where 'the person applying for leave. . .is the child concerned, the court may only grant leave if it is satisfied that he has sufficient understanding to make the proposed application for the section 8 order'. Such applications are heard in the Family Division of the High Court, which accordingly applies a test akin to the *Gillick* competence test (see Chapter 3) to decide whether to allow the application to proceed.

Whilst children are theoretically able to access the courts to seek s 8 orders under this provision, it is clear that this is in practice a very difficult course of action for a child to take. Most children will be ignorant of their legal rights and unaware of how to find a solicitor to act for them. Those who manage to surmount these obstacles have then to persuade the court of their maturity to make the application. Section 10(8) does not, therefore, provide a meaningful mechanism for ensuring that the child's voice is properly heard in most cases affecting them. There has been an increasing awareness of this shortcoming, and of the need for the child's separate representation in cases where parents may be so conflicted that they have lost sight of their children's interests or where the child may seek to voice strong opposition to what the parents are proposing. Although the CAFCASS child and family reporter should include reference to the child's wishes and feelings in the report prepared for the court (see below), this may still be regarded as an inadequate means of ensuring that proper weight is given to these. Increasing recourse has therefore been made to the court's power to make an order directing that the child (regardless of whether the child is of sufficient 'maturity'), be joined as a party to the proceedings and to be represented by a guardian ad litem.[6] In this way, the adults (usually either the child and family reporter or the judge) may identify those cases where the child's individual needs require further recognition through their being put before the court independently of the case being presented by the parents in dispute.

The European Court of Human Rights has held that there is no requirement to hear a child in every case; this must depend upon the particular circumstances and the age and maturity of the child. However, the Court appears to view this issue as concerned as much with ensuring that the parent's interests have been properly weighed by the court, as

---

[6] Family Proceedings Rules 1991, r 9.5. Provision has also been made for s 8 proceedings to be 'specified' under s 41 of the Children Act so as to enable the appointment of a children's guardian to represent the child: Adoption and Children Act 2002, s 122.

with focusing upon the child's wishes.[7] The question of whether to hear the child has also become complicated by a concern, manifested in particular by some American commentators and fathers' lobby groups, that a child's expressed views may reflect the influence of the primary carer and an attempt to alienate the child from the other parent. On this analysis, the child is not a reliable witness to her own 'true' feelings and, for the benefit of her long-term psychological interests, her current objections and fears must be overridden. The scientific basis for such a view, however, has been powerfully challenged (Bruch, 2002) and the English courts have been wary of accepting the thesis.

THE S 8 ORDERS

Under s 8 of the Children Act, a court has a 'menu' from which to choose a variety of orders governing the exercise of parental responsibility.[8]

Residence orders

A residence order 'means an order settling the arrangements to be made as to the person with whom the child is to live'. This order is made most frequently in the context of parental divorce. In such a case, both parents retain their parental responsibility and the order simply determines which one will have the child living with him or her. Where non-parents without parental responsibility, such as relatives, are granted a residence order, the order confers parental responsibility upon them at the same time, lasting for the duration of the order.[9]

The order may be made in favour of more than one person, so it is possible, for example, to provide that a parent and her new partner both have a residence order in their favour. Equally, it is possible to grant a shared residence order whereby the child spends part of her time with one carer, and then moves to the home of the other, perhaps spending alternate weeks with each parent, or term-time with one, and holidays with the other. Such an order was at one time unpopular with the English

---

[7] *Sahin v Germany; Sommerfeld v Germany* [2003] 2 FLR 671.

[8] A court cannot make a s 8 order in respect of a child aged 16 unless the circumstances of the case are exceptional (s 9(7)). Except in the case of a residence order made in favour of a person who is not a parent or guardian of the child, a s 8 order should not remain in effect once a child has reached that age, again unless the circumstances are exceptional (s 9(6), s 12(5), and s 91(10) as amended).

[9] Section 12(2). Where a court grants a residence order to an unmarried father who does not have prior parental responsibility, it must make a s 4 parental responsibility order in his favour at the same time: s 12(1). This order cannot be terminated while the residence order remains in force: s 12(4).

courts, which regard it as preferable for a child to be settled in one secure home rather than be 'shuttled to and fro'. However, they have recognized that it may be appropriate in individual cases and have moved away from permitting it only in exceptional circumstances or where a positive benefit to the child can be shown.[10]

One of the purposes behind the introduction of residence orders (Law Commission, 1988: para 4.5), was to 'lower the stakes' in disputes over children, especially on divorce, so that parents would not see themselves as having 'won or lost' the child if they were granted, or refused, an order. This was a major reason for providing that divorce does not terminate a parent's parental responsibility, even though the child may no longer live with that parent. In practice, notwithstanding the best intentions of the Law Commission, it may well be that a person who has obtained a residence order regards herself, and is seen by others, as having the best claim to make decisions in respect of the child, and as having 'won' the right to possession of the child. This may explain why shared residence orders have become more popular with the courts. Shared residence orders serve to reinforce the notion of 'shared parenting'—the idea that parents living apart nonetheless have, and play, a full part in their children's upbringing. Such a notion has been strongly urged by 'non-resident' parents, usually fathers, as they have sought to acquire more recognition of their rights. A shared residence order, rather than an order giving residence to one parent and contact (see below) to the other, enables the parents to claim 'equality' in their parenting.

The grant of a residence order brings with it the power to determine the child's day-to-day life, including her whereabouts and movements. Smart et al (2003) found that 60 per cent of a sample of s 8 applications in three English courts were for residence, compared with national statistics of *orders* granted, which show that twice as many orders were for contact as for residence (Lord Chancellor's Department, 2003: Table 5.3). They found that mothers were more likely to apply for residence and fathers for contact, with the fear that the non-resident parent would take the child away from her a particular motivation for the mother's application. Shared residence orders would clearly do nothing to ease such mothers' worries.

The powers granted to the holder of a residence order, and the motivations of parents seeking the order, in essence reflect the view of the child as being under the control of the person with residence. Section 2(7) of

---

[10] *Re F (Shared Residence Order)* [2003] EWCA Civ 592, [2003] 2 FLR 397.

the Children Act at first sight appears to reinforce this view. It provides that:

Where more than one person has parental responsibility for a child, each of them may act alone and without the other (or others) in meeting that responsibility. . . [subject to the operation of any enactment requiring the consent of another in a matter affecting the child].

This would seem to allow a person with parental responsibility, and hence also a person with a residence order in their favour, a wide discretion to take decisions in respect of the child, without the agreement, or even the knowledge, of anyone else with parental responsibility. However, both statute and case law have imposed some limitations on this power. First, certain fundamental legal steps are not available to those who only have parental responsibility by virtue of a residence order. For example, such a person cannot agree to the child's adoption, or appoint a guardian for the child.[11] Section 13 of the Act also provides that, while a residence order is in force, the child's surname may not be changed, and the child may not be removed from the United Kingdom for any period or periods of more than one month, without the written consent of every person with parental responsibility, or the leave of the court. Case law has gone further, by holding first, that even *parents* with joint parental responsibility cannot act unilaterally to change the child's surname (see Chapter 3). Secondly, a parent (or person with a residence order) cannot unilaterally agree to non-therapeutic medical treatment, such as ritual male circumcision, without the other's consent.[12] Where those sharing parental responsibility are in dispute as to whether a child should be immunized or inoculated, they must refer the matter to court for a 'specific issue order' (see below).[13] And finally, it also seems that there is no right to decide on the child's education without at least consulting the other parent first.[14]

Contact orders

Disputes over whether contact is to take place between a child and a non-resident parent, or other relative such as a grandparent, are often the most bitterly contested and acrimonious of all family disputes.

A contact order

---

[11] Section 12(3).
[12] *Re J (Specific Issue Orders: Child's Religious Upbringing and Circumcision)* [2000] 1 FLR 571, CA discussed in Chapter 3.
[13] *Re C (Welfare of Child: Immunisation)* [2003] EWCA Civ 1148, [2003] 2 FLR 1095.
[14] *Re G (A Minor) (Parental Responsibility: Education)* [1994] 2 FLR 964, CA.

means an order requiring the person with whom a child lives, or is to live, to allow the child to visit or stay with the person named in the order, or for that person and the child otherwise to have contact with each other.

The provision makes clear that contact may be 'indirect' rather than face to face, so that letters, telephone calls, and e-mail messages all constitute contact. Direct contact involves the child visiting or staying with the person named in the order or that person coming to visit the child, but no guidance is given on what constitutes 'contact' beyond this bare outline. Indeed, little is known about what children and parents or relatives actually *do* during 'contact'.

Although courts have the power to lay down detailed directions on how, when, and where contact is to take place, the preferred order is for 'reasonable contact', with the parties sorting out the details for themselves. This is largely because of the minutiae involved, and the need to respond to changing circumstances (ranging from sudden illness to a child's involvement in the school play, to the child's 'growing up' and wanting to spend more time with friends) that may require an alteration of previous arrangements.

Prohibited steps and specific issue orders

Prohibited steps and specific issue orders are intended to enable courts with family jurisdiction to determine precise questions governing the future of a child and to control particular aspects of parental responsibility. A prohibited steps order

means an order that no step which could be taken by a parent in meeting his parental responsibility for a child, and which is of a kind specified in the order, shall be taken by any person without the consent of the court.

The 'step' must relate to an aspect of parental responsibility, but the order may be made against a non-parent. For example, the order might prohibit a third party from having contact (which is clearly an attribute of parental responsibility) with the child. The aim of the order is to restrain future acts, and this may be particularly important where there is a risk that the action taken might be effectively irrevocable. Thus, a prohibited steps order may be granted to forestall the removal of the child from the jurisdiction or to prevent a medical procedure from being carried out. A specific issue order

means any order giving directions for the purpose of determining a specific question which has arisen, or may arise, in connection with any aspect of parental responsibility for a child.

Where parents disagree on an aspect of the child's upbringing and future, for example, as to the school she should attend, the court may be asked to decide by making a specific issue order. A good example is *Re A (Specific Issue Order: Choice of School: Parental Disagreement)*[15] where the Court of Appeal upheld a decision to order that two children of a French father and British mother should attend a French-speaking school in London so that they would maintain their French cultural and linguistic background.

ORDERS IN CASES OF CHILD ABDUCTION

While s 8 orders may be largely concerned to *control* the exercise of parental responsibility and thus the effects of the possessory power of the carer over the child, a court order may also be necessary to *uphold* possessory rights, and the concomitant right to respect for family life, for example in cases of child abduction.[16] These may amount to criminal offences,[17] but where the removal of a child can be anticipated, it is preferable for the carer to take pre-emptive action, if necessary by seeking a prohibited steps order or making the child a ward of court. Where the child has been abducted, the carer may seek the courts' help in achieving her return. If the abduction is within the jurisdiction of England and Wales, the abductor may have broken the terms of a s 8 order and may be in default or contempt.

INTERNATIONAL PARENTAL CHILD ABDUCTION

However, as populations have become more mobile, with individuals and whole families moving to different countries to work and settle, the problem of *international* child abduction has increased (Lowe, Everall, and Nicholls, 2004). When a parental relationship breaks down, one parent may wish to return to his or her home country with the children. If the other will not agree, the parent may unilaterally remove the children, return to the other country, and hope that the courts of that jurisdiction prove amenable to his or her case for retaining possession of the children. To deter abduction and such forum shopping, two international Conventions may be invoked to try to effect a recovery: the Hague Convention on Civil Aspects of International Child Abduction and the European Convention on Recognition and Enforcement of Decisions

[15] [2001] 1 FLR 121, CA.   [16] See, e.g. *Hansen v Turkey* [2004] 1 FLR 142.
[17] Child Abduction Act 1984, s 1 (which is subject to the operation of s 13 of the Children Act 1989 discussed above) and s 2.

Concerning Custody of Children. The United Kingdom has ratified both, and enacted their provisions in the Child Abduction and Custody Act 1985, although in practice the Hague Convention is used more often because more states have ratified it and its provisions appear more straightforward. However, a Convention can only apply as between the states that have ratified it. Where the child has been removed to a 'non-Convention' country, the carer must use that state's legal processes to attempt to obtain her return. If the child has been brought here from such a state, the child should be made a ward of court. The High Court will then determine whether the child should be returned, applying the welfare principle (discussed below).

Under the Conventions, where a child has been taken from a state where she was 'habitually resident' to another country, then provided the relevant criteria are met, the courts of the latter should generally order her immediate return so that the courts in the former can resolve the parents' dispute on its merits. A judge in the Family Division (which hears all international child abduction cases in this country) deciding whether to order such return will not, therefore, apply the welfare principle which would determine an application in wardship or under s 8 of the Children Act. The policy behind the Conventions is to deter abduction and uphold the 'welfare' of all children, collectively, in having disputes about their upbringing and care determined in the courts of the state where they have been living prior to the abduction. This is regarded as taking priority over the interest of an individual child to have her case reviewed thoroughly by the court in the country to which she has been taken, although the Conventions provide for exceptional circumstances where the court may decline to order the child's return.

PUBLIC LAW ORDERS AND POWERS

The law's emphasis on the prior claim of the parents to exercise powers over the upbringing of a child is particularly important in relation to the 'public law' orders that a court may make. The ideological attachment to the privacy and autonomy of the family has been reasserted in the years since the enactment of the Children Act 1989. Before then, the law enabled local authorities to 'assume' parental rights by administrative act, and courts were empowered in exceptional circumstances to grant public law orders (known as care or supervision orders) even when hearing private law disputes. Once a child was 'in care', parents appeared to have little voice in what was to happen to her, even to the point of being unable to challenge the refusal of the authority to permit contact between them. The breadth of the local authority's powers and the lack of any means of challenging them were eventually held to be a breach of parents' rights under Articles 6 and 8 of the European Convention on Human Rights.[18]

The 'child care' system that had evolved over the course of nearly a century from the late nineteenth century appeared, by the 1980s, to be an amalgam of differing policies, philosophies, and understandings of what might be best for children. It carried the remnants of punitive approaches to dealing with unruly children, failed initiatives at integrating services for both 'depraved and deprived' children, and half-hearted attempts at 'preventative' measures aimed at keeping children in their birth families rather than removing them to children's homes or foster care. On the one hand, the law was too broad and intrusive. It had, for example, permitted the 'Cleveland Crisis' (Butler-Sloss, 1988) to develop during 1987, when over 100 children were removed from their parents because of doctors' suspicions, based on a controversial diagnostic technique, that they had been sexually abused. On the other, the law appeared to be too narrow, with limited and outdated grounds for obtaining care orders, and ineffective at protecting children from serious abuse or neglect. A succession of tragic cases involving children murdered by their parents or step-parents revealed that social services departments had, despite the legal mechanisms available to them, failed to act robustly enough in responding to concerns about their well-being.

A thorough review of the law, conducted in the 1980s (DHSS, 1985), accordingly sought to address these many problems and to arrive at a better balance between preserving the integrity of the family unit and safeguarding the interests of the vulnerable child within that unit. The hallmark of the public law provisions now contained in the Children Act is the delicate balancing of these two concerns, reflecting the similar exercise in balancing competing rights and interests required by Article 8 of the European Convention on Human Rights. Unfortunately, as continuing tragedies unfolded in the years after the 1989 Act came into operation, it became clear that substantive legal changes may have limited impact in a system where social workers are in short supply, resources to assist families better meet the needs of their children are scarce, and lack of co-ordination, poor levels of expertise, and a failure to share information are the continuing hallmarks of bad practice in too many authorities (Laming, 2003). A further attempt to improve the system was therefore

---

[18] *W, R, O, B and H v United Kingdom* [1988] 2 FLR 445, ECHR.

made through the introduction of the Children Bill in 2004, with a focus on amalgamation of expertise through the merging of health, education, and social services for children in England, the creation of a database containing details on all children to enable professionals to check and share data about them and the designation of a director of children's services in every relevant local authority, health board, or trust in England and Wales.[19]

SERVICES FOR FAMILIES

As part of the attempt to protect family autonomy from coercive intervention, Part III of the Children Act 1989 contains a variety of provisions to enable local authority social services departments to work with families in 'partnership' for the benefit of their children, without the necessity of seeking a court order. Section 17(1) imposes a duty on the authority

(a) to safeguard and promote the welfare of children within their area who are in need; and

(b) so far as is consistent with that duty, to promote the upbringing of such children by their families,

by providing a range and level of services appropriate to those children's needs.

This section empowers authorities to provide, or arrange, services to assist families with children, including home helps, nurseries, family centres, accommodation for children whose parents cannot look after them, and even cash (although this is very limited in availability). But it should be noted that the *duty* to provide such services extends only to children 'in need' and is a general duty not enforceable for the benefit of any particular child.[20] Under s 17(10), a child 'shall be taken to be in need' if he is unlikely to achieve or maintain a reasonable standard of health or development without the relevant services, or his health or development is likely to be significantly or further impaired without them, or he is disabled. This definition enables authorities to prioritize those groups of children to whom restricted resources should be channeled. In practice, most efforts are directed towards children who would otherwise potentially be the subjects of coercive court orders because of the degree of abuse or neglect they are at risk of suffering. Perhaps in partial recognition

---

[19] The Bill also contains provisions for the creation of a Children's Commissioner for England, to catch up with those already established in the other constituent parts of the United Kingdom.

[20] *R (G) v Barnet LBC; R (A) v Lambeth LBC; R (W) v Lambeth LBC* [2003] UKHL 57, [2003] 3 WLR 1194.

of this, for the much wider group of children who are generally disadvantaged or socially excluded, Government initiatives have been established directing money for the provision of services both to public authorities such as health services, social services, and education, and to the voluntary sector.[21]

The most important of the local authority's services under Part III is the provision of accommodation. Under s 20(1) of the Act, the authority are under a duty to provide this for any child in need within their area who appears to them to require accommodation as a result of—

(a) there being no person who has parental responsibility for him;
(b) his being lost or having been abandoned; or
(c) the person who has been caring for him being prevented (whether or not permanently, and for whatever reason) from providing him with suitable accommodation or care.

The main situation where a child needs to be accommodated is where a parent is temporarily unable to care for her and there is no one else able to do so; where, for example, a single parent may have to go into hospital. But the section is also used where the parent is an inadequate carer and the child is at risk. The legislative objective of working co-operatively with the family enables the authority to offer accommodation as an alternative to seeking a care order. To encourage take-up of the facility, under s 20(8), any person with parental responsibility may at any time remove the child from the accommodation being provided.[22] This is intended to underline the importance attached to the prior claim of the parents to the possession of their child.

Where possible, 'accommodation' will take the form of care in a family.[23] If the child's own wider family is unable to care for her, she will be placed in foster care rather than in a children's home, unless there are special circumstances making this undesirable or unfeasible. Concern about the quality of care in children's homes and a belief in the superiority of care

---

[21] 'Sure Start' provides family support to parents with pre-school children in disadvantaged areas; the 'Children's Fund' works with families of children aged 5–13 who are showing signs of difficulty in school or disruptive behaviour; 'Connexions' provides advice and support to young people aged 13–19 to encourage them to acquire qualifications.

[22] There are exceptions where the child was placed in accommodation by a person with a residence order or special guardianship order in their favour, since such a person is regarded as having a better claim to determine what is to happen to the child than a non-resident parent (s 20(9)), and where the child is 16 and agrees to being provided with the accommodation (s 20(11)).

[23] Section 23(2).

within the family setting have been vindicated, both by psychological research (discussed below) and by the discovery of shocking levels of physical, emotional, and sexual abuse carried out in homes in the past (Waterhouse et al, 2000).

INVESTIGATIVE POWERS AND ORDERS

Where there is a need to investigate whether a child is at risk, there are two means by which the matter can be referred to the local authority for investigation. First, under s 37 of the Children Act, where a court hearing a private law matter is concerned about the child's well-being in the family unit, it may direct the local authority to investigate and report back to it. However, should the authority decline to apply for a public law order after the investigation, the court cannot make such an order of its own motion. The boundary between private and public is thereby preserved (though this is not without difficulty where the court is convinced that direct state involvement is necessary, but cannot persuade the authority to agree).[24] In many instances, concern about a child is brought to the authority's attention by private individuals, such as neighbours, relatives, teachers, or doctors. Under s 47, the authority must then investigate and establish whether they should take any further action such as applying to the court. In determining the future course of action, a child protection conference will be called, bringing together representatives from the various professions and agencies concerned with the child. In addition to social workers, the police, health authority, primary health care team, education authority, and relevant voluntary organizations will all be involved in contributing to what is known about the child and how matters should proceed, but once again, it is for the local authority to decide whether to do so and they cannot be compelled to act.[25] The parents are not entitled to attend the conference, although there must be strong reasons for excluding them and their legal representatives.[26] The child may be permitted to attend part of the conference, if considered of

[24] See *Nottingham County Council v P* [1994] Fam 18, CA.

[25] The authority owe a duty of care to the child (but not to the parents) in relation to the investigation of suspected child abuse and the initiation (or failure to initiate) and pursuit of care proceedings: *JD v East Berkshire Community Health NHS Trust* [2003] EWCA Civ 1151, [2004] 2 WLR 58. There is potential liability under s 8 of the Human Rights Act 1998 to both parents and children for such decisions as a result of rulings by the European Court of Human Rights: *Z and others v United Kingdom* (2002) 34 EHRR 3; *TP and KM v United Kingdom* (2002) 34 EHRR 2.

[26] *R v Harrow London Borough Council ex parte D* [1990] Fam 133, CA; *R v Cornwall County Council ex parte LH* [2000] 1 FLR 236.

suitable age and understanding. These limitations on the family's ability to participate fully in the conference may be subject to challenge under the Human Rights Act. Although the main purpose of the conference is to decide whether to place the child on the 'child protection register', such action will have implications for the future attitude and actions of the local authority. It may therefore arguably interfere with the family's Article 6 (right to a fair trial in the determination of one's civil rights) and Article 8 rights.

Where the authority are unable to carry out the investigation because of obstruction by the child's carers, they may apply to the court for an emergency protection order, granted under s 44. This authorizes the removal of the child from her home (or prevents her removal to the home from, say, a hospital) for a period of up to eight days. Alternatively, s 44A enables the court to exclude an alleged abuser from the home, so that the child does not have to be removed. Should this period be inadequate to carry out preliminary investigations, the court may extend the order for a further seven days.[27] Since this is a clear interference with the autonomy of the family, an order may only be granted where the court is satisfied that there is reasonable cause to believe that the child is likely to suffer significant harm if the order is not made. The order gives the applicant parental responsibility for the child while it remains in force, but to limit the interference that this may entail with the parents' own parental responsibility, s 44(5)(b) provides that the applicant may only take such action in meeting his parental responsibility for the child as is reasonably required to safeguard or promote the child's welfare 'having regard in particular to the duration of the order'. Thus, one would not expect major life-changing decisions over the child to be taken by the applicant during the brief pendency of an emergency protection order.

CARE AND SUPERVISION ORDERS

Where, in the light of their investigations, the local authority decide to seek a longer-term order in respect of the child, they must apply to the family proceedings court under s 31 of the Children Act 1989.[28]

---

[27] While any person, and not just a local authority, may seek an initial order, only a local authority (or other person authorized to apply for a care order—in practice, only the NSPCC) may seek an extension: s 45(1), (5).

[28] The proceedings are governed by the *Protocol for Judicial Case Management in Public Law Children Act Cases* [2003] 2 FLR 719, a detailed procedural guide, akin to the protocols introduced under the Civil Procedure Rules 1998, which aims to reduce delay and improve efficient disposal of the case.

Two public law orders may be granted: a care order, or a supervision order.[29]

A care order imposes a duty on the authority to receive the child into their care and keep her in their care for the duration of the order. The authority acquire parental responsibility for the child, which they share with any parent, guardian, or special guardian. In this way, the child's parents are intended to retain a say and interest in her future; indeed, the child may even be placed back at home with them. However, under s 33(3)(b), the authority are 'in the driving seat' since they have the power to determine the extent to which the parent or guardian may meet their parental responsibility for the child. The parents are not allowed to constrain the authority's discretion to do what the authority consider necessary to safeguard or promote her welfare. But they—and others including the child—may challenge local authority decisions regarding the restriction or refusal of contact, under s 34 of the Children Act. They may also use the authority's internal complaints procedure to complain about other decisions and actions taken by the authority, apply for the order to be discharged or seek a remedy under the Human Rights Act 1998.

Before the court may make a care order, it must first consider a 'care plan' presented to it by the local authority.[30] This sets out what they plan to do, for example, as to the type of placement the child will have and whether they plan to rehabilitate the child with the birth family or intend to seek adoptive parents for her. The House of Lords has held that it is not open to a court to seek to maintain scrutiny over the authority's implementation (or non-implementation) of the care plan by requiring the non-performance of key events or decisions, as identified by the court, to be referred back to the children's guardian (see Chapter 1 and below) with a view to that officer returning the case to court.[31] However, s 26 of the Children Act, as amended, provides that a local authority must appoint an independent person to participate in the regular reviews that must be held of the child's case and may, where he or she considers it

[29] A care or supervision order cannot be made in respect of a child who has reached the age of 17: s 31(3). A care order lasts until the child is 18, unless discharged sooner: s 91(12). A supervision order lasts for up to one year in the first instance, and may be extended to a maximum three years' duration: Sch 3, para 6. Either order may be made as an interim or final order. An interim order cannot last for more than eight weeks in the first instance, and four weeks on further renewals: s 38. An exclusion requirement may be attached to an interim order, requiring the alleged abuser, rather than the child, to leave the home: s 38A.

[30] Children Act, s 31A.

[31] *Re S (Minors) (Care Order: Implementation of Care Plan); Re W (Minors) (Care Order: Adequacy of Care Plan)* [2002] UKHL 10, [2002] 2 AC 291.

appropriate, refer the case to a CAFCASS officer who may then decide to initiate legal proceedings.

Whereas a care order clearly concerns the possession of the child and is a potentially severe interference with parental responsibility, a supervision order is intended to offer support to the parents to enable them to *meet* their parental responsibility. By s 35(1)(a) and Schedule 3 to the Children Act, the order places a supervisor (a local authority social worker) under a duty to 'advise, assist and befriend the supervised child'. The supervisor may give directions to the child, for example, as to where to live, or to participate in appropriate activities. Such provisions appear to imply that it is the child's behaviour that is the subject of attention, but in many instances, it may be the parents' conduct that is of concern. Accordingly, the Act provides that, if the 'responsible person' (that is, a person with parental responsibility, or with whom the child is living) consents, the order may include a requirement that he comply with any directions given by the supervisor. These may relate both to the child's fulfillment of directions, and to the person's own attendance and participation in appropriate activities. For example, the supervisor might require a parent to attend a family centre or nursery with the child.

The position of the child in the proceedings

Proceedings for a public law order are unusual not only because the state is bringing the case, but also because the respondents are both the child and her parents. At one time, a quasi-prosecutorial model applied with the local authority acting 'against' the child alone. Her parents, as an aspect of their parental authority, were permitted to represent her interests in the proceedings. However, in most cases, it is the parents' care of the child that is in issue and there may be a conflict of interests between them and the child. The child's voice should therefore be heard independently of that of the parents. The law was accordingly amended to provide that parents and child should be regarded as separate parties to the proceedings. Under s 41 of the Children Act, the child is represented by a children's guardian, a CAFCASS officer whose duty is to investigate and report to the court on the case, to inform the court of the wishes of the child, and generally to safeguard the child's interests. The guardian appoints a lawyer to act for the child, if the court has not already done so, and gives instructions to the lawyer on the child's behalf. Where the child disagrees with the guardian's instructions and recommendations, she may, if of appropriate age and understanding, instruct the lawyer herself, in which case the guardian may seek separate legal representation or conduct her case herself.

THE 'THRESHOLD CRITERIA'

Since the family is regarded as having the best claim to the possession of a child, it is deemed necessary in public law cases to require the state to justify its intervention beyond the simple application of the welfare principle (discussed below). This approach ensures compliance with the jurisprudence of the European Court of Human Rights, which has repeatedly stressed the gravity of actions which result in the removal of a child from the family and in particular, those which entail cutting off contact between the child and her birth family.[32] Section 31(2) therefore lays down 'threshold criteria' that must be satisfied before, having subsequently applied the welfare principle, a care or supervision order can be made. But it should be noted here that the court may, in its application of the welfare test once the threshold criteria have been satisfied, decide instead to make a s 8 order, depending on what it considers will be best for the child.

Satisfying the criteria

Section 31(2) provides:

A court may only make a care order or supervision order if it is satisfied—

(a) that the child concerned is suffering, or is likely to suffer, significant harm; and

(b) that the harm, or likelihood of harm, is attributable to—

  (i) the care given to the child, or likely to be given to him if the order were not made, not being what it would be reasonable to expect a parent to give to him; or

  (ii) the child's being beyond parental control.

The first part of the test the authority must satisfy is that the child is suffering, or is likely to suffer significant harm. Section 31(9) as amended defines harm broadly, to mean 'ill-treatment or the impairment of health or development', including 'impairment suffered from seeing or hearing the ill-treatment of another'; and these terms are themselves broadly defined. Physical, sexual, and emotional abuse, and physical, intellectual, emotional, social, or behavioural development are all included. The

---

[32] *P, C and S v United Kingdom* (2002) 35 EHRR 31.

degree of harm must be significant, but this is not defined in the section, leaving it to the courts to apply its ordinary meaning of 'considerable or important'. In deciding whether the relevant harm amounts to the impairment of the child's health or development, s 31(10) directs the court to compare the condition of the child with that which could reasonably be expected of a similar child. This enables the intellectual development of a Down's Syndrome child, for example, to be compared with that of another such child, rather than imposing a 'norm' which would be unfair in the particular circumstances. However, social and cultural differences may not be relevant to this question. In *Re D (Care: Threshold Criteria: Significant Harm)*[33] the court suggested (but did not have to decide) that it would be wrong to hold that what amounts to significant harm might vary according to the child's ethnic or cultural background. This seems correct. A child subjected to severe physical punishment or neglect because of her gender, say, should not be denied protection because that is the cultural norm in her family's ethnic or cultural group. In practice, it has not been difficult for courts to determine whether the requisite degree of harm is established. Much more problematic has been the requirement to show that the child either *is* suffering, or *is likely* to suffer, such harm. This, in essence, requires a degree of parental fault or at least failure, to be established. The case law has shifted as the courts have sought to balance the competing interests of the parents and the child.

'Is suffering'
The reason for requiring the authority to show either that the child is suffering, or is likely to suffer, significant harm, rather than that she *has suffered* such harm is to ensure that the state does not intervene in a family where the harm is purely in the past and there is no danger of its recurrence. But the difficulty with establishing that the child *is suffering* harm is that by the time the case comes to court for the full hearing, it is most likely that the child will have been removed from the harmful family environment and is currently *not* suffering harm. One would hardly expect the authority to leave the child in a dangerous situation, after all. The question therefore arises whether, given the language of the provision, it must be shown that the child is suffering harm *at the date of that hearing*. Not surprisingly, the House of Lords has held that this is not

---

[33] [1998] Fam Law 656.

necessary. In *Re M (A Minor) (Care Order: Threshold Conditions)*[34] the court had to consider the fate of a baby whose father had murdered the mother. The child's half-siblings went to live with the mother's cousin, but she felt unable to care for the baby as well. By the time the care proceedings were heard, the child was thriving in foster care, and the cousin had changed her mind and wanted to look after him. The House of Lords held that a care order could still be made. Lord Mackay held that:

> where, at the time the application is to be disposed of, there are in place arrangements for the protection of the child by the local authority on an interim basis which protection has been continuously in place for some time, the relevant date with respect to which the court must be satisfied [that the child is suffering significant harm] is the date at which the local authority initiated the procedure for protection under the Act from which these arrangements followed.[35]

It does not follow from this that, in a case where the danger to the child has completely disappeared, the court would still be entitled to have regard only to the situation which had triggered the authority's actions in the first place. Lord Mackay recognized that if the need for the protective arrangements 'had terminated, because the child's welfare had been satisfactorily provided for otherwise' it would not be possible to found jurisdiction on the original situation. Take, for example, the case of a child who has been removed from home because of suspected sexual abuse. If the abuser subsequently died in a car crash, then provided there were no concerns about the remaining carer's ability to protect the child, it would not seem that the threshold condition would be satisfied, because there would be no continuing situation of risk.[36] By the same token, however, even if a lengthy period had elapsed between the authority's original action and the final hearing, provided the 'protective arrangements' were still regarded as necessary, the court would be able to refer back to the past situation to base its finding of significant harm. This need to show that there is a *continuing* risk to the child's well-being underlines the ideological belief that coercive state interference in the family should ultimately be grounded in a concern for the child's future welfare. If there is no continuing risk, an order should be unnecessary. But on this basis, there seems little point in having the 'is suffering' test at all; the fact

---

[34] [1994] 2 AC 424.   [35] At 433–4.
[36] But cf *Re SH (Care Order: Orphan)* [1995] 1 FLR 746, where it was held that, even where suspected abusers had died, the child could still be said to be suffering harm by reference back to his initial removal from home. This seems to ignore Lord Mackay's proviso.

that a child 'is likely' to suffer harm would seem to be sufficient to ensure protection for the child.

'Likely to suffer'

A child may need protection even though she has not yet suffered, and is not presently suffering harm, if there is a risk that she is likely to do so. Here again, there has been uncertainty in interpreting the scope of the provision, this time regarding how such likelihood is to be assessed. In *Re H (Minors) (Sexual Abuse: Standard of Proof)*[37] the question arose whether children were at risk of sexual abuse in the light of an allegation of rape made by their elder half-sister against their father. Their Lordships all agreed that the word 'likely' in s 31(2)(a) means 'a possibility that cannot sensibly be ignored', but does not mean 'more likely than not' or 'probable'. They also all agreed that the standard of proof in care proceedings is the normal civil standard of the balance of probabilities and not a higher standard. The trial judge had therefore been wrong to hold that a 'high' standard of proof must apply to the truth of the girl's allegation. These rulings suggest that the test for satisfying this part of the threshold is not particularly onerous. Past facts need only be proved to have occurred on the balance of probabilities, and the harm which may be inferred from those facts as 'likely' to occur in the future need not be a *probable* outcome.

However, the majority considered that, in the words of Lord Nicholls:

the inherent probability or improbability of an event is itself a matter to be taken into account when weighing the probabilities and deciding whether, on balance, the event occurred. The more improbable the event, the stronger must be the evidence that it did occur before, on the balance of probability, its occurrence will be established.[38]

Furthermore, they held that the inference of likely harm in the future may only be based on facts as *proved* in accordance with this probability test. If the facts cannot be so proved, then there is no basis from which to infer a future risk. Acting on mere suspicion would not be acceptable, as this would shift the burden of proof onto the alleged abuser to prove that he had not carried out the suspected act. Applying their test, therefore, the majority held that the father had not been found to have sexually abused the eldest child. There was no *proven* evidence from which to suggest that the younger children were likely to suffer significant harm. The threshold criteria had therefore not been satisfied.

[37] [1996] AC 563, HL.　　　[38] At 586G.

The problem with this view, as recognized by the minority, is that, the graver and more unlikely the past event, the harder it is to prove it, *even on the balance of probabilities*, and the harder it will therefore be to infer the likelihood of future harm. But this may have grave consequences if the child is indeed at risk. Take the example of so-called 'satanic abuse'. The suggestion that children might be 'sacrificed' as part of some satanic ritual is fundamentally far-fetched and therefore, on the majority's view, strong evidence will be required to prove on the balance of probabilities that it has occurred. But if the practice is in fact going on, a child may be in grave danger and yet will remain unprotected because of the difficulty of satisfying this test.

Some recognition of this dilemma appears in the speech of Lord Nicholls. He accepted that there might be cases where 'a combination of profoundly worrying features' can be proved, even though a specific allegation of maltreatment (such as the rape) cannot. In such a case, the court could infer, from these other features, that there is a real possibility of future harm and thus find the test satisfied. It would seem, therefore, that so long as an authority base their case on a combination of factors, enough of which they *can* prove, and do not rely on one instance alone, they should still succeed. Moreover, the Court of Appeal has rejected the view that the need to have regard to the inherent improbability of an allegation does in fact amount to imposing a higher standard of proof where the alleged harm is very severe or unusual. In *Re U (Serious Injury: Standard of Proof); Re B* it reiterated the difference in the standard of proof between civil care proceedings and criminal prosecutions for child abuse and confirmed that an acquittal or successful appeal on a criminal charge would not necessarily lead to the dismissal of care proceedings. As the President noted, the 'strict rules of evidence applicable in a criminal trial which is adversarial in nature is to be contrasted with the partly inquisitorial approach of the court dealing with children cases in which the rules of evidence are considerably relaxed.'[39]

The harm is attributable to the care given to the child
Having established the requisite harm, it is then necessary to show that this is 'attributable to the care given, or likely to be given, to the child.. . .not being what it would be reasonable to expect a parent to give to him' or to the child's being beyond parental control. The latter limb

---

[39] [2004] EWCA Civ 567, [2004] 2 FLR 263, para 13.

has not caused difficulty, but the first has created problems, no doubt because its focus is on parental default. The rationale is clear enough; a child should not be removed from her family unless there is a causal connection between the harm and the quality of their care.

With both parents working, many children are today cared for in a shared arrangement between the parents and others, such as nurseries, nannies, and child-minders. The question that has arisen is *whose* care is relevant to the threshold test in such cases? In *Lancashire County Council v B (A Child) (Care Orders: Significant Harm)*[40] a child was placed with a child-minder, and later suffered physical abuse leading to brain damage. At first instance, the judge held that it had to be shown that the harm was attributable to the care of the parents against whom the care order was sought. Since it could not be determined whether the parents or the child-minder had inflicted the injuries, the test was not satisfied. The House of Lords rejected this opinion. Lord Nicholls, once again, gave the main speech. He attempted to find a middle way between holding on the one hand, that only the care provided by the parents or primary carers was relevant, and on the other, that it is irrelevant who might cause the harm. He concluded that

The phrase 'care given to the child' refers primarily to the care given to the child by a parent or parents or other primary carers. That is the norm. . .Different considerations from the norm apply in a case of shared caring where the care given by one or other of the carers is proved to have been deficient, with the child suffering harm in consequence, but the court is unable to identify which of the carers provided the deficient care. In such a case, the phrase 'care given to the child' is apt to embrace not merely the care given by the parents or other primary carers; it is apt to embrace the care given by any of the carers.[41]

The key to his Lordship's opinion was the concern that unless this approach were taken, the child might remain at risk because of the inability to identify the perpetrator of the harm. Indeed, he recognized that

the effect of this construction is that the attributable condition may be satisfied when there is no more than a possibility that the parents were responsible for inflicting the injuries which the child has undoubtedly suffered. . .parents who may be wholly innocent, and whose care may not have fallen below that of a reasonable parent, will face the possibility of losing their child, with all the pain and distress this involves.[42]

---

[40] [2000] 2 AC 147, HL.   [41] At 166.   [42] Ibid.

'Uncertain perpetrator' cases
The precise problem of identifying which of a range of possible abusers
may have been responsible for inflicting injury on a child was not resolved
in the *Lancashire* case. But these 'uncertain perpetrator' cases have caused
difficulties for both the civil and criminal courts. In the criminal law,
where parents 'cover' for each other, and refuse to divulge what really
happened so that it cannot be determined which of them actually caused
the harm to the child, it has not been possible for either of them to be
convicted for the abuse (Law Commission, 2003). To attempt to rectify
this situation, the Domestic Violence, Crime and Victims Bill proposes a
new criminal offence where a child (or vulnerable adult) dies as a result of
the unlawful act of a person who was a member of the same household
and had frequent contact with him. Where there was a significant risk of
serious physical harm being caused to the child by the unlawful act
of such a person, then if the defendant was, or ought to have been, aware
of the risk to the child, yet he failed to take reasonable steps to protect the
child, and the act occurred in circumstances of the kind that he foresaw,
or ought to have foreseen, he will be guilty of an offence punishable with
up to fourteen years' imprisonment. The objective is to enable the prosecution to secure a conviction even though it cannot identify the actual
perpetrator, liability being based on the defendant's unreasonable failure
to protect the child. But it may be noted that the offence only arises
where the child has died, not where she has suffered serious injury, which
appears to be a major omission.

In the child care system, it has, as the *Lancashire* case demonstrates,
been possible to satisfy the threshold test in such circumstances anyway.
But it may be unfair to fix a range of people with possible responsibility
for harm to a child, and difficult to determine how the case should then
be dealt with. After all, if there are a number of possible perpetrators how
is the court to decide how the child is to be protected in the future if it
cannot reliably narrow down the scope of the risk? In *Re O and another
(Minors) (Care: Preliminary Hearing); Re B (A Minor)*[43] the House of
Lords had to decide this question. In one of these conjoined appeals, the
Court of Appeal had held that, since it had not been proved on the
balance of probabilities that the mother had been responsible for any of
the child's injuries, the welfare stage should proceed on the basis *that she
did not pose a risk* to the child. In the other, another division of the Court
held the opposite—since it had not been possible to prove whether the

[43] [2003] UKHL 18, [2004] 1 AC 523.

mother or her partner had caused the injuries, *she should not be disregarded as a risk to the child in the future.* It can be seen that, in the former case, the Court focused on the *Re H* approach—that is, it sought to rely only on what had been *proved* to have occurred—while in the latter, the Court took the *Lancashire* approach—that what is of concern is the *possibility of risk*, projecting back into the past in considering what might have happened, as well as into the future in evaluating what might recur.

The House concluded that

The preferable interpretation of the legislation is that in such cases the court is able to proceed at the welfare stage on the footing that each of the possible perpetrators is, indeed, just that: a possible perpetrator.[44]

The question remains as to how the court is to handle the issue of how many possible perpetrators to take into account at the prior, threshold stage? In *North Yorkshire County Council v SA*[45] the potential abusers of a young baby were the parents, the night nanny whom they employed, and the maternal grandmother. The trial judge considered that he should only exclude someone from this list if there were 'no possibility' that they could have inflicted the injuries the child had suffered. On the facts, none of them could thus be excluded. The Court of Appeal held that this approach was wrong, and adopted Lord Nicholls' test in *Re O; Re B*. Dame Elizabeth Butler-Sloss P considered that notwithstanding his Lordship's reference to dealing with the welfare stage of the case,

In his observations about the likelihood of future risk and the likelihood that carers were possible perpetrators of past injuries to children he was, in my judgment, applying the same test of *real possibility*. . .the test of no possibility is patently too wide and might encompass anyone who had even a fleeting contact with the child in circumstances in which there was the opportunity to cause injuries. . . .I would therefore formulate the test set out by Lord Nicholls of Birkenhead as, 'Is there a likelihood or real possibility that A or B or C was the perpetrator or a perpetrator of the inflicted injuries?'[46]

The Court of Appeal seems here to be attempting to carve yet a further middle way between fixing responsibility for abuse on too wide a range of potential perpetrators and exculpating those for whom proof of responsibility cannot be established. It is not entirely certain that this should follow from what was held in *Re O; Re B*. Lord Nicholls made it very

---

[44] Ibid per Lord Nicholls at para 28.
[45] [2003] EWCA Civ 839, [2003] 2 FLR 849.
[46] Ibid, paras 21–26, emphasis added.

clear in that case that he adhered to his earlier view, in *Re H*, that 'given the purpose of the threshold criteria, both limbs of the "significant harm" condition call for proof of facts'.[47] But he also recognized that an inroad had been made into this stance in the *Lancashire* decision, in order to avoid the otherwise unacceptable consequence that the child would remain unprotected. The two later House of Lords decisions therefore represent a rowing-back from the logic of *Re H* in order to ensure the child can be protected. *North Yorkshire*, ironically, adopts the same departure from strict 'proof' in order to exculpate those the Court deems less likely to have been responsible for the child's injuries.

It is important to recall once again, however, that it does not follow from the fact that the threshold criteria are satisfied that a care or supervision order will be made. The court has still to apply the 'welfare principle' (see later in this Chapter) in deciding how to dispose of the case.

THE 'HYBRID' JURISDICTIONS

THE INHERENT JURISDICTION OF THE HIGH COURT

The inherent jurisdiction stems historically from the position of the sovereign as 'parens patriae' who had a duty to protect those of his subjects, such as children, unable to protect themselves. Originally, the main concern of the sovereign as feudal ruler was to control the property of infants whose fathers had died. Such infants were known as 'wards'. Although the history is uncertain, it is generally understood that this power was delegated to the Lord Chancellor and in turn to the Court of Chancery, exercising what became known as its 'wardship' jurisdiction. The clear basis of the sovereign's interest in the child can be seen to lie in his control over the child's inheritance during the child's minority. However, over time, the general well-being of the child was also taken into account, and by the end of the nineteenth century, the welfare of the child was regarded as the governing factor in determining issues arising in wardship.

During the first half of the twentieth century, the wardship jurisdiction was a forum whereby private law disputes over a child could be resolved, such as in the case of parents seeking to try to prevent their teenage daughters from making unsuitable relationships. But by the 1980s, a significant use of the jurisdiction was as a public law device. It was used by local authorities concerned about children at risk of abuse or neglect

---

[47] [2003] UKHL 18, [2004] 1 AC 523, para 17.

where they were unable to satisfy the criteria of the legislation then governing the grant of 'public law' orders. Because the wardship court could exercise its powers on the basis of what was in the child's best interests, it was unconstrained by such criteria. However, these restrictions were important in attempting to preserve a degree of family autonomy from state interference. Accordingly, when the Children Act was passed, social services departments were prohibited by s 100(2) from using this jurisdiction to have a child placed in their care or under their supervision or to make a child already subject to a care order a ward of court.

Under the modern law, the inherent jurisdiction appears to have two facets. First, there is a general inherent jurisdiction to decide particular questions where the child's welfare is in issue. The High Court may determine a very broad range of matters, from deciding whether medical treatment can be carried out on a sick child, to restraining a third party from contacting the child. Secondly, there remains the 'wardship jurisdiction', the key distinguishing feature of which is that control over all important questions affecting the child's future vests in the court for as long as the child remains its 'ward'. Until the Children Act 1989, these two facets were blurred and all cases were handled under the ambit of 'wardship' proceedings. Now, *wardship* has become once again primarily a private law jurisdiction, useful in cases of urgency, such as child abduction, because an application automatically makes the child a ward until the court determines otherwise. This renders any unauthorized action affecting the child, such as removal from the jurisdiction, a contempt of court.

The *inherent jurisdiction* apart from wardship remains available for use in both private and public law matters, although s 100(3) provides that a local authority seeking to use it must have the leave of the court to make an application. Such leave may only be granted if the court is satisfied that the result the authority wish to achieve cannot be obtained by the making of another order and there is reasonable cause to believe that the child is likely to suffer significant harm if the jurisdiction is not exercised.[48] This filter ensures that the autonomy of the family is still preserved but enables the state to act where there is serious concern. Leave has been granted where, for example, a local authority is seeking authorization for medical treatment of a severely anorexic child in care.[49]

---

[48] Section 100(4).
[49] *Re W (A Minor) (Medical Treatment: Court's Jurisdiction)* [1993] Fam 64, CA, also discussed in Chapter 3.

The inherent jurisdiction therefore represents an anomaly in the general scheme regarding court orders relating to children. It straddles the private/public divide in terms of its subject matter, and is available to any applicant. Persons concerned about a child have been able to invoke the jurisdiction even where their relationship with the child is tenuous. Perhaps the most striking example can be seen in *Re D (A Minor) (Wardship: Sterilisation)*.[50] There, an educational psychologist made a child, who had some learning difficulties, a ward of court to prevent her being sterilized, even though the child's mother and doctors agreed that the operation should proceed. The Court prohibited the operation from taking place. Finally, the inherent jurisdiction was the first to recognize the separate status and interests of the child in family proceedings, by requiring that the child be separately represented by the Official Solicitor, displacing the parents or others with parental responsibility.

ADOPTION

Like private law proceedings, adoption proceedings are brought by private individuals, the prospective adopters. It was noted in Chapter 2 that around one quarter of adoptions involve step-parents and are family 'reconstitutions'. But the state has an interest in adoption which has always been thought to justify a more direct involvement than that provided simply by the court acting as adjudicator of the application. This is because, under the Adoption and Children Act 2002, s 46,[51] adoption constitutes the complete substitution of one set of legal parents for another. The child ceases to be a member of one legal family, and becomes part of a new one. To guard against trafficking in children and to prevent exploitation of vulnerable parents who are unable to cope, attempts have been made to ensure that adopters are suitable carers and that those arranging adoptions act ethically. To this end, s 92 of the Act[52] makes the private placement of a child with a view to adoption, other than by leave of the High Court, a criminal offence, unless the prospective adopters are the parents, relatives, or guardians of the child (or one of them is) or the prospective adopter is the partner of a parent of the child. Only adoption agencies (local authorities or registered adoption societies) may place children with unrelated adopters. Furthermore, as psychological theory stressing the importance of permanency and stability for children has gained ground, so adoption has come to be seen as the

---

[50] [1976] Fam 1985.   [51] Previously the Adoption Act 1976, s 12.
[52] A similar but less broad provision was contained in s 11(3) of the 1976 Act.

preferred goal of the public law system for many children once rehabilitation with the birth family has been rejected as an option by social services (Department of Health, 2000: para 1.13). The state therefore has a direct interest and role in adoption proceedings, as facilitating and promoting the adoption of children who would otherwise remain in the care system.

Although prospective adopters do not have to seek the leave of the court to apply for an order, they will have been thoroughly 'vetted' before the substantive hearing is held. A private adopter must give written notice to the local authority of their intention to seek an order under s 44 of the Adoption and Children Act 2002,[53] and the authority must investigate and report to the court. A would-be adopter who seeks to adopt from an adoption agency or local authority must be approved by the agency's adoption panel, and will be the subject of very close scrutiny before this is given.

Welfare of the child in adoption

Before the 2002 Act, an adoption order was not determined by a court in the same way that it would approach proceedings for an order under the Children Act, because of its fundamental interference with the rights of the birth parents. The welfare of the child was *not* the court's paramount consideration. Rather, s 6 of the Adoption Act 1976 provided that 'first consideration [shall be] given to the need to safeguard and promote the welfare of the child throughout his childhood'. In practice, this made little difference to the court's view of the matter since the court would still regard the child's welfare as the most important factor.

Placing less emphasis on the welfare of the child in adoption decisions may be justified as a means of giving greater weight to the parents' right to respect for their family life with the child under Article 8 of the European Convention on Human Rights. The European Court has been particularly concerned to recognize the continuing interest of birth parents in the future upbringing of their child and to protect parents' rights where children are adopted after having been in public care.[54] But it does not make sense to downgrade the child's interests in relation to one of the most important decisions that could possibly affect a child's well-being. Section 1(2) of the Adoption and Children Act 2002 accordingly brings adoption law into line with the Children Act by providing that

---

[53] Replacing Adoption Act 1976, s 22.
[54] *Johansen v Norway* (1997) 23 EHRR 33. Different considerations may apply in step-parent adoptions, according to *Soderback v Sweden* [1999] 1 FLR 250.

The paramount consideration of the court or adoption agency must be the child's welfare, throughout his life.

Section 1(4) of the Act attempts to ensure compatibility with the Convention, notwithstanding the introduction of the paramountcy principle, by requiring the court or adoption agency to have regard to a 'checklist'[55] of factors designed to balance the Article 8 rights of the birth family and the child. They include the likely effect on the child (throughout his life) of having ceased to be a member of his original family and become an adopted person; the relationships the child has with birth relatives or others, and the likelihood and value of such relationships continuing; and the wishes and feelings of such relatives or other persons. When placing a child for adoption, an adoption agency must also give due consideration to the child's religion, racial origin, and cultural and linguistic background, to help ensure that his sense of identity (also protected under Article 8) is properly safeguarded.

The agreement of the birth parents

The other way in which an adoption order is distinct from other orders relating to children lies in the fact that it can only be made where each parent with parental responsibility expressly consents, or where the court overrides that parent's refusal to consent. The consent of an unmarried father without parental responsibility is not required, although such fathers should usually be traced where possible and invited to participate in the proceedings, and a failure to permit them to do so may be a breach of their Article 8 right.[56]

Before a child can be adopted, she will have spent a period of time (the length depending upon whether the adoption has been arranged by an agency or not)[57] with the prospective adopters to test whether the placement is likely to prove successful. The decision to place a child with prospective adopters is highly significant. It indicates that those responsible for planning the child's future consider that this lies with a new family and not with the birth parents. The decision may be taken by the birth parents themselves, as when, for example, a young mother gives up her child feeling that she cannot care for it adequately herself, or by a

---

[55] A rather different checklist applies in proceedings under s 8 and Part IV of the Children Act 1989: s 1(3) discussed below.

[56] *Keegan v Ireland* (1994) 18 EHRR 342; *Re H; Re G (Adoption: Consultation of Unmarried Fathers)* [2001] 1 FLR 646, CA.

[57] Adoption and Children Act 2002, s 42, replacing and amending Adoption Act 1976, s 13.

local authority looking after the child, either as part of its original care plan as presented to the court when a care order was granted, or, after having attempted to work with the family but finding that rehabilitation of the child is not going to succeed. In contrast to the prior law, where the local authority could place the child with prospective adopters without parental consent or the court's sanction, under the 2002 Act, there must be parental consent or express endorsement by the court through the making of a 'placement order',[58] before the child can be placed, in order to ensure due regard to the parents' Article 8 rights. Such an order can only be made if the child has no parent or guardian, is already subject to a care order, or the threshold criteria under s 31(2) of the Children Act 1989 are satisfied. While the child is placed (either by consent or under an order), the adoption agency and prospective adopters are given parental responsibility, which they share with the birth parents, but the adoption agency may determine whether and how the exercise of such responsibility by either the birth parents or prospective adopters is to be restricted.[59]

If the placement is successful and the prospective adopters decide to adopt the child, the court must be satisfied that the birth parents consent to the adoption or that their consent should be dispensed with. The parent may give advance consent to the child's eventual adoption.[60] This is intended to enable the prospective adopters to have a child placed with them with a view to adoption, secure in the knowledge that the birth parent cannot go back on her decision and thus disrupt the placement. Otherwise, dispensing with consent, either to placement itself or to the actual adoption, may only be done on proof of either of two grounds set out in s 52(1) of the Adoption and Children Act 2002.[61] The court must be satisfied that either

(a) the parent or guardian cannot be found or is incapable of giving consent, or
(b) the welfare of the child requires the consent to be dispensed with.

The introduction of a 'welfare' ground as the basis for dispensing with parental consent to this fundamental decision is highly controversial. Given that s 1(2) of the 2002 Act makes the child's welfare the court's paramount consideration when coming to any decision regarding the adoption of the child, it is hard to see how, once the court has concluded that it is in the child's best interests to be adopted, it could then go on nonetheless to decide that the birth parents' consent should not be

---

[58] Ibid, s 21.   [59] Ibid, s 25.   [60] Adoption and Children Act 2002, s 20.
[61] Replacing and amending s 16(2) of the Adoption Act 1976.

dispensed with. Surely, the child's welfare must inevitably so require? If that is so, there is a danger that the parents' Article 8 right to respect for family life will be given insufficient weight. However, it has been noted above that the welfare checklist contained in s 1(4) of the Act is intended to help the court to balance out the competing family members' rights. Moreover, the European Court of Human Rights has stressed that Article 8 has a procedural, as much as a substantive, element to it. By this, the Court means that a parent must be given an adequate opportunity to participate in the decision-making process and put their case.[62] The provision is therefore Convention compliant. Moreover, it *is* possible to envisage situations where the court could find in favour of the parent. In *Re M (Adoption or Residence Order)*,[63] the Court of Appeal held that a mother's refusal to agree to her 11 year old child's adoption should not be dispensed with (on the test which then applied, of being unreasonably withheld) where it had been based on the child's own wish not to be adopted. Although the mother, a former drug addict, could not currently care for her daughter, the Court considered that it would 'require fortitude bordering on indifference for a mother to shut her ears to what her child has said' in the face of the child's steadfast opposition to the adoption. There seems no reason to think that the same view would not be taken under the test set out in the 2002 Act.

Re M suggests that the child's own views may be decisive in a difficult case. The former Conservative Government proposed that the agreement of a child aged 12 or over should become mandatory to an adoption, unless she is incapable of giving such consent (Department of Health, et al, 1993: para 4.3), and this is already the law in Scotland. This reflects the growing recognition of the child's autonomy rights and her individual interest in asserting these regardless of the parents' possessory claims. However, the 2002 Act does not introduce this requirement, no doubt because of the concern expressed by many involved in adoption work that this is too onerous a decision for a child to have to make.

THE WELFARE PRINCIPLE

THE HISTORICAL DEVELOPMENT OF THE PRINCIPLE

At common law, the father of a legitimate child was seen as having a prior and stronger claim to possession of the child than the mother (or others)

---

[62] *McMichael v United Kingdom* (1995) 20 EHRR 205.   [63] [1998] 1 FLR 570.

in disputes concerning the custody of the child. The onus was therefore on those opposing the father to satisfy the court that this superior right should be overridden in the circumstances of the particular case. This was a difficult task since the courts also assumed that remaining in the father's possession would indeed generally be in the child's best interests. This dual logic extended to other jurisdictions dealing with children. Even in wardship proceedings, where, as noted, the child's welfare had become the primary consideration by the end of the nineteenth century, social and moral opinions influenced ideas about welfare and mingled arguments based on parental rights with those based on children's interests.

Under pressure from feminist campaigners in the era when female suffrage was finally won, the Guardianship of Infants Act 1925 provided that the welfare of the child should be the court's 'first and paramount consideration' when it was considering her custody or upbringing (Cretney: Chapter 16). This provision was intended to satisfy women that they would henceforth be treated as equal to men in custody disputes. But the statute did not define what was meant by 'welfare'. This enabled the courts to use their previous understandings of what would be best for a child, and hence to maintain an approach ultimately based as much on 'justice' between the parents as on the 'welfare' of the child.

INFLUENCES ON THE LEGAL CONCEPTION OF WELFARE

Over time, broader influences led to an apparent shift away from this approach. First, there was an acceptance of the child as a person with separate interests from her parents. This meant that decisions about the child's future could not be based on parental rights alone.

Secondly, new insights from psychology and sociology shed light on how children's development and well-being may be harmed or helped by what happens to their family relationships. Three main strands of research appear to have been particularly important in influencing social and legal policy. First, John Bowlby's theories of 'maternal deprivation', published after the Second World War, emphasized the need of a child for a primary caretaker to provide a stable emotional attachment (Bowlby, 1953). Bowlby considered that only the child's mother could fulfil this role. This was controversial. Feminists rejected the argument that women should stay at home to care for their children, and further research suggested that a child might in fact be able to form close attachments to persons other than the mother, so long as stability and security were maintained. Nonetheless, the idea that young children, at least, are best

162   *An Introduction to Family Law*

off with their mothers, remained influential in judicial decision-making affecting children.

In the 1970s, Goldstein, Freud, and Solnit (1973) argued that the primary need of the child is for a 'psychological' parent. Once the bond is formed between the child and such a parent (who need not be the biological parent at all), it is harmful to disrupt it, and the child's 'sense of time' means that, for a young child, such an attachment can be formed quickly. Delays in decision-making over children can lead to them being damaged by uncertainty and instability; equally, moving a child from a secure attachment will be damaging to the child. They therefore argued for laws which would place whoever was the child's psychological parent in control over the child's relationships with others, including the absent parent in situations of marriage breakdown and the birth family where a child is in secure foster care. While this particular proposal was highly controversial, their findings on the speed at which attachments can form and the damage that can be done from breaking them proved extremely influential. The desirability of avoiding delay in reaching a decision and the importance of recognizing the child's 'status quo' have been reiterated by other researchers, and have affected judicial and social work approaches in both private and public law cases. Courts seek to reduce avoidable delay in procedures as far as possible, and social work planning seeks to find secure placements for children removed from birth families as quickly as possible.

In the 1980s and 1990s, research[64] into the effects of parental separation and divorce on children suggested that conflict and distress experienced by the parents impacts upon children and may precipitate behavioural and emotional problems. Furthermore, good continuing contact with the non-resident parent may help children adjust to the divorce. These findings have influenced attempts to make legal procedures less antagonistic and adversarial and have resulted in the promotion of conciliatory approaches and offers of mediation to help parents settle their differences. They have helped non-resident parents to argue strongly for the law to recognize their continuing role in the child's life, both through the maintenance of parental responsibility and the grant of contact. They have also strengthened the view, strongly held since the 1960s by most policy-makers in relation to divorce, that legal labels of blame or default attached to the child's parents may be harmful to the child's future well-being.

[64] Reviewed by Rodgers and Pryor (1998).

But as with earlier ideas of children's 'welfare' that we would now find patriarchal and out-moded, one should be aware of two things. First, 'scientific' insights produced by one disciplinary profession—child psychology—are applied selectively and reinterpreted to fit social and legal understandings of the world and to meet social and legal priorities in ways that can run counter to the original intentions of the researchers (King and Piper, 1995). Secondly, research findings based on 'science', may themselves be influenced by social and cultural factors. Bowlby's views on maternal deprivation, as much as the nineteenth century judges' views on fathers' rights, were products of his time and the society in which he worked. Findings about the value of non-resident parents' (primarily fathers') continuing input into their children's emotional lives fit a social and political agenda seeking to reinstate men's centrality in the nuclear family. They would have been inconceivable as research issues at a time when a father's role was understood as appropriately confined to being the breadwinner and head of household.

WELFARE AS THE COURT'S 'PARAMOUNT' CONSIDERATION

The best example of how these various influences led the law away from its preoccupation with parental rights to a concern for the child can be seen in the leading case, *J v C*.[65] The child was a ward of court, born to Spanish parents who had worked in England for a time. Unable to care for the child because of poverty, they had entrusted him to English foster parents, with whom he remained, apart from some time spent as an infant in Spain. When the child was about five years old, the parents became concerned that the foster parents wished to keep him, and they demanded his return. The child was warded but the case did not reach the House of Lords until he was aged ten and a half, and had not seen his parents since he was three. The parents could not be regarded as having neglected their child, but on the contrary, had always acted in what they perceived to be his best interests. Nonetheless, the House ruled that the child should remain with the foster parents, and held that there was no presumption in law that a child's welfare is necessarily served by being brought up by his 'unimpeachable' parents. The case established that the welfare principle applied not only to disputes between parents in situations of marital breakdown but also to disputes between parents and third parties, and regardless of parental 'fault'. Lord MacDermott also

[65] [1970] AC 668, HL.

provided an important interpretation of the words used in the legislation then in force—that the child's welfare is 'first and paramount':

[these words] must mean more than that the child's welfare is to be treated as the top item in a list of items relevant to the matter in question. I think they connote a process whereby, when all the relevant facts, relationships, claims and wishes of parents, risks, choices and other circumstances are taken into account and weighed, the course to be followed will be that which is most in the interests of the child's welfare as that term has now to be understood. That is the first consideration because it is of first importance and the paramount consideration because it rules upon or determines the course to be followed.[66]

It was this elevation of the child's interests clearly above the possessory claims of the birth parents that made the case so important in marking out the potential scope of the welfare principle. After *J v C*, the courts often showed themselves willing to disregard notions of 'justice' as between parents, or parents and third parties or the state, in ensuring that the child's welfare would be best served. In the private law sphere, the guilt or default of the parent in a marriage breakdown was regarded as usually irrelevant in determining who should have the care of, or contact with, the child.[67] In the public law field, the courts have been prepared to cut ties between the child and birth family, notwithstanding the parents' blamelessness in relinquishing care of the child. In *Re KD (A Minor) (Ward: Termination of Access)*,[68] the House of Lords rejected the argument that such action conflicted with the mother's right under Article 8 of the European Convention, considering that the child's interests must always ultimately prevail over those of the parents. In fact, the European Court has accepted that the best interests of the child may override the rights of the parent, although it still requires a 'fair balance' to be struck between them.[69] Similarly, Article 3(1) of the UN Convention on the Rights of the Child requires that the best interests of the child shall be 'a primary' but not 'the paramount' consideration, leaving scope for the parents' interests to be weighed in the balance.

This balancing exercise can sometimes be accommodated by a redefinition of what will be in the child's welfare, by equating this with the parents' possessory claim. In *Re KD* itself, although the House rejected the mother's argument to preserve contact, they nonetheless emphasized that

[66] At 710–11.
[67] *Re K (Minors) (Children: Care and Control)* [1977] Fam 179, CA.
[68] [1988] AC 806, HL.
[69] *Johansen v Norway* (1997) 23 EHRR 33; *L v Finland* (2001) 31 EHRR 30.

The best person to bring up a child is the natural parent. It matters not whether the parent is wise or foolish, rich or poor, educated or illiterate, provided the child's moral and physical health is not endangered.[70]

A striking example of the application of this approach is *Re M (Child's Upbringing)*,[71] the facts of which are remarkably similar to those in *J v C*. A White South African woman agreed to take into her home the eighteen-month-old son of her Zulu servant. She later moved to England with the child and the rest of her family. When there was talk of her adopting the boy, the parents demanded his return and he was made a ward of court. Once again, litigation was lengthy and the boy was ten by the time the case reached the Court of Appeal. They ordered his immediate return to South Africa, emphasizing 'the strong supposition' that it is in a child's interests to be brought up by his natural parents, and by the need to preserve his cultural heritage as a Zulu child. While the language of the decision turns on the notion of welfare (and also on the child's right, under Article 8 of the United Nations Convention on the Rights of the Child, to preserve his identity), there is also recognition of the prior claim of the parents.

When the law relating to children was being overhauled in the 1980s, the Law Commission recommended that welfare be regarded as the court's *sole*, rather than 'first and paramount' consideration. This was rejected and instead s 1(1) of the Children Act provides as follows: When any court determines any question with respect to:

(a) the upbringing of a child; or
(b) the administration of a child's property or the application of any income arising from it, the child's welfare shall be the court's paramount consideration.

It might be thought that this wording is incompatible with Article 8 of the European Convention on Human Rights because it appears to leave no rooms for any consideration of parental interests. However, as has been noted above, the European Court has agreed that the child's welfare should be capable of overriding the parents' rights, and with hindsight, the rejection of welfare as the 'sole' consideration seems to have been wise. The use of the term 'paramount', if interpreted in accordance with Lord MacDermott's explanation in *J v C* (above), provides a little leeway to take into account the parents' separate interests, as required by the

---

[70] Per Lord Templeman [1988] AC 806 at 812.
[71] [1996] 2 FLR 441, CA.

European Convention, while still ensuring that the resulting decision is ultimately determined by what is best for the child.

WHEN IS THE WELFARE PRINCIPLE APPLICABLE?

Before considering *how* the welfare principle is applied, it is necessary first to note that numerically, it is only relevant to a minority of cases where children's interests are affected. This is because, as set out in s 1(1) above, it applies only where a court must determine a question with respect to the upbringing of a child (or the administration of a child's property). In its other formulation in the Adoption and Children Act 2002, s 1(2), it applies to courts and adoption agencies taking decisions regarding a child's adoption. Thus, it does not affect those other than courts or adoption agencies, such as parents in particular, who take decisions affecting a child. Secondly, it does not apply where the child's interests are only indirectly affected, such as in deciding whether to make an occupation order under Part IV of the Family Law Act 1996 (see Chapter 4) or in determining whether to direct a DNA test to ascertain the child's parentage (see Chapter 2). Thirdly, it does not apply where excluded by other legislation applying a different test, for example, in relation to matters of financial support or divorce (although the courts do consider children's interests in deciding whether to delay the grant of decree absolute—see Chapter 6).

PROVIDING EVIDENCE FOR ESTABLISHING WHAT WILL BE IN THE CHILD'S WELFARE

Evidence directed to the question of what will be best for the child may be provided by a welfare report compiled by an officer of CAFCASS (see Chapter 1). Expert evidence may also be submitted, with leave of the court, most commonly by child psychiatrists and paediatricians. The child is not usually present in court, and judges have traditionally been reluctant to accede to children's requests to speak to them in private, although they occasionally exercise their power to do so. As noted above, difficult questions can arise concerning the applicability of the child's right to be heard under Article 6 of the European Convention on Human Rights and of Article 12 of the UN Convention on the Rights of the Child. If a judge sees a child in private, the parties to the proceedings have the right to know what was said, so that no confidentiality can be promised. A refusal to hear the child, on the other hand, may be a breach of the child's right.

THE MEANING OF 'WELFARE'

There is no statutory definition of 'welfare'. One of the major criticisms of the law prior to the Children Act 1989 was that courts had no guidance on what they were supposed to take into account, or what was supposed to be conducive to a child's welfare. It was left to the virtually unfettered discretion of each court to attach its own meaning to the term and to arrive at outcomes influenced as much by personal prejudice as by legal principle or scientific evidence. To provide a measure of guidance to the courts, s 1 of the Children Act sets out a number of factors identified as relevant in arriving at a decision as to what is in the child's best interests. These factors draw on the psychological findings discussed above as well as previous judicial pronouncements. Section 1(4) of the Adoption and Children Act 2002, as we have already seen, also provides a set of criteria relevant to the context of adoption. These largely reflect the factors set out in the Children Act, coupled with particular emphasis upon the child's birth ties, and are not discussed further here.

Delay

Section 1(2) states that there is a 'general principle that any delay in determining [a question relating to a child] is likely to prejudice the welfare of the child'. Courts are required to set a timetable for proceedings to ensure the effective management of the litigation. Although proceedings are still subject to significant delays, one would not expect to see many cases taking as long as *J v C*. Delay also has human rights implications. Protracted litigation may jeopardize the effective exercise of a person's Article 8 right to respect for family life, for example.[72]

The necessity for an order

Section 1(5) is potentially of even greater significance to the way in which legal disputes over children are handled. It provides that, in considering whether to make an order under the Act, a court shall not make an order 'unless it considers that doing so would be better for the child than making no order at all'. The rationale for this was to discourage the making of unnecessary orders. It was felt that this new approach would 'lower the stakes' between the parties and the level of conflict between them so as to reduce the damage to the child. For example, while it might well be right in a given case that the mother should have her children

---

[72] *Sylvester v Austria* (2003) 37 EHRR 17.

living with her, there might be no reason why she should automatically be granted a residence order stating this. The *need* for the order must be proved to the court's satisfaction. Clearly, where the parties are able to agree the arrangements for the child, as they are strongly encouraged to do, it may be difficult to explain why an order is still necessary.

The welfare 'checklist'

Section 1(3) sets out a list of factors to which a court must have regard when it is considering whether to make a s 8 order which is opposed by any party to the proceedings, or whether to make a care or supervision order. There is nothing to stop a court applying the checklist outside these particular instances, but it is not obliged to do so.

The ascertainable wishes and feelings of the child
Inclusion of the child's wishes and feelings in the checklist serves to ensure compliance with Article 12 of the UN Convention on the Rights of the Child. But it is arguable whether that obligation is best fulfilled by treating the child's wishes and feelings as an aspect of her welfare. It may well be the case that the more informed the court is about the child's emotions towards what is happening to her, the better it will be able to ascertain where her best interests lie. But by subsuming the child's views within the welfare checklist, the court is enabled, as with the common law application of the *Gillick* competence test (discussed in Chapter 3), to discount her views where they appear to conflict with its own conception of her interests. Since Article 12 should best be understood as a child's *autonomy* or *participation* right, arguably it should stand as a consideration to be taken into account by the court distinct from the child's welfare.

There is no minimum age below which a court would refuse to take account of a child's expressed views and quite young children's wishes and particularly their feelings may be regarded as significant. At the other end of the age range, the older the child, the more weight her views may carry, simply because the court may have to recognize that the child may 'vote with her feet' if she refuses to abide by the court's decision. However, it is clear that the child's opinions cannot dictate the court's decision. Ultimately, the test is what will be best for the child, not what will best satisfy the child.[73]

---

[73] See, e.g. *Re W (A Minor) (Residence Order)* [1993] 2 FLR 625, CA. But note that in *Re M (Child's Upbringing)* (above n 71), the child wished to remain in England, and, after a few unhappy months in South Africa, returned with the agreement of his parents.

The child's physical, emotional, and educational needs
Establishing what the child's needs are and how they should be met is not
straightforward and can reveal the influence of cultural and social percep-
tions as much as 'objective' scientific advice. For example, material considerations may appear to carry little weight and one parent will not
obtain the care of his child simply because he can provide a better standard of living than the other. But 'middle class' conceptions of what a child
needs may incline a court to prefer a more traditional lifestyle to one that
appears 'bohemian'.

A controversial question has been whether, following Bowlby's theory,
a young child should be placed with her mother rather than father. The
courts have eschewed the notion that such a view carries any presumptive
weight, yet babies and infants are still likely to be regarded as best cared
for by their mothers, at least where they have been in the mother's care in
the past. Thus, in a Scottish House of Lords decision, *Brixey v Lynas*,[74]
Lord Jauncey considered that 'where a very young child has been with its
mother since birth and there is no criticism of her ability to care for the
child only the strongest competing advantages are likely to prevail'.

In line with the evidence presented by Rodgers and Pryor (above) a
child is also likely to be regarded as 'needing' a good continuing relationship with a non-resident parent and the wider family. Indeed, Article 9(3)
of the UN Convention on the Rights of the Child recognizes this view. It
requires states to respect the right of a child separated from one or both
parents to 'maintain personal relations and direct contact with both parents on a regular basis, except if it is contrary to the child's best interests'.

A strong 'assumption'[75] that contact should take place has influenced
the courts' approach to applications for contact, even in cases where the
absent parent is alleged, or found, to have committed domestic violence
against the carer. The courts tended, until recently, to be 'robust' in
dismissing the objections of carers as based on 'implacable hostility' or
irrationality, and to have ordered contact, and enforced their orders, *even
to the point of imprisoning a recalcitrant mother for contempt of court.*[76]
Concern that they were thereby disregarding the genuine and serious
fears of mothers eventually led to a review of the evidence and the issues
by the Children Act Sub-Committee (CASC) of the Lord Chancellor's
Advisory Board on Family Law (2000). The Sub-Committee, while

[74] 1996 SLT 908, 911.
[75] As distinct from a 'presumption'—see Thorpe LJ in *Re L (A Child) (Contact. Domestic Violence)* [2001] Fam 260, 295C, CA.
[76] *A v L (Contact)* [1998] 1 FLR 361.

considering that there was no need for any statutory amendment to the law to provide better protection to carers and their children, did consider that it would be desirable for the courts to follow Good Practice Guidelines. These should indicate how the courts should investigate and approach allegations of violence so as to ensure that all the potential issues and effects of making an order or its refusal are properly weighed. The Court of Appeal effectively incorporated these guidelines into a decision given on four conjoined appeals, all upholding refusals of contact based on the violence of the non-resident parent.[77] How to make contact 'work', in the face of research (Trinder et al, 2002) that suggests that taking court proceedings to enforce contact is more likely to damage, rather than enhance, its prospects of success, was the subject of a further major report by the CASC (2002). The Board proposed a range of measures intended to 'educate' parents into better understanding the value of contact to the child and the need to put the child at the heart of their thinking. Translating such principles into effective action is an ongoing task of the Department for Constitutional Affairs, through initiatives such as the promotion of 'parenting plans' (in which parents set out the detailed arrangements they will make for matters ranging from contact visits to washing sports kit and dealing with birthdays and Christmas) and early access to mediation when parents are in dispute.

The likely effect on the child of any change in his circumstances
The psychological evidence has placed considerable emphasis on the need to preserve the child's 'status quo'. In other words, where a child is in a settled and stable situation, there must be good reasons for disrupting this. (But equally, an unsatisfactory status quo may require change, and this of course justifies the removal of children from situations of neglect and abuse.) The courts applied this approach in their judicial reasoning prior to the enactment of the welfare checklist, and it remains an important consideration. Even in *Brixey v Lynas*, as we have seen, the House of Lords noted that the child had been in the mother's care from birth, and hence their decision was justified as much by a desire to avoid damaging the child's routine as by a 'maternal preference'. Indeed, whilst fathers' groups lobbying for more 'shared care' claim widespread gender bias in the courts, the much more likely explanation for the tendency to award residence to mothers is that the courts are upholding the status quo by leaving the child with the mother who has been the primary carer.

---

[77] *Re L (A Child) (Contact: Domestic Violence)* [2001] Fam 260, CA.

The child's age, sex, background, and other relevant characteristics
This provision enables the court to consider wider factors in the child's situation and could once again, for example, justify the placement of a baby with her mother. Equally, it could justify placing an adolescent boy with his father if the need for a male role model were felt to be important to the child. The child's cultural, ethnic, and religious background may be taken into account and may be given weight as part of the court's wish to recognize obligations under Articles 8 (preservation of identity) and 30 (enjoyment of minority culture and religion) of the United Nations Convention on the Rights of the Child. But these factors may be overridden by other needs. In *Re P (Section 91(14) Guidelines) (Residence and Religious Heritage)*,[78] the Court of Appeal declined to disturb a decision refusing the return of a Down's Syndrome child to an orthodox Jewish family. They had been unable to care for her and had asked the local authority to find a Jewish foster home for her, but this proved impossible and she was placed with a secular Roman Catholic family. The Court agreed that the child's satisfactory 'status quo' with that family took priority over both the view that a child is best off with her natural family and with the desire to ensure an environment in which she could retain her Jewish heritage.

Any harm the child has suffered or is at risk of suffering
The meaning of 'harm', and the way in which it is to be proved, are the same as in relation to care proceedings (discussed above). Harm may cover a wide spectrum, ranging from direct physical or sexual harm from an abusing parent, to emotional harm or 'moral' harm from exposure to undesirable life-styles such as drug-taking or (mainly in the past), homosexuality. In particular, there has been a new recognition that, even where domestic violence is directed only against the carer, the child may be psychologically damaged by witnessing or knowing about it, or by the detrimental impact it has on the carer. This has led to a more subtle consideration of the risks involved than was the case in the past.[79]

The capability of the child's parents, or others, in meeting his needs
This factor overlaps with the previous ones. For example, a mother may be regarded as better able to meet a baby's needs than a father. A parent's ability to appreciate the child's position and to recognize the child's

---

[78] [1999] 2 FLR 573, CA.
[79] Section 120 of the Adoption and Children Act 2002 amends the definition of harm in s 31(9) of the Children Act to include 'impairment suffered from seeing or hearing the ill-treatment of another'.

individual needs and wishes may be important where, for example, the child has been at risk of neglect and the question is whether the parent can be entrusted to provide adequate care.

The range of powers available to the court in the particular proceedings
The court must consider the range of orders it may make (and, by virtue of s 1(5), whether it should make any order at all). This provision enables the court to have regard to the requirement under Article 8 of the European Convention on Human Rights that any interference with the parents' right to respect for their family life must be 'necessary in a democratic society'. In other words, it must be 'proportionate' to the legitimate aim of protecting the child.[80] This may be particularly important in public law proceedings. A court satisfied as to the threshold criteria (discussed above) may still decide that a public law order is unnecessary, or opt for a supervision order, as being less invasive than a care order, even though the local authority argue for the latter. In private law proceedings, a court hearing a contact dispute might choose to make a 'family assistance order' under s 16 of the Children Act to enable a CAFCASS officer or local authority social worker to help a family comply with the substantive order.

Competing 'best interests'

Finally, it is necessary to address an inevitable limitation of the welfare principle. A court may be required to determine the best interests of more than one child at the same time, resulting in a decision which potentially places the welfare of one child over that of the other. The starkest illustration of this problem arose in the unique and tragic case, *Re A (Children) (Conjoined Twins: Surgical Separation)*[81] (discussed in Chapter 3), concerning the conjoined or 'Siamese' twins, 'Jodie' and 'Mary'. There, the Court of Appeal had to determine whether it would be lawful to separate the twins, thereby bringing about Mary's death. This inevitably required the judges to weigh the competing interests of the two children. While it was clearly in Jodie's interest to give her the chance of survival, their Lordships differed as to whether it could be said to be in Mary's interest to cause her to die. Johnson J, at first instance, and Robert Walker LJ in the Court of Appeal, both considered that it *would* be, since she had no quality of life while conjoined and would, at least, achieve the dignity of bodily autonomy (albeit only on death) if separated. Ward and

---

[80] *Re C and B (Care Order: Future Harm)* [2001] 1 FLR 611, CA.
[81] [2001] Fam 147, CA.

Brooke LJJ, by contrast, accepted that the operation would not be in her best interests. As Ward LJ put it, the 'best interests of the twins is to give the chance of life to the child whose actual bodily condition is capable of accepting the chance to her advantage, even if that has to be at the cost of the sacrifice of the life which is so unnaturally supported'.[82] The case illustrates how notions of welfare may ultimately come down to the court's determination of the moral justice of the case. Usually, this is camouflaged because the court need simply focus on the child's interests over and above those of the parents. In *Re A*, there was no legal (as distinct from public) controversy surrounding the question of overriding the parents' wishes. Instead, the balancing of one child's right to life against that of the other could not be avoided. Ultimately, the Court had to make a moral choice one way or the other. Its preference for saving the life of the stronger child could not necessarily be predicted from previous judicial articulations of the welfare principle. Another court could decide the opposite with equal justification. This essential uncertainty and inconsistency may be both the greatest strength and greatest weakness of the 'welfare principle'.

[82] At 197.

6

Ending Family Relationships

STATUS AND CONSEQUENCES

When family relationships come to an end, the law may be required to
deal with two different issues. First, it may be invoked to change the legal
status of those involved, to reflect the change in their social relationship.
For example, a married couple who have separated will usually seek a
divorce to bring a legal end to their marriage tie; or, as noted in the
previous Chapter, an adopted child ceases to be a legal member of one
family and becomes that of another. Secondly, the law may be needed to
deal with the consequences of the termination of the relationship. There
may be emotional and social consequences, and Chapter 5 considered the
potential use of orders regulating the exercise of parental responsibility to
protect the position of children. But very often, the consequences will
also be financial—a widow may seek support from her deceased
husband's estate because he left her nothing in his will; a parent with care
of children may require child support from the absent parent for their
maintenance.

The legal formation of marriage[1] and parenthood, as discussed in
Chapter 2, takes place within a framework of law but without recourse to
the legal system. One does not need to go to court to get married and
parental status is usually evidenced by means of birth registration alone.
But where the relationship is terminated during the lifetime of one or
more of the parties, only the courts can give legal effect to any consequential change of status that they may seek. It is arguable that the requirement of a court order for this is an unnecessary historical relic. Nearly all
divorces are uncontested and the majority of adoption orders are also
made with parental agreement. Simple registration procedures could be
introduced to record the desired change in legal status, leaving the legal
process to handle just the consequences where the parties could not

---

[1] Civil partnerships would, under the proposed legislation, be handled in largely the same
way as marriage, and are not discussed in detail in this Chapter.

resolve these themselves (as is the case with divorce in Japan and Russia). However, the rationale for retaining court control over change of status is to ensure that the public interest is safeguarded, both in relation to society as a whole and the individuals concerned. The political fear that marriage will be taken too lightly if divorce is made too simple requires that a person seeking a divorce must prove her entitlement to it to a judge (although, as will be shown below, the task is not an onerous one). Moreover, the respondent to a divorce, and any children of the family, have financial and emotional interests that the state regards as worthy of protection. It therefore reserves the right to scrutinize the proposed arrangements for these to try to ensure that harmful consequences are minimized. But the effectiveness of the legal system in achieving this goal is open to question. This is because couples end their emotional relationship with each other regardless of the requirements of the legal process. Until they choose to engage with the legal system, there is no mechanism whereby the needs and interests of the individual family members can be checked. A cohabiting couple need not go to court to end their relationship and the legal process may therefore never be aware of any need to protect the interests of the weaker partner. A married couple do not *have* to seek a divorce; they may simply separate from each other and the legal process may know nothing about them and their needs. And such needs may be as great and as pressing when a relationship has been ended by death as by divorce, yet there is no obligation to go to court to resolve problems concerning the guardianship of children.

It is therefore necessary to bear in mind that there are multiple aspects to the ending of family relationships. First, there is the social, economic, and emotional reality that affects those involved, regardless of their present or future legal status. Secondly, there is the legal framework which governs their position and which may control aspects of status and the legal consequences of the termination. Finally, there is the legal process which operates through the courts to resolve particular problems arising from the first two.

This Chapter considers first of all how the law deals with the change in status brought about by divorce. It then examines the financial and property consequences arising out of the ending of a relationship, looking at the termination of marriage and non-marital relationships and then at how the law determines rights to the estate of a person who has died. In both cases, a tension exists between two different models of the parties' relationship with each other. As suggested in earlier Chapters, one may categorize marriage or cohabiting relationships as based either on a 'partnership of equals' or 'joint enterprise' model. The adoption of the separate property system in the reform of marital property in the nineteenth century has enabled the partnership of equals model to predominate. This means that where a party to the relationship seeks to obtain a (larger) share of the other's property, she has to justify this either by arguments effectively embodying the joint enterprise model, or by demonstrating that she is in a weaker and dependent position which demands protection. While the latter approach may be appropriate for a child or other relative, it may be queried whether it is appropriate in the case of a spouse or partner.

TERMINATING MARITAL STATUS

Divorce[2] is one of the most politically sensitive aspects of family law. The rate of divorce is used by politicians as a measure of the social health of the nation; a 'high' divorce rate is regarded as indicative of moral and social decline. Yet, as was discussed in Chapter 1, it is unclear what is actually meant by a 'high' divorce rate. Moreover, the divorce rate does not measure the rate of marriage breakdown but only the rate of recourse to the divorce courts. There may in fact be higher rates of separation or disenchantment in countries with lower divorce rates than the United Kingdom, but these are less susceptible to measurement.

The political significance attached to divorce has always made it a highly controversial area for legal reform. After all, one must recall that the foundation of the Church of England stemmed from a 'divorce' case (although in fact it concerned whether Henry VIII's marriage to Catherine of Aragon could be *annulled* rather than terminated by divorce). After the Reformation, the Church continued to accept the Roman Catholic doctrine of the indissolubility of a valid marriage, so that although the ecclesiastical courts could annul a marriage, they could not pronounce a divorce as we understand it. An alternative route for those wishing to end a marriage between the seventeenth and nineteenth centuries was to obtain a private Act of Parliament (Stone, 1990) to that effect, but this was difficult for all but the wealthiest. When a judicial process for obtaining a divorce was finally introduced in 1857, it continued to reflect the view that divorce was a remedy for a wronged spouse and a punishment of the guilty party. It was an adversarial, almost quasi-criminal contest in

[2] A 'judicial separation', which terminates the obligation on the spouses to cohabit, but not the status of marriage, may be granted under s 17 of the Matrimonial Causes Act 1973.

which the petitioner (the person seeking the divorce) had to prove the marital misconduct of the respondent.

THE DEVELOPMENT OF DIVORCE LAW

Extraordinarily, in nearly a century and a half of the most profound social change, the substantive law of divorce in England and Wales has only been reformed on four occasions since judicial divorce was introduced—and the last of these was abandoned before it was even brought into force. In 1857, the law reflected the Victorian sexual double standard and the practice that had obtained in Parliament. It permitted husbands to divorce their wives on the ground of adultery alone, while the wife had to prove that the husband had committed adultery *and* some other aggravating offence such as cruelty or desertion. Moves toward formal gender equality placed husbands and wives on an equal footing in 1923, and made the sole ground for divorce the adultery of a spouse. In 1937, there was the first recognition that a divorce might be justified notwithstanding that the respondent was not guilty of adultery. It permitted either spouse to petition on the basis of the other's cruelty or desertion alone and, more significantly, it allowed a divorce to be granted because of the respondent's insanity. This meant that, for the first time, a spouse could be divorced even though he had committed no matrimonial offence at all. As an attempt to encourage the parties to 'work at' their marriage and attempt to mend any early breakdown in the relationship, rather than to rush to the divorce courts, the Act also introduced a bar (subject to the court's discretion) on petitions for divorce being presented during the first three years of the marriage. These two measures marked the beginning of a debate that has yet to be conclusively resolved as to whether divorce should be based on the breakdown of the marriage or the failings of a spouse.

THE CURRENT LAW

The Divorce Reform Act 1969, now consolidated in the Matrimonial Causes Act 1973, attempted to deal with this question by providing that the *sole* ground for divorce is the 'irretrievable breakdown' of the marriage. The Act provides, however, that such breakdown may only be evidenced by proof of one or more of five 'facts', three of which are manifestations of matrimonial misconduct.[3] The other two 'facts'

---

[3] The basis for dissolution of a civil partnership would also be irretrievable breakdown, but adultery will not be a relevant fact for establishing this, since the act is defined in heterosexual terms.

demonstrating irretrievable breakdown are differing periods of separation. Where the respondent consents to the divorce, the necessary period of separation is two years. Where she refuses her consent, the period is extended to five years. To maintain the view that divorce should not be granted too quickly after the wedding, the time bar on presenting petitions was reduced to one year, but was made an absolute prohibition by the Matrimonial and Family Proceedings Act 1984. This compromise has proved workable but intellectually unsatisfactory. Those who believe that marital fault should be the basis of divorce are unimpressed by references to irretrievable breakdown. Those who support the concept of irretrievable breakdown consider it confusing nonetheless to require the parties to bring their case within one or more of five categories, three of which are still based on fault.

Since the Divorce Reform Act came into force, the annual number of divorces has climbed (from around 45,000 in 1968), and then stabilized in the 1990s, to around 140,000 per annum (Lord Chancellor's Department, 2003: Table 5.5). Around two-thirds of these are based on the 'fault' facts and around 70 per cent are sought by wives rather than husbands (ONS, 2003*b*: 87). The reason for the continuing preference for reliance on matrimonial fault is the speed with which the divorce may be obtained; rather than wait for two or five years, the divorce may be granted within a matter of months. The predominance of wives among petitioners is due to their greater financial dependence. They need to resolve matters of finance and property and the care and support of the children because they lack the economic autonomy to manage without some form of assistance from either their husbands or the state. They cannot, therefore, remain too long in legal and financial limbo, but must bring the breakdown of the marriage to some form of conclusion so that arrangements for the future can be made. The legal consequences of the ending of the marriage are therefore as important to them as the alteration of their legal status.

Adultery and intolerability

Under s 1(2)(a) of the 1973 Act, the first of the facts that may be relied on is that the respondent has committed adultery and the petitioner finds it intolerable to live with him or her. The reason for requiring the petitioner to show 'intolerability' as well as adultery was the belief that adultery should be seen as a symptom, rather than the underlying cause, of the breakdown of the marriage and that it should not suffice, of itself, to justify a divorce. However, it has been held that the petitioner need not find it intolerable to live with the respondent *because of* his adultery.[4] In practice, it is doubtful that the subtlety is appreciated by many petitioners, who probably assume that the law is allowing them to divorce their spouse because of the adultery.

The respondent's behaviour

Replacing the old-fashioned concept of 'cruelty', s 1(2)(b) provides that irretrievable breakdown may be established where the petitioner shows that the respondent has behaved in such a way that the petitioner cannot reasonably be expected to live with him. In contrast to 'intolerability', the question of what it is reasonable to expect the petitioner to put up with is not a matter of assertion by the petitioner. Rather, it is to be answered by the court, assessing the personalities and circumstances of the individual couple. As it was put in *Livingstone-Stallard v Livingstone-Stallard*:[5]

Would any right-thinking person come to the conclusion that *this* husband has behaved in such a way that *this* wife cannot reasonably be expected to live with him, taking into account the whole of the circumstances and the characters and personalities of the parties?

A very broad range of conduct has been taken into account, from the obvious examples of domestic violence or drunkenness to an obsession with (ineptly) carrying out DIY jobs around the house.[6] Furthermore, while 'behaviour' might appear to connote willed activity on the part of the respondent, it has been held that involuntary conduct brought on by mental illness will suffice.[7] In practice, because very few divorces are contested, there is no real opportunity for a court to assess the severity, or even the truth, of the allegations made against the respondent. However, a petitioner may feel obliged to dredge up every act or omission of the spouse that can possibly be the subject of criticism and put the worst possible gloss on all of these in order to be sure of satisfying the court that the fact is made out. Lawyers may try to tone down allegations made by their clients, aware that these may only serve to encourage the respondent to resist claims over finance, property, and the children. The Law Commission (1990: para 2.16) certainly criticized the scope of the fault 'facts', behaviour in particular, for contributing to the hostility and bitterness felt by the parties as they go through the breakdown process.

---

[4] *Cleary v Cleary* [1974] 1 All ER 498, CA.   [5] [1974] Fam 47, 54.
[6] *O'Neill v O'Neill* [1975] 3 All ER 289, CA.
[7] *Thurlow v Thurlow* [1976] Fam 32.

Desertion

The fact most rarely relied upon is that in s 1(2)(c): that the respondent has deserted the petitioner for a continuous period of at least two years. Desertion is a matrimonial offence, effectively amounting to an unjustified separation from the other spouse, with the intention of remaining permanently apart, and without his or her consent. It will usually be possible to rely on one of the other facts, either fault-based, in which case there will be no need to wait for two years, or the neutral separation periods.

Separation for two or five years

Regarded at the time of their enactment as extremely liberal, the introduction of neutral separation periods was intended to provide a more 'civilized' way of obtaining a divorce and it was hoped that the two-year separation period would become the normal fact relied upon. However, it is less popular than reliance on behaviour, and more likely to be used by those in the higher socio-economic groups. The main reason is that only the better off may be able to afford to move into separate accommodation and wait for two years before reaching a property settlement in the divorce suit. In fact, the courts will accept that the parties have been living apart even though they remain under the same roof, but it may be difficult to establish the proof that they are leading sufficiently separate lives to have formed two distinct 'households'.[8] The more modest the accommodation, the harder it will be to satisfy this test; the more lavish the living standards of the parties, the easier it will be for one of them to move out in any case.

Section 1(2)(d), which enables irretrievable breakdown to be established on proof of two years' separation together with the respondent's consent to the divorce, was the first introduction into English law of overt divorce by mutual consent. Even though, as noted, most divorces are— and have for long been—undefended, it has been regarded as undermining the institution of marriage to permit the parties to obtain a divorce simply because they decide that they both want it. Requiring them to show that they have separated for a fixed period was intended to demonstrate that their wish to end the marriage is not simply a temporary whim but firm evidence that it has broken down and cannot be mended.

The parties may separate, or one spouse may technically be in desertion, but the other may refuse to consent to the divorce or petition on her

[8] *Mouncer v Mouncer* [1972] 1 All ER 289.

own behalf. In that case, it was eventually conceded that it would be unfair to prevent the spouse wishing to end the marriage from ever being able to do so. Indeed, it was thought that cohabitation outside marriage would decline if spouses trapped in dead marriages could obtain a divorce and marry the partners with whom they were otherwise forced to 'live in sin'. Accordingly, it was decided that, where the spouses have lived apart for five years, the petitioner should be able to terminate the marriage without the other's consent. It was assumed that petitioners in such cases would usually be men who had left their wives and formed relationships with younger women and there was concern that s 1(2)(e) would be used as a 'Casanova's Charter'. To safeguard the interests of such wives, s 5 of the Matrimonial Causes Act provides that a petition may be dismissed if the respondent satisfies the court that dissolution of the marriage will result in grave financial or other hardship to her, and that it would be wrong to end the marriage. Such arguments have rarely succeeded. The financial hardship resulting from divorce will usually stem from the fact that the change of status will prevent the respondent from becoming the widow or widower of the other spouse and thus lose pension entitlements. But provided there are other financial assets that can be made available to the spouse under the divorce settlement, or via other sources such as state benefits, the court is unlikely to refuse the divorce.[9] 'Other' hardship, such as the stigma of divorce in certain ethnic minority communities, is usually found to arise from the professed failure of the marriage rather than from its legal termination, and hence to fall outside the terms of the section.[10] Basically, s 5 provides a reluctant respondent with a bargaining counter to use in extracting a more favourable divorce settlement from the other spouse. It helps to demonstrate how, under modern divorce law, the focus of attention, of both the law and the parties, is on the 'ancillaries'—the financial and other consequences—rather than on the divorce decree itself.

Divorce procedure

The special procedure
This position is reinforced by the divorce process. Procedural reforms introduced during the 1970s accomplished a far more profound shift away from an emphasis on proving the ground for divorce, than a reading of the Matrimonial Causes Act by itself can reveal. To control the public

---

[9] See, e.g. *Archer v Archer* [1999] 1 FLR 327, CA.
[10] *Banik v Banik* [1973] 3 All ER 45, CA.

costs of a seemingly ever-increasing number of divorce petitions, all undefended petitions (virtually all divorces) are dealt with by means of the 'special procedure'. This means that there is no court hearing of the petitioner's claim for the divorce. Instead, the district judge in the county court scrutinizes the petition and accompanying documents, and if satisfied with the contents, certifies that the petitioner is entitled to a decree. Unless the respondent challenges any of the documentation, there can be minimal scope to check on whether what the petitioner states is true.[11] Assuming there are no complications, decree nisi is then pronounced in open court, with the petitioner able to obtain the decree absolute six weeks later.[12] It is this latter decree which legally terminates the marriage and enables the parties to remarry.

Where there are children under the age of sixteen in the family, under s 41, the petitioner must file a 'statement of arrangements' setting out what she (or both spouses) propose for the children's future upbringing and care. The district judge may hold up the decree absolute if he or she is not satisfied as to these and considers that powers under the Children Act 1989 (see Chapter 5) may need to be exercised, although this is rare.[13] More often, the district judge may call for further evidence, or bring the spouses in for a hearing, to clarify what is proposed.

Mediation

When the current law was introduced, provisions were included to encourage the spouses to try to reconcile before proceeding to divorce. For example, under s 6(1), the petitioner's solicitor must certify whether the possibility of reconciliation has been discussed with the client. Subsequently, the focus shifted away from attempting to reconcile the parties, toward *conciliation*, or, as it is now more commonly known, mediation. This entails assisting the spouses to come to terms with the ending of the marriage, to reach agreement on how the consequences should be handled, and to reduce the degree of conflict between them. Unlike lawyer negotiation, mediation is conducted by one (or two) neutral mediator(s) who does not 'act' for either party, but holds the ring between them. The mediator's role is to open up possible lines of communication between the parties and explore avenues of compromise with them.

---

[11] For a rare example of court staff detecting fraudulent petitions, see *Bhaiji v Chauhan (Queen's Proctor Intervening)* [2003] 2 FLR 485.

[12] If the petitioner does not apply for the decree absolute, the respondent may do so three months after decree nisi: s 9(2).

[13] Where one of the spouses is already seeking an order under the Children Act alongside the divorce decree, this step in the procedure is omitted.

Unlike a judge, the mediator does not impose a binding settlement on the parties; they must agree this (or fail to agree) for themselves. Most areas have established mediation schemes, either operating separately from the courts, or as part of their internal processes, but these have depended on local initiative and precarious funding. The possibility that mediation might be a cheaper option for the public purse than the funding of lawyers' services through the Community Legal Service Fund (legal aid) led the Government to explore the scope for allowing mediation to be publicly funded, and according it a more central role in the divorce process. This might also help divorcing couples reach agreement which could reduce the level of conflict between them and hence (as we saw in Chapter 5) the consequential disruption to their children. The Government accordingly amended the law governing legal aid to provide that any applicant for aid from the Fund in proceedings relating to family matters must generally first provide information to an approved mediator to determine whether his or her case is suitable for mediation. If so, funded assistance may be refused if the litigant declines to engage in mediation.[14] However, mediation depends upon the willingness of *both* parties. Where the other (who may not be legally aided and hence able to choose how he or she wishes to proceed) is unwilling to come to mediation, there will be no real option open to the Legal Services Commission but to grant the applicant aid for legal representation.

REFORM PROPOSALS

Although the current law is in some ways a careful compromise between those wishing to retain the doctrine of the matrimonial offence and those wishing to move to a concept of irretrievable breakdown, it can be criticized as intellectually incoherent. By retaining 'fault', and enabling divorce to be obtained more quickly if such fault is 'proved', the law undermined the attempt to move people to a view of divorce as a recognition of the breakdown of the marriage rather than as a penalty for misbehaviour. Blame and guilt continue to permeate the parties' dealings with each other, but because there is no real attempt to investigate the truth of allegations, these feelings are displaced onto the way the spouses negotiate the 'ancillaries'. The procedures of divorce, and the way they are handled by solicitors, also seem to produce a conveyor-belt effect.

---

[14] Access to Justice Act 1999, s 8(3) and Community Legal Service Funding Code Part II Procedures, Section 7—Referral for Family Mediation. The requirement relates to most types of family matters and not just divorce.

The parties may feel that once proceedings have been initiated, there is no opportunity to step back and reflect before the point of no return at which the marriage has been dissolved (Davis and Murch, 1988).

The Law Commission (1990) proposed a new system that would eliminate notions of fault from the divorce process once and for all and which would also allow the parties time to consider if they really wish to proceed to the termination of the marriage. They recommended that the irretrievable breakdown of the marriage should remain the sole ground for divorce, but that this should only be evidenced by the passage of time—ideally twelve months. So that the parties would have a better idea of what divorce might entail, they would be given a comprehensive information pack at the start of the twelve-month period, which would point them to sources of advice, support, and help, including counselling and mediation as well as legal services. The parties would use the passage of time to test out whether their marriage was really over, and, if it were, could then negotiate the terms of any financial and property settlement and any arrangements for their children. At the end of the twelve months, the divorce could therefore be granted with all the ancillary matters settled at the same time.

THE FAMILY LAW ACT 1996

The Government of the day accepted the main thrust of the Law Commission's proposals (Lord Chancellor's Department, 1993, 1995). But they also made some important changes, intended to ensure that couples understood the implications of commencing proceedings, to boost further the role of mediation (which were duly brought into force through the amendments to the legal aid system described above), and to require that the ancillaries were completed before the divorce was granted. The resulting Family Law Act 1996 introduced, in Part I, a set of general principles applicable to divorce and in Part III provisions governing publicly-funded mediation (see above). These were brought into force. Part II, however, which set out the new divorce law, was eventually abandoned. We need to consider why, given the professed inadequacies of the current system, the Government nonetheless declined to implement the reforms.

The 'general principles'

The courts, and any person exercising functions in relation to divorce (such as lawyers and mediators), must have regard to s 1 of the Act, which provides as follows:

(a) that the institution of marriage is to be supported;
(b) that the parties to a marriage which may have broken down are to be encouraged to take all practicable steps, whether by marriage counselling or otherwise, to save the marriage;
(c) that a marriage which has irretrievably broken down. . .should be brought to an end
  (i)   with minimum distress to the parties and to the children affected;
  (ii) with questions dealt with in a manner designed to promote as good a continuing relationship between the parties and any children affected as is possible in the circumstances; and
  (iii) without costs being unreasonably incurred in connection with the procedures to be followed in bringing the marriage to an end; and
(d) that any risk to one of the parties to a marriage, and to any children, of violence from the other party should, so far as reasonably practicable, be removed or diminished.

One can see here the ideological messages that the legislators attempted to communicate to those facing divorce. First, divorce law must not undermine the institution of marriage. Somehow, though this never seems to be clearly explained, it must still 'support' marriage, presumably by not making divorce too easy. Secondly, irretrievable breakdown of the marriage is the only basis for divorce, hence the parties must be assisted to try to save their marriage, and divorce should only be granted when all such attempts have failed. Thirdly, divorce should be a 'civilized' process. Bitterness and antagonism should not be made worse by the legal procedures that parties must go through. The adults should be reminded that their children's interests demand that conflict between them be reduced as far as possible; and that it is in their own interests, as well as those of the state, to avoid unnecessary costs incurred through protracted and unreasonable litigation. Finally, however, there must be a recognition that domestic violence may force some spouses to end the marriage. They must not be left unprotected by what might in their case be an undue concentration on attempting to keep it in existence.

Divorce under Part II of the Act

Parliament made the Law Commission's original scheme for obtaining a divorce more complicated, in attempts to insert further 'breathing spaces' and obstacles in the path to divorce to try to encourage the parties to save the marriage. Although the irretrievable breakdown of the marriage would remain the sole ground for divorce under the 1996 Act, it would no longer be necessary to demonstrate any 'facts' tending to prove such breakdown. Instead, passing a series of procedural hurdles would provide the necessary evidential basis.

The starting point would be for a spouse contemplating divorce to attend an 'information meeting'. At this, information would be given about counselling, marriage support, mediation and the legal process, the likely consequences of divorce for the parties and their children, the financial implications, and means of obtaining protection from violence. This information meeting replaced the Law Commission's proposed 'information pack' and was intended to deal with the problem, revealed by earlier research, of couples' ignorance of the options open to them and of the possibilities for stopping short of final divorce.

To provide a 'cooling off' period, and to enable a spouse to absorb the information given in the meeting, a person wishing to proceed with the divorce would then have to wait at least three months before moving to the next stage. This would entail filing a 'statement of marital breakdown' with the court. The filing of the statement would 'start the clock' running for the passage of time that must elapse before the divorce could be granted. The basic period that the spouses would have to wait would be nine months, but where there were children of the family under the age of 16, or the other spouse applied for further time for consideration, the period would usually be lengthened by six months. The reason for imposing a longer time period where there are children involved was the assumption that their interests require the parents to try harder to achieve a reconciliation. This view prevailed over what had been the prior received wisdom that requiring parents to wait longer than others would simply add to their bitterness and ultimately be damaging to the children.

By the end of the period, the parties would be expected to have reached a settlement or to have obtained appropriate orders concerning the financial and property consequences of their divorce and arrangements for their children's future upbringing. The aim would be to ensure as far as possible that the divorce marked the end of the legal proceedings between the spouses, representing the culmination of their dealings with each other and avoiding the necessity for further negotiation and argument which are a feature of the existing law. Instead of a two-stage pronouncement of the divorce, a single order would terminate the marriage and enable the spouses to marry again.

Evaluation of the 1996 scheme
The process as enacted in Part II was so controversial that the Government launched a pilot programme intended to test the key features of the new

law, before introducing it on a national scale. The pilot research testing out different modes of delivering the information meetings found, to the Government's disappointment, that only small proportions of those attending had gone on to marriage counselling or mediation. By contrast, nearly 40 per cent had indicated that they were more likely to consult a lawyer as a result of the information they had received. Since the ostensible purpose of the meeting was to present options rather than to dictate choices, it is hard to see why these results should be either unexpected or unwelcome. More profoundly, the researchers pointed out that it may be difficult to combine 'marriage saving' messages with encouragement toward mediation, and that the individual circumstances of the divorcing couple will affect how information is received. A person who has already thought long and hard and decided on divorce may need different information to that required by someone who is still uncertain about what should happen (Walker et al, 2001). Making mediation more central to the process also appeared to have limited effect in either improving rates of resort to mediation or reducing costs (Davis et al, 2001). The Government therefore decided in 2001 that Part II would not meet the objectives either of saving more marriages, or of helping divorcing couples to resolve their problems with less acrimony. One imagines that the political unpopularity that would have followed the introduction of a scheme which would have made many couples wait longer to obtain their divorce, and the potentially huge costs of implementing the information meetings, may also have played a part in this decision.

Apart from the political imperatives, there are further objections to the law as it was enacted in 1996. Far from reducing scope for disagreement between the parties, it provided ample opportunities for litigation, as spouses might seek to curtail the extended period of reflection, for example, or seek an order (akin to that currently available under s 5 of the Matrimonial Causes Act 1973, but applicable in all divorce cases) preventing divorce, if only as a bargaining counter to extract a better financial settlement from the other party. It also assumed that all—or most— divorcing couples behave in similar ways and can therefore be steered down the same path (via the provision of information dictated by the state, counselling, and mediation) to reconciliation or settlement.

On the other hand, the scheme would have encouraged parents to pay greater attention to their children's interests by informing them of children's needs at the outset and throughout the process. A clearer obligation would have been imposed on the court granting the divorce to take account of the importance of children's welfare and their wishes and feelings. The scheme would have marked a break with notions of blame. These, at least, are elements of the scheme that should be salvaged for the future. In the meantime, the Family Advice and Information Networks (FAInS) initiative (see Chapter 1) is intended to test how the clear need to provide a wider range of advice and support services to couples facing relationship breakdown can best be met. The researchers monitoring these pilot schemes will need to determine whether solicitors are the most appropriate gate-keepers to these services, and whether clients can obtain access to them at the most appropriate stage in the breakdown process, given that they may only consult lawyers when they are already some way down the track of deciding that their relationship is in difficulties.

THE FINANCIAL AND PROPERTY CONSEQUENCES OF DIVORCE

Notwithstanding the fate of Part II of the Family Law Act, its emphasis upon the need for the parties to consider the future position of the family highlighted the fact that it is the 'ancillary' matters, rather than the divorce decree itself, that have the most impact on the parties themselves and on their children. The arrangements for the children may be relatively easy to settle; in the majority of cases the child will live with the mother and have contact with the non-resident father, reflecting the pattern established when the parties initially separate. Such arrangements may change or prove difficult to sustain and disputes may continue to arise over the years as the children's needs and their parents' circumstances alter, but at the time of the divorce process it is likely to be the financial and property arrangements that cause the parties more difficulty. In most cases, there will not be enough money to sustain the standard of living enjoyed by the family before the breakdown of the marriage; the question will then be who should bear the loss. Clearly, there is considerable scope for conflict in such cases, and this may undermine the 'civilized' message that the law's focus on irretrievable breakdown attempts to send. Many couples nonetheless resolve their disputes privately and without recourse to the courts. They may receive legal advice and support which enables them to reach agreements largely in line with what they might have received from a court, or they may sort things out for themselves and remain relatively ignorant of the legal framework which exists to deal with this issue. That framework has two particular characteristics which mark it out clearly from the legal regime governing the *ownership* of property that was discussed in Chapters 3 and 4. First, the court[15] has exceptionally wide powers to distribute the spouses' financial resources and property between them, regardless of who was originally the legal owner. Secondly, the court has an exceptionally wide discretion as to how those powers should be exercised.

THE PURPOSE OF THE JURISDICTION

One reason why the courts exercise a very wide discretion is that the legislation does not set out any overriding objective they should seek to achieve in any given case. Beyond the requirement to achieve as fair an outcome as possible,[16] all they are required to have regard to are all the circumstances of the case, including a list of factors, rather like the welfare checklist in the Children Act (see Chapter 5). Under the law prior to the 1970s, orders were usually only made in favour of wives and the purpose of such orders, at least in respect of an 'innocent' wife, was to 'enable the wife to support herself in the rank of life to which she has been accustomed'.[17] Under the reformed law, this aim was broadened to apply to either spouse. The purpose of the jurisdiction was expressed to be 'to place the parties, so far as it is practicable and, having regard to their conduct, just to do so, in the financial position in which they would have been if the marriage had not broken down'.[18]

However, this 'minimal loss' principle was removed in 1984. It was regarded as unachievable except in the case of very wealthy couples and incompatible with the changing economic position of women who were no longer necessarily dependent upon their spouses for support. Moreover, it was seen as unfair, given that a husband might be divorced by his wife against his will, and yet still required to support her. But there was disagreement as to what, if anything, should replace it and in the end, nothing was put in its place. Instead, the courts are now enjoined, in an amended s 25(1) of the Matrimonial Causes Act 1973, to give 'first consideration. . .to the welfare while a minor of any child of the family'. Section 25A(1) requires them to consider whether it would be appropriate to exercise their powers so that 'the financial obligations of each party towards the other will be terminated as soon after the grant of the decree as the court considers just and reasonable'.

---

[15] Jurisdiction is exercised in the first instance by the divorce county court.

[16] Per Lord Nicholls in *White v White* [20001] 1 AC 596, 599H, HL.

[17] *Edwards v Edwards* (1868) 17 LT 584. 'Guilty' wives might obtain an order in their favour, although these were reduced to take account of their misconduct.

[18] Matrimonial Causes Act 1973, s 25 as originally enacted.

The first of these criteria was intended to encourage the courts to pay more attention to the needs of any dependent children rather than to regard these as an issue to be dealt with *after* resolving the position of the spouses. In practice, the major factor the court must settle concerning the children is their housing need—and this in turn will necessarily resolve the housing position of the parent with care.[19] The second criterion gives statutory effect to what has become known as the 'clean break' principle. This derives from the House of Lords' judgment in *Minton v Minton*. There, Lord Scarman said:[20]

There are two principles which inform the modern legislation. One is the public interest that spouses, to the extent that their means permit, should provide for themselves and their children. But the other—of equal importance—is the principle of 'the clean break'. The law now encourages spouses to avoid bitterness after family break-down and to settle their money and property problems. An object of the modern law is to encourage each to put the past behind them and to begin a new life which is not overshadowed by the relationship which has broken down.

In effect, a 'clean break' means a settlement whereby no continuing support is given to the financially weaker spouse or, more broadly, where there is no continuing financial relationship between the parties. Instead, the wife (usually) is expected to become self-supporting—or, in many instances, to turn to a new partner or to social security for her continuing support. The courts have frequently proclaimed that a clean break of this kind may be inappropriate where the dependent spouse is caring for young children and is therefore unable to work full-time, or where she is elderly and has not been in paid employment for many years. But in practice, ongoing spousal support is now relatively rare, at least in the guise of regular periodical payments (described below). A wife will usually trade off her claim to such payments in return for the transfer into her sole name of the former matrimonial home, or for a larger share of the capital assets.

The question of what objective should inform the courts' exercise of their powers in this jurisdiction remains unresolved. Many different goals might be proposed, but there are three basic positions. First, the law can assume that the marriage was a partnership of equals. This could either

---

[19] The children's support needs will usually be dealt with either by the Child Support Agency, or by the parties' consent, taking account of the formula applying under the Child Support Act, discussed below.
[20] [1979] AC 593, 608F–G. Now see *McFarlane v McFarlane*; *Parlour v Parlour* [2004] EWCA Civ 872 paras 57–67 per Thorpe LJ.

result in each spouse walking away with whatever they owned in their own right, following the doctrine of separate property, or with the assets split 50:50 between both, and each thereafter having no further claim on the other. This latter is the basic 'community of property' approach adopted by many civil law systems. It can be highly advantageous to a financially dependent spouse married to a very wealthy partner (which is why many community jurisdictions permit spouses to opt out of the system by making pre-nuptial agreements limiting the extent of the wealthier spouse's liability). On the other hand, it can be highly detrimental where assets are limited and each spouse ends up with very little (Weitzman, 1985). Secondly, there is the joint enterprise model, which could seek to achieve substantial equality of outcome and if necessary require the party in the stronger financial position to compensate the other for the loss she had incurred in, for example, giving up her career to care for the family. Such compensation might be in the form of ongoing support or of a larger share of the available capital. Thirdly, the law could focus on the parties' respective needs and seek to allocate resources and assets between them in the way most likely to meet those needs.

The current law contains elements of all three approaches. For example, it adopts a partnership of equals model in so far as it is gender-neutral. Either spouse may seek an order against the other and there is no restriction on a husband, say, seeking support or a capital order from his wife. Furthermore, the clean break principle assumes that either spouse is capable of immediate or future financial independence so that each could 'walk away' from the other with no continuing or long-term expectation of support.

On the other hand, the law adopts a joint enterprise model by drawing no distinction between different kinds of assets or resources depending upon their ownership or provenance. All of the parties' assets are open to redistribution between them as the court sees fit. The fact that an item of property was inherited, or brought into the marriage by one spouse, or acquired through the paid efforts of one spouse, does not *necessarily* affect how the court may decide to allocate it, although the court may take this into account. Most significantly, a spouse's non-financial contributions, in the form of caring for the children, looking after the home, and otherwise performing the role of a spouse (or in reality, a 'wife'), may be taken into account in determining that spouse's entitlement to an order against the other (see further below). This is in strong contrast to the position pertaining under strict property law, as discussed in Chapter 4. The fact that a husband has been the main or even sole breadwinner throughout the marriage does not enable him to 'trump' the wife's claim to a share of the capital he has produced. Each is regarded as having contributed, albeit in different ways, to the joint enterprise of the marriage and the family they have created and thus to be entitled to share in its profits.

This approach is illustrated to some extent by the House of Lords' decision in *White v White*. There, the House emphasized that 'there is no place for discrimination between husband and wife and their respective roles'.[21] The couple had run a farming business, begun with some financial assistance from the husband's father, throughout their thirty-year marriage, during which they raised three children. Their total assets were worth some £4.6 million, of which the wife had some £193,300 in her sole name and the husband had £1,783,500 in his name.

The first instance judge awarded the wife a lump sum of £800,000 in addition to the property already in her sole name, justifying this by estimating that this would be sufficient to meet her 'reasonable requirements'. The result was to leave her with just over one-fifth of the total assets. The award was increased on appeal to £1.5 million, to recognize her contribution to the family as well as to running the farm. However, the House of Lords, while upholding this award, held that the reasoning of the Court of Appeal had been flawed. Instead, the House held that where there is substantial wealth available, which will exceed meeting the parties' needs, equal division of capital assets should be used as a yardstick against which the court should check a proposed settlement. Nonetheless, they rejected the view that there should be a *presumption* in favour of equal division, regarding this as going beyond the permissible bounds of interpretation of the statute. In fact, in 1998, the Government asked an expert advisory group to consider the merits of introducing a *statutory* presumption of equal shares in property on divorce, at least after the needs of the children and any question of spousal maintenance had been settled. The Lord Chancellor's Ancillary Relief Advisory Group (1998) unanimously opposed any presumption of equal shares and the Government subsequently dropped the idea from its legislative agenda.

This rejection has enabled English law to avoid the danger that formal equality, under the partnership of equals model, may produce, of ignoring women's factual economic inequality. Instead, it leaves scope for a court to embrace the joint enterprise model and thus to achieve closer equality of outcome between the parties. However, it must be recognized that it also leaves discretion, albeit one which the Court of Appeal has

---

[21] [2001] 1 AC 596, 605C, per Lord Nicholls.

attempted to circumscribe (see below), to the court to continue to give one spouse the larger share of the assets. Indeed, even in *White v White*, the House of Lords upheld an award resulting in the wife's receiving only two-fifths of the joint assets. Moreover, in the majority of cases, the limited resources available to the parties mean that the courts can do little more than attempt to meet their basic needs for accommodation and support, including, of course, for the children.

THE COURT'S POWERS[22]

The discussion in this part of the Chapter focuses upon orders in favour of spouses. The position regarding children is dealt with later.

Periodical payments orders

'Maintenance' is primarily conceived as meeting the ongoing financial *needs* of the recipient and thus is an example of continuing dependence upon the former spouse. Under the Matrimonial Causes Act 1973, 'periodical payments' (the statutory vehicle for maintenance) may be paid at any regular interval, including annually. Any amount may be ordered to be paid, including a purely nominal amount (such as £5 per annum), intended to preserve the recipient's right to return to the court for an increase should her circumstances so require. The payments may last indefinitely or for a fixed duration only. The latter may apply where the recipient needs time to adjust to financial independence, perhaps to (re)train for a career, or to tide her over while she is caring for young children. In setting a defined duration to the order, the court may also direct, under s 28(1A), that no extension of that term is to be permitted. This does not preclude an application to vary the *amount* of the payments. If no such direction is attached, then a party can return to court, before its expiry, to seek an extension of the order.[23]

Spousal periodical payments orders are becoming rare, with most wives settling for a clean break and a larger share of the family assets in lieu of ongoing support. The main reasons for this decline are probably, first, that there is a strong ideological message contained in the legislation encouraging clean break settlements. Secondly, the recipient may prefer

---

[22] The powers are set out in s 21 of the Matrimonial Causes Act 1973 and subsequent sections. Similar powers have been proposed for civil partnerships. Only periodical payments orders may be made on an interim basis before a final order is reached. They may also be varied subsequent to a final order. This does not apply to lump sum or property adjustment orders.
[23] *Richardson v Richardson* [1994] 1 FLR 286.

the security of a capital sum or asset in her name than dependence upon the uncertain and potentially unreliable goodwill of the payer to keep making periodical payments. Related to this, other sources of support—a new partner, or the social security system—may be more reliable. Thirdly, the assessment of how much should be paid by way of maintenance has been highly unscientific. Traditionally, the courts adopted a 'one third' approach, whereby the payer could expect to pay a sum which would bring the payee's income up to one third of the couple's joint income.[24] But there is no logic linked to the payee's *need* which justifies this proportion as distinct from any other, and it is now no more than one among many starting-points for negotiation between the spouses.

Lump sums

As well as continuing payments, the court may also order the payment of a lump sum (including by instalments). This may be raised from available capital or may necessitate a loan, or the sale of an asset to realize the amount required. For very wealthy couples, a lump sum may be calculated by reference to the annual income it would produce when invested for the beneficiary, taking account of interest rates, inflation, and life expectancy. This may then be used as the basis for negotiation on the amount required to meet the recipient spouse's support needs.[25] In this way, the spouse can be assured of a continuing income, but can avoid any continuing dependence upon the ex-spouse.

Orders in relation to pensions

In recent years, it has been realized that a person's pension may be a highly valuable form of property that will make the difference between a comfortable retirement and one lived in poverty. Since women are less likely to have access to a full pension because of their interrupted working lives, they are particularly vulnerable to poverty in old age. Adopting a joint enterprise model of marriage, it may be argued that the husband's pension should be regarded as a form of jointly acquired property, since the wife's contribution to his family life has enabled him to concentrate on his career and hence to build up his retirement fund. Furthermore, but for the divorce, the wife would have benefited from that fund and would, if she survived the husband, have received the widow's benefits

---

[24] *Wachtel v Wachtel* [1973] Fam 72, CA.
[25] *Duxbury v Duxbury (Note)* [1992] Fam 62, CA (decided 1985).

thereunder. Accordingly, provisions were introduced into the law[26] to enable pensions to be shared between the spouses. There are two types of order that a court can make to achieve this. First, there is what was originally known as 'earmarking' but is now referred to as 'attachment'. This enables the court to order that part of a pension (such as the lump sum on retirement or the ongoing pension benefits) be paid to the ex-spouse rather than to the pensioner himself when it falls due. The drawback of this mechanism is that the recipient ex-spouse must wait until the other draws his pension and there is uncertainty as to how much this will be worth when it is eventually paid. Moreover, she will not continue to receive any support from the pension scheme after his death, since she will not be his 'widow'.

A preferable alternative is 'pension sharing'. This orders that a person's pension rights—as distinct from pension payments—be shared with the ex-spouse, who may leave them in the pension scheme or reinvest them to build up her own pension elsewhere. Her share of the rights then permits her to take the benefit of the pension as if she herself had accrued them, independently of the circumstances of the other spouse. This approach enables the clean break principle to be maintained while meeting at least part of the future pension need of the ex-spouse.

Property adjustment orders

The court may also order the transfer, settlement, or sale of any of the spouses' property. This power enables it, for example, to transfer the title and equity in the matrimonial home to one spouse absolutely, or to adjust the spouses' respective shares. Alternatively, it might be necessary to order the sale of the home (or other property) and then order a distribution of the proceeds between the spouses or in favour of one of them. Often, this will enable a lump sum payment to be made that could not otherwise be raised. For example, it might be decided that the home should be sold and the equity split to enable each spouse to put down a deposit to enable the purchase of a new home. Sometimes, the court may order that the sale be postponed until a specified event, such as the youngest child of the family leaving school. Such '*Mesher*' orders[27] were

[26] Pension 'earmarking' was originally introduced by the Pensions Act 1995, s 166, inserting ss 25B–D into the Matrimonial Causes Act 1973. Pension 'sharing' came into operation in 2000 under the Welfare Reform and Pensions Act 1999, Sch 3, which further amended the 1973 Act.
[27] *Mesher v Mesher and Hall* [1980] 1 All ER 126n, CA (decided 1973). The specified event might be different, such as the death of the wife, thus ensuring that she has a secure home for as long as she wants it: *Martin v Martin* [1978] Fam 12, CA.

popular for several years as a means of keeping the children's home secure for them until they had grown up while enabling the absent parent to retain a share of the capital value of the home to be realized at that future point. However, they fell out of favour. First, children may need a home long after they leave school, or even university. Secondly, the order precludes a real 'clean break' between the parties because they will have to co-operate over the sale, perhaps several years after the divorce. Thirdly, the order may cause difficulty to the resident parent when the house has to be sold. The absent parent would by then have rehoused himself (albeit perhaps with difficulty) and would see the capital sum as a windfall. By contrast, the carer would be required to use it to acquire a new property, perhaps at a time of life when she would find it difficult to obtain a mortgage to finance the balance of the purchase.[28]

THE EXERCISE OF THE COURT'S DISCRETION

Whilst the goal of the jurisdiction has been said to be to achieve as fair an outcome as possible,[29] as noted above, there is no overriding *legislative* objective set to direct the exercise of the court's discretion. All the court is required to do is to give first consideration to the welfare of any dependent children of the family, and to have regard to the desirability of a financial clean break between the spouses. It must then take into account all the circumstances of the case, and in particular the eight different factors contained in the 'checklist' in s 25(2), but, as with the welfare checklist considered in Chapter 5, these are not ranked in order of priority. They are, perhaps, the 'obvious' factors that the parties themselves would consider were relevant to reaching a decision as to how the financial and property consequences of the divorce should be dealt with.

The factors contained in s 25(2)

Clearly, the court cannot make orders in respect of resources the parties do not have, so the starting-point must be to consider their 'income, earning capacity, property and other financial resources'.[30] The court may also take account of how these are likely to change in the foreseeable future. For example, a full-time carer of young children may be able to go back to work when they are older, while an older spouse may be soon due

---

[28] *Hanlon v Hanlon* [1978] 2 All ER 889, CA.
[29] *White v White* [2001] 1 AC 596, HL.   [30] Section 25(2)(a).

to retire from work. It must also consider whether it is reasonable to expect a spouse to increase his or her earning capacity, perhaps by working longer hours, or training to acquire a higher-paid skill.

There may be major difficulties in obtaining a reliable picture of each party's resources. They are under a duty to make full and frank disclosure,[31] and the courts have power to order the disclosure of financial information. However, delay and obstruction may be considerable as one spouse attempts to prevaricate and obfuscate in order to protect his or her position and perhaps drive the other into a reduced settlement, rather than incur legal costs in forcing the information to be produced. Settlements reached without the benefit of good legal advice may be especially susceptible to one spouse's refusal to 'play fair' in this respect.

The corollary to this information is the parties' respective 'financial needs, obligations and responsibilities', both now and in the foreseeable future.[32] The spouses have their own needs to meet, and those of their children, other partners, and other relatives. The courts draw no distinction between legal and moral obligations that a spouse may owe—if the reality is that a husband supports his new partner, this is taken into account even though they cohabit and he owes her no legal duty of support. Assessing what a party's 'reasonable' needs or requirements are is difficult and may be highly contested, sometimes to the level of querying the amount of money to be spent on a spouse's pet dog.[33] For most couples it is the more basic costs of living that nonetheless can be the subject of considerable dispute.

• In practice, as noted above, it is the family members' respective housing needs that are dealt with first. In many cases the house must be kept for the children and their carer or must be sold to enable them to be rehoused. The husband in such cases may walk away with very little, if any, capital, notwithstanding the investment he may have made in its acquisition during the marriage. Not surprisingly, in such cases, he may resist any claim to make periodical payments to the wife and may also, nowadays, refuse to consider pension sharing. Frequently, the wife will forgo a claim to his pension in order to ensure that she has the benefit of

---

[31] *Livesey (formerly Jenkins) v Jenkins* [1985] AC 424, HL.
[32] Section 25(2)(b). The parties' respective ages and any physical or mental disability they may have are also taken into account: paras (d) and (e).
[33] *F v F (Ancillary Relief: Substantial Assets)* [1995] 2 FLR 45—£4,000 for pet Labrador regarded as excessive.

198 *An Introduction to Family Law*

the house being transferred to her name now. She thus trades her financial security in the future, for stability now.

The 'joint enterprise' model of marriage is apparent in some of the factors in the checklist. The court must take account of 'the standard of living enjoyed by the family before the breakdown of the marriage'[34] and its duration.[35] However, these last can also be viewed as related to the needs model. A wealthy wife will not be expected to assume a humble standard of living if her ex-spouse can afford to keep her in more comfortable circumstances, especially after a lengthy marriage during which she has become accustomed to a certain standard of living. There is also a sense of 'justice' here—a spouse who spent several years in a marriage may well feel, and be adjudged, *entitled* to a generous share of the family wealth. Indeed, Lord Nicholls in *White v White* suggested that, in a 'big money' case where the assets exceed the parties' basic requirements, anything less than an equal share must be justified.[36] The shift towards ordering an equal share is based primarily on the court taking a 'joint enterprise' approach to the marriage, through giving due weight to the requirement that the court consider the parties' contributions to 'the welfare of the family, including any contribution by looking after the home or caring for the family'.[37] It was this factor that the House considered should be treated in a non-discriminatory fashion so that a wife's non-financial contribution to looking after the family and home should not necessarily be valued less than the financial contribution made by the husband bread-winner. However, many cases litigated subsequent to *White v White* involved arguments over when a husband's contribution should be regarded as outweighing that of his wife and justifying a departure from equal shares. For example, in *Cowan v Cowan*[38] the Court of Appeal held that, notwithstanding a marriage lasting over 35 years, the husband's 'stellar' contribution in building up the family's wealth, based on his entrepreneurial acumen in spotting the potential of plastic bin-liners, should be recognized by allowing him to keep more than half of the assets of some £11.5 million. But in *Lambert v Lambert*,[39] recognizing that this ruling had opened a 'forensic Pandora's box'[40] the Court rowed back from its earlier reasoning. As Thorpe LJ put it:

---

[34] Section 25(2)(c).   [35] Section 25(2)(d).   [36] [2001] 1 AC 596, 605G.
[37] Section 25(2)(f).   [38] [2001] EWCA Civ 679, [2002] Fam 97.
[39] [2002] EWCA Civ 1685, [2003] Fam 103.
[40] *Per* Coleridge J in *G v G (Financial Provision: Equal Division)* [2002] EWHC 1339 (Fam), [2002] 2 FLR 1143.

Having now heard submissions, both full and reasoned, against the concept of special contribution save in the most exceptional and limited circumstance, the danger of gender discrimination resulting from a finding of special financial contribution is plain. If all that is regarded is the scale of the breadwinner's success, then discrimination is almost bound to follow since there is no equal opportunity for the homemaker to demonstrate the scale of her comparable success.[41]

But it does not follow that, in a case where assets exceed the parties' needs, an equal share will always now result. The courts are still working through the question of how contributions to welfare sit alongside the other factors set out in s 25(2). In particular, how should the duration of the marriage affect the outcome? Should a 'short' marriage justify a departure from equality, since there has been less opportunity for one spouse to make a 'full' contribution? If not, is it not unfair that a wife who is married for only a few years does as well as the wife who commits her whole adult life to the marriage?

By the same token, a spouse who feels he has been 'wronged' may resent being expected to pay to support his wife who has divorced him against his wishes. An 'innocent' wife may demand to be compensated when her husband leaves her for another woman. Accordingly, s 25(2)(g) provides that the court should have regard to the conduct of each of the parties where it is 'such that it would in the opinion of the court be inequitable to disregard it'. In practice, the courts have steadfastly refused to take cognizance of marital misconduct when assessing financial relief, except in the most extreme cases. In the words of Lord Denning, drawing on earlier case law, only conduct that is ' "obvious and gross". . .so that to order one party to support another whose conduct falls into this category is repugnant to anyone's sense of justice"[42] should be taken into account. An example of such a case is *Evans v Evans*.[43] The wife was convicted of inciting others to kill her husband. Perhaps unsurprisingly, the Court of Appeal upheld the discharge of a periodical payments order (which the husband had faithfully paid for many years since their divorce) in her favour.

The final factor to be considered, in s 25(2)(h), is the value to each of the parties of any benefit which, by reason of the divorce, that party will lose the chance of acquiring. In practice, this usually means the pension that the divorced spouse cannot obtain because he or she will not have the status of widow or widower on the other's death. We have seen that an

---

[41] [2003] Fam 103, para 45.   [42] *Wachtel v Wachtel* [1973] Fam 72, 90.
[43] [1989] 1 FLR 351, CA.

order may be made to deal with sharing pension entitlements and even where such an order is not made, under s 25B the court must still expressly consider the parties' pension position in arriving at its decision. This may entail allocating a larger share of capital or property to one spouse to compensate for the loss of a share in the pension. But where the couple are young with many years of working life before them, the court may simply conclude that it would not be appropriate to let the parties' pension positions affect the orders to be made.

ARRIVING AT A SETTLEMENT

Perusal of the legislation and case law alone does not shed much light on how, in practice, the courts go about determining the sorts of financial outcomes that should be reached on divorce. This makes it difficult for divorcing couples to get a clear idea of what they may expect, and even for lawyers to provide precise guidance on what would represent a sensible compromise and settlement. To address this problem, it has been proposed (Home Office, 1998: para 4.48) that statute should set out an over-arching objective of fairness between the parties and their children, and guiding principles, codifying what the courts currently do. These would place emphasis first on providing a home for the children, then satisfying each spouse's housing needs, and then dividing any residual property fairly, probably in equal shares. Whether this would represent a useful advance can be debated. At least it would give some clue to the parties as to what their priorities should be when negotiating a settlement.

This is important because, in line with the usual ideological emphasis on privacy and family autonomy, and on resolving disputes outside court, the parties are placed under strong pressure to settle their financial differences rather than require the court to adjudicate. But the law sends out conflicting signals in this regard. On the one hand, the case law suggests that parties may be held to an agreement they have reached, at least if it is made with the benefit of independent legal advice and after proper disclosure.[44] Furthermore, the courts frequently seek to deter couples from running up legal costs by highlighting how these can rapidly run out of control. In *Piglowska v Piglowski*,[45] for example, total costs amounted to £128,000, just exceeding the value of the assets in dispute. Even legally aided litigants may face a hefty bill as their contribution to the costs. Where, as is the norm, the result of the case is some form of capital

---

[44] *Edgar v Edgar* [1980] 3 All ER 887, CA.   [45] [1999] 1 WLR 1360, HL.

transfer (such as of the marital home), a 'statutory charge' attaches to the property which will be met, ultimately, from the proceeds of any later sale. The procedure governing ancillary relief proceedings (revised in 2000) is also intended to provide opportunities for the parties to settle rather than fight. It places an emphasis on early disclosure and clarification of the issues, active judicial case management to prevent delay and limit costs, and a 'financial dispute resolution' appointment at which the district judge will act as mediator in attempting to lead the parties toward a settlement.[46]

On the other hand, it is clear that a court exercising its jurisdiction under the Matrimonial Causes Act is not required to accept the parties' agreement as disposing of the case. First, s 34 of the Act provides that an agreement cannot oust the jurisdiction of the court to hear an application for financial relief. Secondly, case law establishes that the parties' rights and obligations must be definitively decided according to the criteria in s 25 and not by ordinary contractual principles.[47] This is because, alongside the principle of family privacy and autonomy, the state is recognized as having the right to ensure that the financial interests of individual family members are properly safeguarded—if only to ensure that the social security system is not required to support them.

The way that these conflicting principles are intended to be reconciled is by the device of a 'consent order'. The couple may present the terms of their agreement to the court for its approval. If this is given, the court embodies the terms in a binding order which then forms the basis of the legal obligation between the parties and is enforceable as any other court order.[48] The court is supposed to exercise independent judgment in scrutinizing the terms of the agreement in accordance with the criteria in s 25. But it is open to question how often this is, or can be, done. First, the parties are regarded as having reached their agreement as responsible adults acting at arm's length.[49] Secondly, there may be insufficient information given to the court to enable the judge to make an informed judgment on the fairness of the proposed settlement anyway. A further problem is that only a minority of divorcing couples obtain any type of binding court order, be it by consent or otherwise. Such couples make their agreements and carry them out without any oversight by the court,

[46] Family Proceedings Rules 1991, as amended, and *Practice Direction (Ancillary Relief Procedure) (25 May 2000)* [2000] 1 FLR 997.
[47] *Xydhias v Xydhias* [1999] 1 FLR 683, CA.
[48] *de Lasala v de Lasala* [1980] AC 546.
[49] *Pounds v Pounds* [1994] 1 WLR 1535, CA.

and often, perhaps, without much input from their lawyers. In such cases, the detailed discretion and broad powers of the courts become irrelevant and the fairness of the agreements reached cannot be scrutinized, still less ensured.

Pre-nuptial agreements

As one solution to this atmosphere of uncertainty, it has been proposed that couples should be encouraged to make agreements, before the wedding, setting out their financial and property entitlements in the event of a divorce. Traditionally, this has been regarded as contrary to public policy, since it contemplates the ending of the marriage by divorce. In recent years, the courts have hesitated over whether to take such agreements into account. On the one hand they may argue that the sole basis of their jurisdiction is the statutory set of requirements laid down in the Matrimonial Causes Act so that any agreement cannot be *binding* on the court. On the other, they consider that the agreement forms part of the 'circumstances' to which they must have regard under s 25.[50] The Government suggested in 1998 that there might be value in permitting spouses to make binding written agreements, either before or during the marriage, 'to give people more choice and allow them to take more responsibility for ordering their own lives' (Home Office, 1998: para 4.21). The Government even thought that encouraging the parties to consider this question before the marriage might lead to more people marrying rather than cohabiting, though it is hard to see why. It seems likely that relatively few couples would in fact bother to make an agreement since most would no doubt assume that their position would be safeguarded by the law. However, there might be some attraction in an agreement for parties of disparate wealth, or where one already had a family from a previous relationship whose interests needed to be safeguarded.

FINANCIAL SUPPORT FOR CHILDREN

Once the housing position of the children is resolved, the question of their ongoing financial support must be determined. Generally, the law has not recognized children as being owed a share of the family wealth

---

[50] Compare *F v F (Ancillary Relief: Substantial Assets)* [1995] 2 FLR 45 with *N v N (Foreign Divorce: Financial Relief)* [1997] 1 FLR 900.

beyond that required for their support[51] and hence, their entitlement is based on dependency. However, the liability of their parents to provide that support embraces both a partnership of equals and joint enterprise approach to the family unit, as is explained below.

Children may need financial support regardless of whether their parents are married or divorcing. While the family is intact, this is provided through the earnings and efforts of the parents, as part of their joint commitment to bringing up a family. These efforts may be supplemented by state support in the provision of tax credits or social security benefits. But where the parents' relationship breaks down and one party leaves, the parent who continues to care for the children may need recourse to outside mechanisms to induce the other, now 'non-resident' parent to help meet the costs of raising the child. As noted in Chapter 3, the obligation to maintain the child in this situation has been enforced by the courts, but growing dissatisfaction with the way the courts exercised their powers led to a fundamental overhaul of the system by the introduction of the Child Support Act 1991.

During the 1980s, the Conservative Government found there were increasing numbers of lone parents becoming dependent upon social security for the basic support of themselves and their children. Even though the courts proclaimed that there could be no 'clean break' from one's children on divorce, the reality was different. Many couples reached settlements (often, it seems, approved by the courts in consent orders) whereby the husband/father provided no ongoing maintenance, not only for the wife but also for the children, in return for giving up his share in the family home. Moreover, even where child maintenance was ordered or agreed, the amounts payable were all too often based on little more than 'gut feeling' as to what it was appropriate to expect the particular parent to pay, rather than on a rational assessment of what the child needed. To add to the inadequacy of the court regime, the Government found widely differing levels of maintenance being set in similar circumstances. As the final straw, they also found that barely a quarter of those required to pay were making regular payments (Department of Social Security, 1990: para 5).

The consequential drain on the social security budget caused by lone parents turning to the state for support tapped into Government hostility to what it perceived as a 'dependency culture'. The Government's solution was to re-emphasize parental obligations to support one's children,

[51] *Chamberlain v Chamberlain* [1974] 1 WLR 1557, CA.

but to enforce these through a more rigorous, predictable, and reliable system than that operated by the courts. Its Child Support Act 1991, which came into operation in 1993, and which was heavily influenced by similar initiatives in Australia, New Zealand, and the USA, represented a radically new approach to enforcing familial obligations. The key features of the scheme were to provide a formula basis for calculating the amount of child support payable, and an administrative, rather than judicial, system for such calculation and the collection of the amounts owed. In this way, it was hoped that child support awards would be predictable and consistent as between decision-makers, since all would be applying a formula in their calculation, and readily and efficiently collected through an administrative machinery which could be pro-active in ensuring that awards were complied with.

Court jurisdiction to award periodical payments was severely curtailed, although not abolished. So long as parents are able to agree on the arrangements for supporting the child, the court may continue to make a consent order based on such arrangements. Moreover, as will be described below, the court may sometimes make capital awards for a child, and these are unaffected by the Child Support system. In practice, this system will only be activated where the couple cannot reach an agreement or where the resident parent becomes dependent on certain benefits, when she is obliged to authorize the Agency to recover maintenance on her behalf. The result has been to produce a two-tier, two-class, system, with wealthier families, who are unlikely to trouble the Benefits Agency, contracting themselves out from child support, while the poorer are brought within its scope.

THE CHILD SUPPORT SCHEME

The basis of the scheme

The Child Support Act bases the liability to support a child on both the partnership of equals and the joint enterprise models, as applied to parenting. Under s 1, each parent is regarded as equally obliged to support that child. A parent looking after a child may apply for child support unless she had already obtained a court order for periodical payments before the implementation of the 1991 Act or has done so at any time since by means of a consent order. Where such a parent claims income support or job-seeker's allowance, then under s 6, she is obliged to authorize the Child Support Agency to pursue the non-resident parent for maintenance, unless she can show 'good cause' (such as the risk of violence from him) for not doing so. Under the original scheme, each parent's income and needs were assessed according to a formula and their obligation to the child was intended to be as equal as possible after taking such individual circumstances into account. Once the scheme came into operation in 1993, it rapidly became clear that this was an unrealistic way of conceiving the carer's discharge of her support obligation. Around 90 per cent of those seeking child support under this system were in fact dependent upon means-tested social security benefits, making it impossible for them to make any significant cash contribution to their child's financial needs.

The original formula approach to calculating the award primarily applied a *needs* model to the child's entitlement. This was to be assessed by reference to social security scale rates, which are themselves intended to meet basic subsistence needs. However, where a wealthy parent could afford to pay more, the child's award would be increased to enable the child to share in the family's greater prosperity. In this way, the 'joint enterprise' model could also be applied to the parent's obligation to support.

It was hoped that using a detailed mathematical formula based on social security rates would enable a more precise calculation of the child's actual needs than the broad-brush attempts at awarding maintenance used by the courts. At the same time liability would be tailored more accurately to the payer's ability to pay. Once this formula was applied, many men indeed found themselves liable to pay significantly higher amounts of maintenance than they had been accustomed to doing under the court system. This underlined how far the courts had under-estimated—or chosen to ignore—the true cost of supporting children.

The scheme proved highly controversial and was opposed by payers and recipients alike. The former resented the fact that little account was taken of new family responsibilities assumed after separating from the parent with care, and objected to paying an element in the formula ostensibly to meet the costs of child care but which appeared instead to amount to maintenance of the parent with care. Nor were debts and liabilities taken into account, even where they may have been assumed in consequence of the break-up of the relationship. A final example of the inflexibility of the formula was its failure to take account of any financial settlement reached between the parents on a divorce whereby the couple had traded the on-going liability to maintain against the transfer of capital.

Parents with care were equally hostile. They objected to being required, once they were in receipt of income support, to co-operate with the Child Support Agency's pursuit of the non-resident parent. This was because failure to comply without good cause is penalized by a significant cut in the level of the parent's benefit, thus reducing the family's standard of living.

The current scheme

After a series of alterations to the basic approach by the Conservative Government, the new Labour Government carried out a fundamental overhaul of the scheme in the Child Support, Pensions and Social Security Act 2000. This represented an effective abandonment of the needs model as the basis for assessing the child's entitlement, in favour of asserting a *symbolic* joint enterprise approach to the parental obligation.

The Government found (Department of Social Security, 1998: 23) that the complexity of the calculations necessary under the original formula meant that 90 per cent of the time of Child Support Agency staff was being spent on assessing the amount of maintenance to be paid, and only 10 per cent on ensuring its collection. To simplify the process, Sch 1, para 1 to the 2000 Act provides that a non-resident parent with a net income (after deductions for tax, national insurance, and pension contributions) of over £200 per week should pay 15 per cent of that net income if he has one qualifying child, 20 per cent for two, and 25 per cent for three or more. A 'reduced rate' is payable where the parent's net income is between £100 and £200, and a flat rate of £5 per week payable by a parent with income below this or where he is himself dependent upon social security. It can be seen that, by applying a percentage basis to the payer's net income, the new formula ceases to attempt to tailor the payment to the child's own actual financial requirements. Furthermore, the only consideration given to the payer's *own* needs is an allowance for each child (whether his own or not) whom he is in fact financially supporting in his new home, which reduces pro rata the amount of his net income from which the percentage deduction is made.

Some of the partnership of equals aspects of the original scheme were also dropped. No attempt is now made to compare the payer's contribution to that of the parent with care, whose own income and circumstances are no longer to be taken into account. This has been strongly criticized as leading to the situation where a very wealthy parent with care will receive an amount of money based on the non-resident parent's net income even though she has no need of any contribution from him to support the child. Moreover, the application of a standard percentage deduction from the parent's net income will be made regardless of the level of that income until it hits a ceiling of £2,000 per week. This, again, has been strongly criticized as being unrealistic—how can a child really 'need' a weekly level of support above the average adult male wage? But this is to miss the symbolic message that the child represents the product of that parent's joint parenting enterprise with the other parent. She is entitled to share in the non-resident parent's wealth, as part of that parent's family, in the same way that she would have shared in it while they were living together.

The effect of the fundamental shift to a percentage basis of calculation is likely to mean that the majority of non-resident parents should pay less in child support than under the 1991 scheme. This may dampen much of the opposition of such parents to meeting their liability and the Government must assume that this will therefore increase their level of compliance, which is hardly any better than under the discredited court-based system operating before 1993. But by contrast with this attempt to appease absent parents, parents with care on benefits will continue to be compelled, except in extreme cases, to comply with the Agency's attempts to trace non-resident parents (although they will at least be given an incentive to co-operate, by being permitted to keep up to £10 per week of child support before their benefits are reduced). The Conservatives' dislike of the dependency culture has now given way to the Labour Government's assumption that lone parents should wherever possible be in paid employment. As an incentive to such parents to return to work, those receiving working tax credit are exempt from the obligation to comply. They may therefore avoid involvement with the Agency at the cost of having to take on more work outside the home.

THE ROLE OF THE COURTS

Consent orders for child maintenance

Under the 2000 reforms, the courts still retain their jurisdiction to make periodical payments orders for child maintenance *by consent*. However, even where the parent with care is not dependent upon benefits and therefore not obliged to co-operate with the Child Support Agency, she will be able to apply to the Agency for a maintenance calculation one year after the making of such a consent order.[52] This appears to give the recipient of such an order a powerful bargaining tool against the

---

[52] Child Support Act 1991, s 4(10) as amended by the 2000 Act, s 2(3).

non-resident parent anxious to avoid a child support calculation. But, by the same token, he may be less willing to give up capital if he thinks that the Agency may become involved in the near future in any event. Clearly, therefore, the interaction of the child support scheme with the divorce jurisdiction will remain an important factor in the final settlement between the parents.

The courts' residual jurisdiction

The Child Support scheme does not apply where payment is sought from a step-parent. It also excludes the provision of special payments such as for school fees or other training and expenses connected with the disability of the child. Finally, it only provides for regular payments of 'maintenance' rather than lump sums or capital. The courts retain jurisdiction under the Matrimonial Causes Act 1973 and the Domestic Proceedings and Magistrates' Courts Act 1978 to make orders against step-parents where they have 'treated' the child as a 'child of the family', and to order parents to make periodical payments intended to meet school fees and so on. Schedule 1 to the Children Act 1989 makes similar provision and also enables a court to make lump sum and property orders. This latter power was first enacted in 1987, under the Family Law Reform Act, which was intended to improve the position of children born outside marriage. The purpose was to enable the court to arrive at outcomes, such as settlements of property, in favour of the child, with the same flexibility as is possible on divorce if the parents were married. In such cases, the courts are clear that the aim, as on divorce, is not to give the child a windfall in adulthood. Even where a house may be provided for the child and her parent to live in, this is usually required to revert to the other parent once the child has ceased to be financially dependent.[53]

UNMARRIED COUPLES

By definition, a couple who acquire no legal status by virtue of their relationship, do not have to undergo any legal process of recognition of the ending of that relationship. But their financial and property affairs may result in exactly the same kinds of disputes that arise between married couples. No regime akin to the Matrimonial Causes Act applies to cohabiting or other unmarried couples (although if the Civil Partnership law is implemented, such partners will be subject to a regime akin to that

[53] *A v A (A Minor) (Financial Provision)* [1994] 1 FLR 657.

on divorce). Instead, they must rely on the usual property laws, outlined in Chapter 4. As was noted in that Chapter, there is now less objection to cohabitants making their own binding contracts to determine these issues, although the legal significance of such contracts has yet to be authoritatively tested. There is an irony in comparing how the law is moving in relation to married and unmarried couples on this issue. For some spouses at least, it seems that the way forward might well lie in the encouragement of pre-nuptial or nuptial agreements. For cohabitants, by contrast, the debate has moved beyond the role of contracts to considering whether to provide an adjustive regime similar to that applying on divorce so that the joint enterprise and needs models might be utilized rather than a narrower focus on a presumed partnership of equals.

THE DEATH OF A FAMILY MEMBER

Finally, we need to consider the way the law deals with relationships terminated by the death of a family member. Chapter 3 discusses the position regarding the *guardianship* of a child whose parent has died. Here, the issue considered is what is to happen to a deceased person's property. There are basically three sets of rules governing this question. First, there are rules governing the devolution of property by will. Secondly, there are rules determining how an estate is to be distributed where the deceased died intestate. Finally, there are provisions enabling a person to challenge the effect of either of these. It will be seen that the three approaches to family relationships—the partnership of equals, the joint enterprise, and the fulfilment of needs—may all be discerned in how these rules are determined and applied. Moreover, ironically perhaps, it is where there has been a death in the family that the law is most open to recognizing relationships going beyond the narrow nuclear model of spouses, cohabitants, parents, and children.

DEVOLUTION OF PROPERTY BY
WILL—PARTNERSHIP OF EQUALS?

The common law reflected an attempt to uphold an ethos of family solidarity that is common throughout European succession law, and limited the extent to which a person could dispose of their property by will. It laid down rules governing the inheritance of real property, for example, to ensure that as much as possible of the family's wealth was passed on to the next generation (or at least, to the male heir). To safeguard the needs of landowners' widows, provision was made to ensure that they would be supported during their lifetimes. However, the nineteenth and twentieth century property law reforms abolished the last vestiges of these rules and substituted an approach heavily weighted towards the individual interests and preferences of the property holder. With marriage regarded as a partnership of equals, and husband and wife entitled to their own separate property, no special provision was seen as necessary for a surviving spouse. The principle of 'freedom of testation' leaves a person free to choose who should benefit from the estate, and there is nothing to prevent him bequeathing everything to charity. It does not follow that family members are left without a remedy—they may seek what is termed 'family provision' despite the terms of the will, as explained below.

INTESTACY—JOINT ENTERPRISE?

By contrast with the position regarding wills, where a person dies intestate, the law distributes his or her estate to members of the family, depending upon the closeness of the relationship. Here, one might see the family viewed in one sense as a joint and continuing enterprise—much as the common law sought to secure the transmission of property down through the generations, so intestacy rules seek to recognize the familial tie.

Under the Administration of Estates Act 1925, the surviving spouse has the first claim on the estate, being entitled to all the personal chattels of the deceased, and then a 'statutory legacy' of variable amount depending upon which other relatives have survived the deceased. Where there are no other surviving relatives, the widow(er) inherits the entire estate.

Although the bulk of the value of most intestate estates will go to the widow(er) and may well be used to meet their financial needs (including the need to preserve the family home), these rules are not intended to fulfil such needs, in any scientific way. Rather, they provide a symbolic recognition of the family bond between the deceased and the survivor. However, they still exclude cohabitants from their scope. The Law Commission (Law Commission, 1989) rejected the view that cohabitants should be treated like spouses on the grounds that this could complicate the administration of the estate and would cause difficulties if the deceased were survived by both a spouse and a cohabitant. They instead recommended that cohabitants should be given greater rights to claim family provision, and these were later duly enacted (see below). The intestacy rules, therefore, continue to construct the 'family' in terms of formal family relationships established by blood or marriage ties.[54] The content of family life and relationships based on that shared life are not yet recognized here (by contrast with the limited situation governing succession to certain types of tenancy, as shown in the *Fitzpatrick*[55] and *Ghaidan*[56] cases discussed in Chapter 2).

FAMILY PROVISION—DEPENDENCY OR JOINT ENTERPRISE?

Whether a person makes a will or dies intestate, the disposal of their property may be challenged by those who feel that they deserve a (larger) share. The possibility of seeking a court order to require that some provision be made for a family member out of the deceased's estate was first given in the Inheritance (Family Provision) Act 1938. Its focus was on those who had been dependent on the deceased and who continued to require 'maintenance' by way of periodical payments or lump sums. Reflecting the assumptions of the time regarding financial dependency, eligible applicants were limited to the surviving spouse, unmarried daughters, sons under the age of 21, and disabled children of the deceased. The legislation was the subject of major reform in the 1970s, resulting in the passage of the Inheritance (Provision for Family and Dependants) Act 1975. This Act continues to focus primarily on dependency as the basis of a claim, but it gives broad powers to the court, akin to those available on divorce, to make not only periodical payments and lump sum orders but also transfers and settlements of property. It also includes some de facto family relationships within its scope.

Who may apply?

Section 1(1) of the Act provides that the following may apply:

(a) the surviving spouse;[57]
(b) a former spouse who has not remarried;
(ba)[58] a person who was living with the deceased as husband and wife for a period of two years immediately before his or her death;
(c) a child of the deceased;
(d) a child treated by the deceased as a child of the family in relation to his or her marriage;

[54] Or, in future, civil partnership.
[55] *Fitzpatrick v Sterling Housing Association Ltd* [2001] 1 AC 27, HL.
[56] *Ghaidan v Godin-Mendoza* [2004] UKHL 30, [2004] 3 WLR 113
[57] A surviving civil partner will also be eligible to apply in future if the Civil Partnership Bill is enacted.
[58] Inserted by the Law Reform (Succession) Act 1995, s 2.

(e) any person who, immediately before the death of the deceased was being maintained, wholly or partly, by him or her.

A former spouse is unlikely to succeed in a claim, as generally their financial affairs are considered settled once and for all at the time of their divorce.[59] Claims by children are not limited to those made during their minority; an adult child may seek an order. The most problematic category concerns a person who was 'being maintained' by the deceased. Section 1(1), (3) provides that a person shall be treated as being maintained 'if the deceased, otherwise than for full valuable consideration, was making a substantial contribution in money or money's worth towards the [applicant's] reasonable needs'. In so deciding, s 3(4) requires the court to consider the extent to which, and the basis upon which, the deceased 'assumed responsibility' for the applicant's maintenance. This provision can be liberally construed. In *Re B (Deceased)*,[60] a woman's disabled daughter had received a large compensation award (administered by the Court of Protection) due to clinical negligence during her birth. Part of the award was used to enable the mother to buy a house and care for her daughter. On the daughter's death at the age of fourteen, the mother applied under the Act. The Court of Appeal held that she could be regarded as having been maintained by the daughter, whose compensation fund had provided the financial means to support them both.

The basis of the claim

Under s 1(1), the applicant must satisfy the court that he or she has not received 'reasonable financial provision' from the deceased's estate. However, reflecting the Act's focus on dependency, except in the case of a surviving spouse,[61] such 'reasonable' provision will be limited to that required for the applicant's 'maintenance'. The rationale for treating a widow or widower more generously is that a surviving spouse should not be left worse off than he or she would have been had the marriage been terminated by divorce. Section 3(2) therefore requires the court expressly to have regard to the provision that the applicant might have expected on divorce. In so far as divorce law recognizes a 'joint enterprise' model of the marriage, then so too does the law governing family provision for the

---

[59] *Barrass v Harding and another* [2001] 1 FLR 138, CA. The Court granting the decree of divorce may order that a spouse shall not be entitled to apply for an order under the Inheritance Act: s 15.
[60] [2000] 2 WLR 929, CA.   [61] Or, in future, civil partner.

survivor of the marriage. However, it does not follow that an applicant will receive the same settlement that he or she might have expected on a divorce. There are no financial needs of the deceased to consider, so there may be scope (subject to the position of other applicants and beneficiaries) for the applicant to receive a larger share of the estate.[62]

Assessing the claim

The court takes into account a list of factors set out in s 3 in determining whether reasonable provision has been made and, if not, what orders it should make. These include the size and nature of the estate, the financial resources and financial needs of the applicant as compared with those of any other applicants or beneficiaries of the estate, both presently and in the foreseeable future, and any physical or mental disability they may have. The court must also consider any other matter, including conduct, which it may consider relevant.

When considering claims by surviving or former spouses, or by surviving cohabitants, the court must further consider the duration of the marriage or cohabitation and the 'contribution made to the welfare of the family of the deceased, including any contribution made by looking after the home or caring for the family'. This provision is clearly intended to mirror the court's jurisdiction in a divorce. However, it fits uncomfortably with the requirement that, apart from in respect of a claim by a surviving spouse, the court is only concerned to ensure that the applicant receives provision for his or her 'maintenance'. One might have thought that the applicant's needs would determine the provision to be made, and it is not easy to see how a contribution to welfare can be relevant to these. It may be that it is more relevant to determining the initial question of whether the deceased has failed to make reasonable provision for the applicant.

The court must also have regard to 'any obligations and responsibilities' which the deceased had towards any applicant or beneficiary. This has caused most difficulty in relation to applications by adult children. At one time, it seemed that the applicant would have to show that the deceased owed a moral obligation to provide for the adult child or that there were other special circumstances (such as disability)[63] justifying the grant of an order. Given the basic principle of freedom of testation, that the law usually expects adult children to be financially independent of their parents, and that an order under the 1975 Act can only provide for

---

[62] *Re Krubert (Deceased)* [1997] Ch 97, CA.
[63] See, e.g. *Hanbury v Hanbury* [1999] 2 FLR 255.

maintenance for the applicant (unless he or she is the surviving spouse), this seems to be logical. However, the courts now take a more generous approach. In *Espinosa v Burke*,[64] for example, the elderly father had cared for his daughter's son. The daughter (aged 55 by the time of the proceedings) gave up her job and moved in with them to look after the father. The father supported the family, but disapproved strongly of his daughter, who had been married five times. During the last year of the father's life, she lived mainly in Spain, leaving the father to be cared for by her son and a cleaner. The father left everything to her son and she applied under the 1975 Act. The Court of Appeal held that there is no requirement to establish a distinct moral obligation on the deceased to provide for his child. Instead, the daughter's own financial needs and situation and her limited earning capacity carried sufficient weight to justify awarding her just under half of the estate.

CONCLUSION

In dealing with the consequences of the ending of family relationships, both on divorce and on death, the law appears to be reflecting the same shift of focus away from the form of family ties, to their content, as was seen in respect of their establishment (see Chapter 2). The model of marriage as a partnership of equals, adopted in response to demands for female emancipation, has been seen to fail to respond to the underlying social and economic disadvantage which women experience. But a focus on needs alone ignores the moral case for substantive equality at the end of relationships in which both parties have contributed in different ways. Appreciation of these shortcomings has driven Parliament and the courts to recognize claims for financial relief on divorce based more on a joint enterprise conception of relationships. The extension of this approach to the ending of cohabitation relationships seems likely to follow.

The law governing family provision after death is currently still focused on dependence rather than joint enterprise as the justification for most claims. But it represents an attempt to recognize family ties as deriving, not only from the traditional relationship based on marriage or a genetic link, but also from the emotional and moral contributions made by people to each other in the lives they share. The next step will be for the law to bring together this appreciation of the significance of family life, rather than family form, with a model of families based on 'joint

[64] [1999] 1 FLR 747, CA.

enterprise'. This would enable family law in the twenty-first century to reflect the profound changes that society continues to undergo, and to conceive of families as collectivities of individuals, bound together in intimate relationships in a variety of ways, with both joint and individual needs and interests that deserve recognition and protection.

Bibliography

Barlow, A., Duncan, S., James, G. and Park, A., 'Just a piece of paper? Marriage and cohabitation in Britain' in Park, A., et al, (eds) *British Social Attitudes: The 18th Report—Public Policy and Social Ties* (London, Sage, 2003).

Beck, U. and Beck-Gernsheim, E., *The Normal Chaos of Love* (Cambridge, Polity Press, 1995).

Bowlby, J., *Child care and the growth of love* (Harmondsworth, Penguin, 1953).

Bruch, C., 'Parental Alienation Syndrome and Alienated Children—getting it wrong in child custody cases' [2002] *Child and Family Law Quarterly* 381–400.

Butler-Sloss, Dame Elizabeth, *Report of the Inquiry into Child Abuse in Cleveland 1987*, Cm 412 (London, HMSO, 1988).

Children Act Sub-Committee of the Advisory Board on Family Law, (2000) *A Report to the Lord Chancellor on the Question of Parental Contact in Cases where there is Domestic Violence* (London, Lord Chancellor's Department).

Children Act Sub-Committee of the Advisory Board on Family Law, (2002) *Making Contact Work: A Report to the Lord Chancellor on the Facilitation of Arrangements for Contact between Children and their Non-Resident Parents and the Enforcement of Court Orders for Contact* (London, Lord Chancellor's Department).

Cretney, S. M., *Family Law in the Twentieth Century: A History* (Oxford, Oxford University Press, 2003).

Davis, G. and Murch, M., *Grounds for Divorce* (Oxford, Clarendon Press, 1988).

Davis, G. et al, *Monitoring Publicly Funded Family Mediation* (London, Legal Services Commission, 2001).

Department of Health, *Adoption: a new approach, A White Paper*, Cm 5017 (London, The Stationery Office, 2000).

Department of Health and Social Security, *Review of Child Care Law* (London, HMSO, 1985).

Department of Health, Welsh Office, Home Office, Lord Chancellor's Department, *Adoption: The Future*, Cm 2288 (London, HMSO, 1993).

Department of Social Security, *Children Come First*, Vol II Cm 1264 (London, HMSO, 1990).

Department of Social Security, *Children First: A new approach to child support*, Cm 3992 (London, The Stationery Office, 1998).

Department of Social Security, *Social Security Statistics 1999* (Leeds, Corporate Document Services, 1999).

Edwards, S., *Reducing Domestic Violence...What Works? Use of the Criminal Law* (London, Policing and Crime Reduction Unit, Home Office Research, Development and Statistics Directorate, 2000).

General Register Office, *Civil Registration: Delivering Vital Change* (London, Office for National Statistics, 2003).

Giddens, A., *Modernity and Self-Identity* (Cambridge, Polity Press, 1991).

Glendon, M. A., *The Transformation of Family Law: State, Law and Family in the United States and Western Europe* (Chicago, University of Chicago Press, 1989).

Goldstein, J., Freud, A. and Solnit, A., *Beyond the Best Interests of the Child* (New York, Free Press, 1973).

Haskey, J., 'One-parent families and the dependent children living in them—in Great Britain' *Population Trends 109* (London, TSO, 2002).

Hohfeld, W. N., *Fundamental Legal Conceptions* (New Haven, Yale University Press, 1919).

HM Inspectorate of Constabularies and HM Inspectorate of the Crown Prosecution Service, *Violence at Home* (London, TSO, 2004).

Home Office, *Supporting Families* (London, The Stationery Office, 1998).

Home Office, *Safety and Justice: The Government's Proposals on Domestic Violence*, Cm 5847 (London, TSO, 2003).

King, M. and Piper, C., *How the Law Thinks about Children*, 2nd edn (Aldershot, Arena, 1995).

Laming, Lord, *The Victoria Climbié Inquiry* Cm 5730 (London, TSO, 2003).

Law Commission Discussion Paper, *Sharing Homes* (London, TSO, 2002).

Law Commission, Report No 86, *Third Report on Family Property: The matrimonial home (co-ownership and occupation rights) and household goods* (London, HMSO, 1978).

Law Commission, Report No 118, *Illegitimacy* (London, HMSO, 1982).

Law Commission, Report No 175, *Matrimonial Property* (London, HMSO, 1985).

Law Commission, Report No 172, *Guardianship and Custody* (London, HMSO, 1988).

Law Commission, Report No 187, *Distribution on Intestacy* (London, HMSO, 1989).

Law Commission, Report No 192, *The Ground for Divorce* (London, HMSO, 1990).

Law Commission, Report No 207, *Report on Domestic Violence and Occupation of the Family Home* (London, HMSO, 1992).

Law Commission, Report No 282, *Children: Their Non-Accidental Death or Serious Injury (Criminal Trials)* (London TSO, 2003).

Law Commission, Working Paper No 74, *Illegitimacy* (London, HMSO, 1979).

Lord Chancellor's Ancillary Relief Advisory Group, *Report to the Lord Chancellor by the Ancillary Relief Advisory Group* (London, Lord Chancellor's Department, 1998).

Lord Chancellor's Department (1993), *Looking to the Future: Mediation and the Ground for Divorce: A Consultation Paper*, Cm 2424 (London, HMSO).

Lord Chancellor's Department, (1995), *Looking to the Future: Mediation and the Ground for Divorce: The Government's Proposals*, Cm 2799 (London, HMSO).

Lord Chancellor's Department, (1998), *1. Court Proceedings for the Determination of Paternity: 2. The Law on Parental Responsibility for Unmarried Fathers* (London, Lord Chancellor's Department).

Lord Chancellor's Department, (2003), *Judicial Statistics 2002* (London, TSO).

Lowe, N. V. and Douglas, G., *Bromley's Family Law*, 9th edn (London, Butterworths, 1998).

Lowe, N. V., Everall, M. and Nicholls, M., *International Movement of Children: Law, Practice and Procedure* (Bristol, Family Law, 2004).

Maine, Sir Henry, *Ancient Law* (Oxford, Oxford University Press, 1861, 1931).

Morgan, D., *Family Connections: an introduction to family studies* (Cambridge, Polity Press, 1996).

Mnookin, R. and Kornhauser, L., 'Bargaining in the Shadow of the Law: The Case of Divorce' *Yale Law Journal* 88 (1979), 950–97.

ONS (2001), *Social Trends 31* (London, The Stationery Office).

ONS (2002), *Social Trends 32* (London, The Stationery Office).

ONS (2004*a*), *Social Trends 34* (London, TSO).

ONS (2004*b*), *Living in Britain 31* (London, TSO).

ONS (2004*c*), *Birth Statistics, Series FM1 No 31* (London, TSO).

Pickford, R., *Fathers, marriage and the law* (London, Family Policy Studies Centre, 1999).

Rodgers, B. and Pryor, J., *Divorce and separation: the outcomes for children* (York, Joseph Rowntree Foundation, 1998).

Sarat, A. and Felstiner, W., *Divorce Lawyers and their Clients* (Oxford, Oxford University Press, 1995).

Scottish Law Commission, Report No 135, *Report on Family Law* (Edinburgh, HMSO, 1992).

Smart, C. and Neale, B., *Family Fragments?* (Cambridge, Polity Press, 1999).

Smart, C., May, V., Wade, A. and Furniss, C., *Residence and Contact Disputes in Court: Volume 1, Department for Constitutional Affairs Research Series No 6/03* (London, Department for Constitutional Affairs, 2003).

Stone, L., *Road to Divorce* (Oxford, Oxford University Press, 1990).

Trinder, L., Beek, M. and Connolly, J., *Making contact: How parents and children negotiate and experience contact after divorce* (York, Joseph Rowntree Foundation, 2002).

Walker, J. et al, *Information Meetings and Associated Provisions within the Family Law Act 1996: Final Evaluation Report* (London, Lord Chancellor's Department, 2001).

Waterhouse, R., Clough, M. and le Fleming, M., *Lost in care: report of the tribunal of inquiry into the abuse of children in care in the former county council areas of Gwynedd and Clwyd since 1974* (London, The Stationery Office, 2000).

Weitzman, L., *The Divorce Revolution: the unexpected social and economic consequences for women and children in America* (New York, Free Press, 1985).

Index

Relatives
  child protection applications by 131
  family life and 62–5
Religion
  marriage and 39
  religious education 17
  upbringing of children 89–90
  welfare of child and 171
Reports, children and family reporters
  24, 132
Residence orders 63, 64, 133–5
Restraining orders 125
Rights *see* Human rights

Same sex couples *see* Homosexual
  people
Section 8 orders 133–7
  contact orders 135–6
  prohibited steps orders 136
  residence orders 133–5
  specific issue orders 136–7
Selfhood 8
Separation, divorce and 180–1
Sex
  age of consent 36
  cohabitation and 50
  marriage and 33–4, 71
  rape 70–1
  sex education 17
Social changes 5–8, 31
Social security and welfare system
  16–17
  lone parents and 7, 21, 203
  maintenance within marriage and
  74–5
Social services for families 140–2
Social workers 24, 172
Special guardianship 63–4
Specific issue orders 136–7
Stalking 124, 125
State *see* Government and the state
Statistics
  cohabitation 6
  divorce 6–7, 176, 178
  on family change 5–7
  lone parent families 7
  marriage 5
Step-families
  adoption and 44–5, 62
  step-parents 61–2
Stereotypes 4
Stigma 55
  decline in 9, 31, 48

Succession 3
  cohabitation and 48, 49
  homosexual people 52–3, 62
Supervision orders 144, 145
Surnames
  children 88–9, 135
  marriage and 72
Surrogacy arrangements 45

Taxation, inheritance tax 96
Tenancies, cohabitation and succession
  to 48, 49
  homosexual people 52–3, 62
Totalitarianism 16
Transsexuality
  family life and 47
  marriage and 34–5
Trust of family home 100–4
  based on direct financial contribution
  102–3
  constructive trust based on express
  agreement 100–2
  proprietary estoppel and 103–4

Unmarried couples *see* Cohabitation
Unmarried fathers 10, 42, 54, 56–61, 80
  assisted reproduction and 45–6
  maintenance and 94
Upbringing of children 81, 89–91
  discipline 91
  religion 89–90
  see also Education

Violence *see* Domestic violence
Void marriage 33
Voidable marriage 33, 34, 37

Wardship 154–6
Welfare of children 18–19, 79, 81,
  160–73
  application of welfare principle 166
  ascertaining child's wishes 168
  capability of parents/carers 171–2
  characteristics of child 171
  checklist 168–72
  competing interests 172–3
  effect of change in circumstances 170
  evidence for establishing what will be in
  child's welfare 166
  historical development 160–1
  influences on legal concept of welfare
  161–3
  meaning of welfare 167–73